Advance Praise for Trailbl

"This is a great book about an amazing journey of a woman who went through hell to become the person she is today." - **Monica Helms, creator of the transgender flag.**

"Brave and Important - Don't miss this wonderful book!" – **Laura L. Engel, author of *You'll Forget This Ever Happened- Secrets, Shame, and Adoption in the 1960s***

"We are proud of the work she has done for setting the foundation of today's Nokia's LGBT+ inclusion and being a trailblazer of transgender rights at the workplace." – **Anneli Karlstedt, Head of Inclusion & Diversity NOKIA**

"Mary Ann Horton is indeed a trailblazer: in her professional life as in her life of faith, she has provided us with a model for courageous, thoughtful, principled engagement with questions of life, faith, marriage, and gender identity. My respect for her, and the life she has carved out for herself, is immense." – **The Rev. Guy Erwin, the first openly gay bishop of the Evangelical Lutheran Church in America**

"But transitioning within a job is not always possible. And for those who cannot seamlessly "pass" or "go stealth," there is the question of whether to address the topic directly or wait until a job offer is made. Ms. Horton first faced that choice in 2001, when she looked for a new job ... after a decades-long career in computer administration in Ohio as Mark Horton." – **The New York Times**

It wasn't about being first. Mary Ann just pushed for workplace acceptance and equality. She didn't just do it for herself but blazed the trail by holding down the grass for others to follow." – **Amanda Simpson, former deputy assistant secretary of Defense for Operational Energy for the Obama administration, the first openly transgender woman political appointee of any presidential administration**

"Mary Ann Horton changed how we communicate, pushed companies to add gender identity and gender expression to non-discrimination policies, and fought for transgender health care." – **The Daily Beast**

"Beyond her technical achievements, Horton deserves notice for her efforts in speaking up for the rights of transgender people in the workplace, which started when she was at Lucent in the 1990s. She helped set the stage for some major changes in the corporate world, particularly in Silicon Valley." – **VICE**

"Mary Ann Horton brings a freshness, a delightful honesty, and clarity to her descriptions of self-discovery…"—**Jamison Green, author of *Becoming a Visible Man***

"Mary Ann has been, for nearly 40 years, my invaluable and treasured mentor on transgender issues in the workplace. This very fine book gave me all the personal stories I still needed to fully understand and appreciate her sacred, trailblazing, hero's journey." - **Brian McNaught, author of *Brian McNaught's Guide to LGBTQ Issues in the Workplace***

"Mary Ann Horton is a pioneer of self-discovery. This is one of the most powerful memoirs I've ever had the pleasure of reading, and highly recommend it. Mary Ann's leadership in the workplace and in the LGBTQ community has paved the way for others to be brave as well." **Erin Branscom, Author of *My Level 10 Life***

"...illuminating, enlightening reading highly recommended for memoir audiences." – **Midwest Book Review**

"This exceptional read deals with the fortitude, joy, and often the loneliness of a strong and resilient person going through personal challenges and identity issues. Throughout her story Mary Ann searches for who she really is, and readers walk along side of her as life knocks her down and she pushes forward... Readers will cheer Mary Ann on and rally for the causes of this caring woman as she learns through trial and error how to become the woman her soul demands and deserves." - **Laura L. Engel, President, International Memoir Writers Association**

"Mary Ann Horton ... secured non-discrimination protections for transgender employees, marking a groundbreaking moment for transgender workplace rights." – **VICE**

"This book is a beautiful and practical expression of her faith. Through pain and forgiveness, ignorance, judgments and assumptions of others, Mary Ann chooses to be fully herself and to value others for who they are as she educated others to do the same." - **Beth Allen Slevcove – author of *Broken Hallelujahs – Learning to Grieve the Big and Small Losses of Life***

For Peg
Thanks be to God!
Mary Ann Horton

Trailblazer

Lighting the Path for Transgender Equality in Corporate America

A memoir by

Mary Ann Horton

Trailblazer: Lighting the Path for Transgender Equality in Corporate America
Mary Ann Horton

Published by Red Ace Press
redacepress.com

ISBN: 979-8-9865205-1-3 paperback
ISBN: 979-8-9865205-0-6 ebook

Horton, Mary Ann, 1955-
Trailblazer: Lighting the Path for Transgender Equality in Corporate America
Published in Poway, CA, USA
Library of Congress Control Number: 2022916301

Legal Notices

Photo Credits

Photo of Adam "eeeeg" by Mary Ann Horton.

Photo of transgender lobbyists at US Capitol by Mariette Pathy Allen.

LesBiGaTr graphic by Sarah Fox.

Lucent EEO policy by Lucent Technologies.

It's Time, Ohio! announcement by Mary Ann Horton.

Photos of Mary Ann on first day at Lucent by Chuck Bryant.

Photo of Mary Ann at Transgender Day of Remembrance by Kaizaad Kotwal for the Cleveland Gay People's Chronicle, copyright © 2001 by KWIR Publications.

Photo of Mary Ann "for Mom" by Fay Bass.

Rainbow ice cream cone graphic by Mary Ann Horton.

Photo of group at Usenix 2019 by Geoff Kuenning.

Wedding photo by Kat George.

Table of Contents

For Matt, Adam, and all the grandkids, and all my beloved family.

You can have anything you want,
but what will you have to give up to get it?

— Bill Horton

It's not what you know, but who you know.

— Virginia Horton

1
My First Day

May 1987

I donned my new denim miniskirt and admired myself in the bathroom mirror. I didn't mind how my dark mustache betrayed the long hair of my curly brown wig. As I struck a feminine pose, I saw the headlights from my wife's car turn into the driveway. *Oh, my God.* Karen was home. She had gone to her friend Andi's house to study and said she would be gone for the night. I snatched my pile of male clothes from the floor and raced to the back bedroom to change.

Our young sons, Matt and Adam, were asleep in the adjacent bedroom, and I hoped Karen wouldn't wake them as she strode down the hall. I managed to get the forbidden clothes off and into the closet. I'd pulled on my pants and was kneeling shirtless on the carpet when Karen barged into the room. *Busted!*

She knew I'd cross-dressed five years earlier, and I'd stopped at her insistence. Suspicious, she opened the closet door and saw the pile of clothes.

"I come home to pick up a study book, and this is what I find?" she said. "How long has this been going on? Are the boys involved?"

Eww. Did she think I was a pedophile abusing my sons?

Unable to find any words, I shook my head. She stormed out of the house without picking up a book. I felt as if she had come home with a plan to trap me.

Our marriage had been on the rocks for months. Karen had withdrawn emotionally, and of late, had spent much of her time and energy studying with Andi. Misery had become my new best friend. Her discovery made me feel a thousand times worse. Now, she had no doubt I'd been cross-dressing in her absence, and I knew she would not keep it a secret. I couldn't sleep that night, knowing I was in trouble and haunted by my thoughts of what might happen next.

As days went by, I felt a cloud of shame hang over our house. Her mother looked down her nose at me; her sister visibly recoiled when she saw me. They knew.

When I could take it no more, I checked in with her. "Are you okay? You've barely spoken to me."

She glowered in return. "Since you asked, Mark, I'm trying to decide if I want a divorce."

I didn't want a divorce. I wanted my wife back. My cravings to cross-dress came with ramifications that were about to upend my life. I didn't understand my feelings. *There must be something terribly wrong with me*, I thought. *Why do I have this burning desire to cross-dress? Am I some kind of pervert?*

I wrestled with this soul-torturing question. I had never dressed in all female clothes, wearing only a few items at a time, and always when alone or underneath my male clothes. I wondered what it would be like to spend a day dressed completely as a woman. If I could do that, then perhaps I would find out if I loved it or hated it, or even felt something else I couldn't imagine.

I was scheduled to travel to Arizona a few weeks later for the Usenix Summer Technical Conference. The event presented an unexpected opportunity. I could skip the first day of the conference and spend the day as a woman. Once I satisfied my curiosity, I hoped it would dispel these bothersome thoughts. One big problem—my mustache. I'd worn facial hair for a decade, even sporting a full beard as a Berkeley grad student. If I shaved, it would grow to no more than a messy stubble after a three-day conference. No matter how I felt afterward, this action would be the point of no return. Karen would notice and she would tell everyone in her family what I had done. If the experience put my desire to rest, I didn't think she would believe me.

I packed my thirty-dollar K-Mart wig and a pair of size-13 pumps, and boarded the plane from Columbus to Phoenix. Sitting in the airplane, a war raged inside my head. Would I feel exhilarated or terrible to wholly present as a woman? Should I do it or not? If I did it, there would be no end to Karen's harassment. If I didn't, I would never have my answer. I felt an overpowering drive to go through with it, and five minutes later I would wonder if I had the willpower to resist. What if I did it and liked it? As I went to sleep that night in the hotel, I made up my mind. I had to find out. I would do it.

I looked at myself in the mirror and placing my finger over my dark mustache, tried to blur my vision to see what I would look like. There was one way to know. I turned on my Norelco electric with its familiar buzz and went for it. I pressed hard and did the best I could by tucking my upper lip down to flatten the area. I couldn't remember the last time I felt the cool sensation of fresh air across my entire face. The area over my lip had a lighter, pinkish color than the surrounding area. My face looked naked and my upper lip felt itchy. Seeing my face sans mustache quickened my pounding heart.

I dressed in my usual men's clothes. I unpacked the wig and pumps, and would need to buy a full complement of women's clothing. At 9:00 a.m., it was over 100 degrees outside. I drove to the nearby Camelback Mall.

I removed the electronics and papers from my laptop bag, and stashed them in the trunk of my rental car. I carried the emptied laptop bag like a clunky purse. My first stop was Montgomery Ward for ladies' underwear. I picked out a bra, panties, and black opaque tights from the overwhelming selection. I hoped I had the right size because I was terrified to try them on in the store. I avoided looking at the teenaged checkout clerk. I felt relief when she rung up my purchases without any reaction.

I knew my next stop, The Limited, would have a good selection of averaged-sized women's clothing. As I browsed the long denim skirts, a twentyish saleslady approached.

"What size are you looking for?" she asked.

I didn't know what to say. I couldn't say I was shopping for myself. "I don't know…a-about my size?"

She selected a size-16 skirt and a matching denim shirt. I had no idea how they would fit and I didn't want to go back to the hotel to try them on. *Well*, I thought, *I guess it's do or die*. I summoned up my courage. "These are for me. May I try them on?"

She stiffened her back and contorted her face. I didn't know if it was against the law for me to use a ladies' fitting room. She looked around and not seeing anyone else in the store, picked up her key and led the way.

Everything fit. I put my men's clothes back on and paid. Now I had another problem. How would I change into my new clothes for the rest of my day? I couldn't use either mall restroom for a gender change. Shedding my last bit of masculinity, I asked the clerk, "I'd like to wear them out of the store. May I use your dressing room again?"

I could almost hear the wheels in her head turn as she considered my bizarre request. She glanced around and seeing no one, let me into the dressing room. I had brought along extra socks and used them to pad my bra. Black tights covered my hairy legs. I adjusted my wig and took in my entire appearance. I stared at the mirror. This was me, all of me, in complete female presentation. I smiled, my eyes agog, and waved goodbye at myself. I exited and made a beeline for the exit. The clerk ignored me. *Whew!*

I stepped into the central hallway of the mall. It was early, and the mall teemed with retired people walking laps in the air-conditioned hallways. I felt their icy stares as they sized me up, an ungainly six-footer wearing a denim shirt and long skirt, black tights, high heels, and a cheap wig that did nothing to diminish my Fred Flintstone chin. A little makeup would help me look and feel more like I intended. Feeling vulnerable, I spotted a Merle Norman store in the distance. I had never walked far in the shoes and wasn't used to high heels. I wobbled into the store and caught the attention of a middle-aged clerk.

"Hi." My throat went dry and the words caught in my throat. "I think I need makeup."

She gulped and her eyes narrowed as if she was peering at me through mini-blinds. "Um, the woman who does that won't be in until two o'clock."

A makeup store claiming they wouldn't have a makeup person in for hours? I knew when I wasn't wanted. I reentered the mall's open space. The walkers wore exercise clothes and comfortable shoes. I felt out of place. *I need a makeup store*, I thought. *I must keep moving*. I walked around the two corners of the U-shaped mall. I felt the eyes of every mall walker on me as I tried to steady my gait, fearful someone would confront me. The longer I walked, the more comfortable I became in my shoes. *Maybe nobody cares*, I thought. *They're going on with their day*. I began to relax.

At the far end of the mall, I spotted a hippie-style boutique. I caught a whiff of lavender before I pushed aside a beaded curtain. A sweet, young lady offered to help me.

"Uh, I need makeup?"

"We can do a makeover for twenty-five dollars. Would that be okay?"

I didn't know what a makeover was, but I was game. "Sure."

"My name is Stacy. What's yours?"

Until that moment, it had never occurred to me "Mark" wasn't the right answer. I had no idea what to say. In moment of inspiration, I came up with a response. It started like Mark and went femme. "My name is Mary Ann." I always liked Dawn Wells from *Gilligan's Island*.

"What will you be doing today?" she asked. "Do you have a date?"

I didn't understand she needed to know if I wanted to look sexy or have a look appropriate for business. I sure didn't have a date—the thought never entered my mind. I realized I had no idea what I was going to do once I left the mall.

"I guess I'll work on my manuscript," I said, without explaining the technical reference book I was writing about coding.

"Okay, so nothing too flashy then. A day look."

Over the next two hours, the makeup artist worked on my face. I had no idea what she was doing, even as she tried different foundations on the back of my hand to check for color compatibility. We exchanged small talk as she brushed along my eyelids. Overall, I liked how it felt to have someone apply cosmetics to my face. Stacy had a gentle touch and I'm sure she treated me as she would anyone who might wander in. When we were done, I was amazed by my reflection. A pleasant female face smiled back at me. While I was no beauty queen, I looked nice. My face better matched my outfit. I proceeded to Woolworth's for a purse, hairbrush, lipstick, and wallet, I felt much more comfortable. Most of the stares disappeared among the walking crowd. With the morning gone, hunger took precedence.

I drove to a Wendy's drive-through and ordered at the speaker. The clerk thanked me and called me, "sir." I cringed at the sound of the word. I pulled up to the pick-up window, and when he saw my female face, he looked confused. Thinking he had the wrong meal, he verified my order.

For the remainder of the day, I worked on my book in a beautiful public park where no one bothered me. I went to a nice restaurant for dinner and saw a movie. I had enjoyed my time as a woman and felt more comfortable than I had in months.

Back at the hotel, I didn't know if anyone from the conference might recognize me and didn't want to find out. I felt nervous walking through the deserted corridors, fearing someone would come out of a door and I'd have to explain myself.

In my room, I washed off my makeup, put my male clothes back on, and reflected on the day. How did it feel? Was it as exhilarating as I expected? Did it feel great?

The word that came to mind was "boring." After I'd left the mall, the day had been boring, not the rush I had expected. The next year, I realized the correct word to describe my experience that day: "relaxing."

I took all my female clothes, including the wig and heels, and threw them into the trash by the hotel elevator. Purging all my clothes was expensive and I had done it a few times. I resolved not to cross-dress anymore. After the conference ended, I flew back to face Karen and my life as Mark.

This time on the plane, a new question taunted me. "Who am I, really?"

2

Childhood

1965

In the fourth grade, my parents bought a beautiful three-bedroom, two-bath, brick ranch house in a new subdivision in Spokane, Washington. I liked to play with my toy trucks on the bare dirt yard. I was an ordinary nine-year-old boy, or so I thought. We spent that summer planting grass and trees, pouring a patio out back, and setting up gardens and irrigation. It was a big step up from the rented houses we'd lived in.

Virginia, my mom, was an attractive brunette, five feet five, with a slender build. She didn't get along with her mother in their native Arkansas. I never found out the details of what went wrong, but family had commented, "It was terrible what Virginia's mother did to her." My mom resolved to get out of there at her first chance and married at sixteen, divorced at eighteen, and moved to Washington where she met Bill Horton, my father. They married in 1954 and set up their lives in Richland, Washington, on the Columbia River.

Dad worked for Standard Oil of California, now Chevron. He worked his way up from a gas station attendant, and by then, he'd been promoted to sales representative. He traveled for business and drove around Eastern Washington, selling products to the managers of company-owned Standard Oil stations and Chevron franchise owners. He was almost six feet tall with dark hair, an athletic build, and an engaging smile. Blessed with great people skills, Dad was on a fast track to management. He seemed to get a promotion every couple of years, necessitating a move to another town: from Richland, to Lewiston, to Spokane, to Couer d'Alene, to Yakima, and back to Spokane. "He's a good provider," Mom would say.

At nine years old, I noticed women's clothes and thought them more interesting than the boring dungarees I wore. I'd see girls on TV twirling their skirts and it looked like fun. I wanted to do that. This was the first I'd ever noticed anything different about my gender. I knew boys weren't supposed to do that sort of thing, so I did what any red-blooded American crossdresser would do; I sneaked into my mom's room and "borrowed" an outfit, including a dress, underwear, nylons, and shoes. I tried them on in my room. I twirled and smiled at the wonder of it. I hadn't thought through my adventure and left the clothes in a pile on the floor of my closet.

That evening, Mom opened my closet to put away laundry. "What are my clothes doing here heaped up on the floor?" Her eyes exploded with anger. "Were you wearing them? Go get the board."

The board wasn't a traditional paddle, it was a rough, broken floorboard about a half-inch thick by three inches wide, and stretched the length of her forearm. She swung it like a club and wasn't partial to my bottom. I raised my arms over my head to absorb most of the blows. She beat me severely that night.

I had opened Pandora's box, and I knew I had to wear those wonderful clothes again. Going forward, I had to be creative. I learned how to choose items my mom wouldn't miss. I spotted two slinky floral dresses in her underwear drawer in a corner box, and realizing she never wore them, I made them mine. I could stuff the non-wrinkle fabric into my secret stash—the box my baseball glove had come in. I learned to memorize the layout of her drawers. I could borrow clothes and then put them back as if I'd never been there. I couldn't risk another beating.

I remember my first beating around age seven. My dad had to go on a business trip and we saw him off at the Yakima airport. After he boarded, I made a loud, offhand remark like, "No more Dad for a whole week."

My mother became livid. She assumed some man had overheard us and would be invading our home while the man of the house was gone, a point I hadn't considered. In the car, she fumed and yelled, and when we got home, she made me pull down my pants and bend over my bed. She beat me with her board and didn't stop. I didn't know I could feel that much pain. Each stinging blow was only matched by my fear of the dark night.

Mom didn't need much to set her off. She beat me about once a week, whether I deserved it or not. If I crossed her, it would be ten times worse. When the beating was over, she would dismiss me by sputtering, "Get out of my sight."

I wasn't an angel. I acted up and did things I wasn't supposed to, and then I'd get a well-deserved beating. When I'd been good, she would find an excuse and yell at me to get the board, something as simple as eating her Hershey's chocolate or using tape without asking. I saw little point in being good.

My mom didn't believe my father needed to travel as much as he proclaimed. Dad loved to drink, golfed as well as the pros, and made friends easily. While away, Mom was convinced he was "on a toot," meaning he was out boozing it up or in bed with some floozy. He might have been. I think he needed to get away from her.

I was an active kid with scrapes and scabs from playground falls and bike crashes. No one noticed the extra marks and bruises from when Mom whaled on me with the board. My dad didn't see any evidence and I never told him, knowing my mom would make it worse for me.

Dad told me later in life, "I never knew who I'd find when I came home. Sometimes she was the most loving woman in the world. Sometimes she was like a raging tiger." Another time, he confided what he knew about her mental health problems. "Before you were born, she saw a psychiatrist who diagnosed her as paranoid schizophrenic."

As an adult, I came to believe in the accuracy of that diagnosis. She never took meds for it and never trusted anybody. She managed to live without hospitalization.

Mom was also intelligent and determined, and most of the time she was sweet. She read to me when I was young, which fostered my lifelong love of books. She made me fancy birthday cakes, once shaping and frosting one as a lion. She served as den mother for my

Cub Scout pack one year and hosted den meetings in our home. I feared my mother, and I loved her too.

I wished I'd had a brother or sister. I asked my parents if they were going to have another child and Mom refused, saying, "When you were born, it nearly killed me." My parents considered adoption and went through the interview process.

"Virginia, tell me about your relationship with your mother," the counselor asked.

She spat back, "My mother and I do *not* have a relationship," and that was the end of the adoption.

I faced the world alone, an introvert seeking peace from within. Scant visits to out-of-state family meant I never had the chance to find a confidant, someone who might have been able to help or intervene. My refuge was clear; I had to spend time in women's clothing, and I fixated on dresses, slips, stockings, and panty girdles, even though I didn't know why. Whenever my parents went out for the evening, I took the opportunity to wear them, and I felt better.

Across from our house there was a woodsy area full of tall Ponderosa pines where I liked to walk the dog. Sometimes, I would change clothes there, or I'd wear the clothes under my jeans and shirt and then take off my outer garments. I felt protected and safe among the trees with their piney vanilla aroma wafting through the air. *Mmm.* Conversely, I started to feel discomfort being alone in boy clothes. I felt fine being alone in women's clothes, which always felt nice. Looking back, I felt as if those clothes acted like a security blanket, one that wrapped around me offering warmth and safety. I was at peace.

There were many things I didn't understand as a child. At the time, I thought it was all about the clothes. I was wrong.

* * *

In fifth grade, school became my refuge. I dove into books, and when I did well, which was often, I received praise at school and home. Mom pushed me to do extra credit, and I kept busy with additional projects. Part of my success that year had to do with my teacher. We clicked and I thrived with her guidance. She told me I spoke more like an adult than a kid.

Reading became my favorite class. I loved to read textbooks and encyclopedias cover to cover. I would check out books from the school library and made a habit of having a book on hand.

In sixth grade, I saw an ad in the back of a comic book and wrote to the Olympia Sales Club to sell greeting cards door to door. The job was simple. In September, I pitched personalized Christmas cards. Most families refused. The ones that were interested would sign up and pay up, while I earned points I could cash in on a catalog of kid-oriented items. I was gung-ho about it and earned enough points for a ten-speed bicycle.

My bike gave me more mobility, especially in my hilly neighborhood. I was soon riding all over Spokane, earning more money. I learned fast how a cute kid could sell almost anything, for example, butter toffee peanuts to earn money to go to YMCA summer camp. Each box held six tins and most kids sold one or two boxes. In my first year, I sold twelve boxes. I sold about thirty boxes the third year, enough to pay in full for three weeks of camp.

I loved being at Camp Reed, located on a tree-lined lake in the middle of nowhere, blessed weeks away from my mother. I could be a regular kid there and enjoy camp activities: swimming, hiking, crafts, and archery.

My last summer, at age thirteen, I brought my stash of women's clothing with me to camp. One night, I woke up at two in the morning. I took my slinky dress outside the cabin to change and luxuriated in the feel of the fabric. I strolled down a moon-lit trail, and as I savored the experience, a white streak up ahead caught my eye. A skunk trotted along the path toward me, oblivious to my presence.

I froze. *What if he sprays me or bites me? I'll have to explain what I'm wearing.* I felt the hair on my nape stand in alert. Reacting more than thinking, I stopped and let out a quiet, "Hey." The skunk stopped in its tracks and looked at me. He did not appear alarmed. I veered off the path to the right, to go around him. He followed my lead and took a wide circle to his right. Completing our half do-si-do and returning to the path, we both went on our way.

* * *

I had a crush on a pretty girl at school named Sheree. She was nice to me, and we hung out together. We were in the seventh grade, too young for anything serious. One day at lunch, I sat on the bench in the school cafeteria with Sheree and her friends discussing fashion.

"Does your mother let you wear nylons?" one of the girls asked me.

My eyebrows shot up in surprise. I thought, *No, I have to hide them from her.* Knowing I couldn't say that, I wondered what I could say. I felt as if they had accepted me as one of the girls. I would have loved to join this conversation, and knew I couldn't. I didn't look like a girl, at least I didn't think I did, and I had too many secrets to keep. I got flustered and mumbled, "No."

She persisted. "Well, why not?"

"I'm a boy!" The conversation moved on without me. I always wondered if she saw the girl in me.

One day in eighth grade, Sheree wore a wig to school. It had long, straight hair, much like her natural hair, but a different shade of brown. The other girls were trying on the wig and having fun. I felt envious and wanted to join in.

After school, I caught up with Sheree on the sidewalk, and in a small voice, asked, "May I try it on?"

"Sure."

I loved the feel of the long hair brushing my cheeks. I wished I could have seen myself.

"You'd make a good-looking girl," she said. I was happy with the compliment.

Wigs were trendy in the 1960s. Mom rarely wore the few wigs she had, and I could borrow hers for a long time without notice. Once, I felt bold enough to wear a dress, nylons, and a blonde wig to go outside on a bicycle ride. A guy whistled at me from his car. A wave of fear rushed over me. *This is dangerous,* I thought. *I could get beat up, or exposed.* I didn't do it again.

3

Trouble at Home

My mother complained often and was quick to judge, favoring the dark side of human nature. Her motto: "Believe nothing you hear and only half of what you see," summed up her skepticism. While Dad could go on a trip, I couldn't, and I preferred to play on my own. I hung out in the basement and set up configurations using my electric slot car racetrack to stay amused.

Mom griped about Dad. "He's staying out late again." "He didn't come home last night. He must be sleeping with some floozy." "I know he's a homosexual." This last remark was something she shared about her first husband, too, and while Dad was away a lot, I had no idea of the truth in her claims.

Mom planned a divorce and part of it included coaching me. "If the judge asks who you want to live with, say Mom." I was about twelve, and legally, I might have been allowed to choose had they asked. I agreed out of denial and self-protection. I didn't take her seriously, though I should have.

Dad explained what happened. "I was out mowing the lawn when Ginny came out. She said, 'There's a man here to see you.' I went to the door and he served me with divorce papers. 'You have to leave the house,' he said. I was taken totally by surprise. I asked her, 'Do you want me to finish mowing the lawn?' She said, 'I'd sure appreciate it.' I finished up, put my golf clubs in my car, and left."

Dad found a single-room hotel downtown in the low-rent district. I couldn't allow myself to feel the devastation of our family's breakup. For my own safety, I kept my head down and focused on school. I became the ultimate introvert.

I saw Dad from time to time. He would treat me to a yummy cheeseburger lunch followed by seeing a game of our local baseball team, the Spokane Indians. I learned to love baseball from these outings.

Like most men of that era, Dad didn't contest custody. Nobody asked me where I wanted to live and I avoided any courtroom drama. He sent alimony and child support. Mom went to school to learn typing and shorthand to become a secretary.

Mom couldn't afford the house by herself, so she sold it and rented a house in an older neighborhood. My stash of women's clothing, all swiped from my mom, was safer from her prying eyes in my new basement bedroom. I could even sleep in my girl clothes.

I made friends with the kids next door, a girl about my age named Sue Harris and a younger boy. I liked Sue and developed a crush. Her surname stuck in my memory, and I used it later in life.

A rare opportunity arose for my dad. A Chevron gas station franchise became available in the San Diego area. He would have to move out of state. Owning his own station was a big deal, and he jumped at the chance. I wasn't able to see him much for the next few years.

* * *

In the middle of my ninth-grade year, Mom decided living in Spokane wasn't working out for her.

"We're going to move to Little Rock and live near my parents."

In the winter of 1970, I said goodbye to all my friends and packed up my stuff. The moving van took everything away, and Mom and I got in her car to drive to Little Rock. I was fascinated with road maps, and knew all the roads and highways. Arkansas was southeast and we were headed the wrong way. As we exited Spokane, I asked, "Why are we going west?"

"We aren't really moving to Little Rock. We're going to Portland, Oregon. I don't want Bill to know where we live, and I knew you'd blab."

She believed he would come and attack her. I knew Dad was harmless, and it was only her paranoia talking. How was I supposed to blab when we never spoke? I decided it didn't matter where we went. If I didn't keep my big mouth shut, I'd regret it.

Mom rented an apartment in the eastern area of central Portland. I enrolled in Washington High as a freshman. Instead of biking to school, I took a city bus. Washington was an inner city school. Portland was a clean town and the school was okay. The kids were the same as anywhere. I was too introverted to make a lot of close friends.

I signed up for a paper route and thrived on it. I got out of the house and had spending money. In the afternoon, I sold newspaper subscriptions door to door. The *Oregonian* ran a promotion offering a free dictionary. I learned if I only got in one word before the door slammed in my face, it should be "free."

I sold enough subscriptions to earn a trip to Disneyland. This should have been a huge deal, except I'd barely heard of the place. I took home permission papers for Mom. She hit the ceiling and refused to sign. I never went. I shrugged it off and let it go.

* * *

One day that spring, Washington High held an event where students could sample new classes. I loved math and thought the computer programming classroom would be interesting. The teacher demonstrated a strange typewriter-like device set on a pedestal that noisily chugged away as it printed capital letters on a roll of paper.

"This is a model 33 Teletype. See this telephone and modem on the side? When I dial this number, it connects to the General Electric Time-Sharing Service."

I was hooked. My brain flooded with endorphins as I dove in headfirst. I couldn't wait to stay after school each day to use the computer. We could write programs in a language called BASIC, which I picked up in no time. I wrote programs with the other kids to play computer games: blackjack, craps, and shooting artillery shells.

To avoid the boring task of writing out hand printed receipts for my newspaper customers each month, I wrote a program to print it for me. I had a new superpower: I could will a machine to do my bidding.

4
San Diego

1971

I hadn't heard much from Dad since he moved to San Diego. That changed in late August. Mom took great pains to hide from him, but I overheard them talk on the phone. She listened and because she sounded agreeable, I didn't pay much attention. I soon discovered the import of their conversation.

An abdominal aortic aneurysm, known as a triple-A, had almost killed him. They replaced most of his aorta with a tube sewn into place with silk sutures. As a result, he lost his gas station and wouldn't be able to send money for child support. He was sorry, but there wasn't anything he could do about it.

My parents' solution was for me to live with my dad. Looking back, I have no idea how this made sense. Dad wasn't working, and he was going to take care of me? Go figure.

School would start soon and I needed to enroll in eleventh grade where Dad lived. My mom gave me two weeks to get my affairs in order. As usual, I did what they told me to do without argument. Not that I didn't mind getting away from Mom and her moods; I felt reluctant to give up the computer access I loved and that made life tolerable.

I quit my paper routes, my only source of income. I packed up my boy clothes and my computer tapes into one suitcase and with regret, threw away my girl clothes where Mom wouldn't see them. Mom withdrew the $137 I had in my savings account and instructed me to open a bank account when I arrived. I hated to leave behind my trusty bike, my only means of transportation. There was no way to take it with me. She bought me a one-way bus ticket to California, and bade me goodbye.

* * *

I got off the bus in front of a Rexall drugstore in the sleepy beach town of Solana Beach in San Diego's North County. Dad picked me up in his beater car. We drove up US-101 to his home on the northern edge of town.

We entered a neighborhood of nondescript one-story houses. This was pricey real estate in Southern California, even in 1971. We stopped in front of a three-bedroom house two blocks from the beach. Dad introduced me to the owner, an elderly woman. He showed me to a bedroom with two twin beds, one for each of us. We had privileges to use the rest of the house, and shared a bathroom with another man who rented another bedroom. I had no idea what to expect. This sure wasn't it, yet I felt grateful to be far away from Mom.

Though Dad had recovered from his triple-A, he'd lost his business, drank too much, and gave the appearance of a broken man. He took whatever work he could find: working in a gas station, tending bar. Whether away working or out drinking, I didn't see him much. I had an unexpected and welcomed independence. At fifteen, I had no driver's license, no car, and no bike. I had the freedom to come and go if I could get a ride. I had no privacy in our shared room, and even if I had any girl clothes, I could never have hidden them. I stuffed that part of myself deep inside.

He enrolled me in San Dieguito High School, a few miles up the road in Cardiff. I took a regular school bus to get there. Unlike the school in Portland, the San Dieguito High classrooms opened to the outside. San Diego coastal weather was warm and pleasant, even in winter. Seagulls circled the outdoor cafeteria looking for bits of spilled lunches. Most of the students hung out at the beach and had sun-bleached hair. To me, the beach was cold and dirty, and a waste of time.

I signed up for my eleventh-grade classes: calculus, physics, film study, and gym. I liked the calculus teacher. He was all about math, and so was I. Even though calculus was tough, I took it as a challenge. Tucked away in the front corner of the classroom was the school's new gadget. The Typagraph was a Teletype that could also plot graphs. My disappointment over losing computer access evaporated.

Within weeks, half a dozen students lined up after school each day for ten minutes of computer time. I thrived at San Dieguito. School was fun, I made friends, and I got to use computers.

After a year, Dad was able to move us into a nice two-bedroom apartment in Cardiff. I could walk to my minimum wage job at Jack in the Box, and earned enough money to buy an old car and a small stash of girl clothes. With Dad gone much of the time, I had the privacy to wear them from time to time. I felt better about life.

I graduated a semester early after working hard at school. I knew I'd be going to college. I qualified for full financial aid at USC based on my good grades and my parents' low income. Before starting, I worked full-time for seven months in menial jobs, flipping burgers, sharpening saws, washing dishes. It was hard work, and it motivated me to get an education that would prepare me to be a white-collar professional.

In April, I came home to the apartment to find our belongings stored in a utility closet. Dad hadn't paid the rent and we'd been evicted.

Stunned by this setback, the practical, resilient side of me kicked in. I figured I'd sleep in my old Ford station wagon outfitted with shag carpet and curtains. My friends joked it looked like a hearse. At least I had a place to store my stuff, and as a silver lining, I could sleep in my girl clothes. It was a short-term plan until school started; however, soon thereafter, my friend's parents let me use their playhouse built years ago in the wooded backyard of their expansive Rancho Santa Fe home.

Dad couch surfed at various houses, pumped gas and tended bar. We kept in touch through his friends and rarely visited. I was an emancipated minor, self-supporting—albeit rent-free—and loved my independence.

5
USC

1973

I arrived at USC full of hope and in anticipation of a new life as a college student. I had enough financial aid to pay the bills, an old station wagon with a balky transmission, and a love of computer programming. There were no parents to boss me around. I felt pumped, ready for this awesome adventure.

USC was in the middle of Los Angeles, not in a good neighborhood. Friends warned me to be careful off-campus as USC was a "white island" in the middle of Watts. Didn't I remember the Watts riots of 1965? No, I was a kid in Spokane. I felt fortunate to have been assigned a room in Men's Residence West. Each floor of the new eleven-story dorm was divided into four suites, and each of those had four shared bedrooms, a common living room, kitchenette, and bathroom. The dorm across the street was a dump. My room on the fifth floor had a nice view of the parking lot.

As part of my financial aid, I needed to find a campus job. I was thrilled to get a job as an operator at USC's Information Science Institute (ISI), a think tank located across town in Marina del Rey, a fancy coastal community. ISI occupied the top two floors in one of two new twelve-story buildings that towered over the harbor.

As the new hire, I had to work the weekend graveyard shift. That was okay; it didn't conflict with my classes. I'd worked graveyards at Jack in the Box in high school and didn't mind a weird sleep schedule. I had all night to play with the system. There was little to do except reboot if it crashed. I resolved to learn the system and get into techie mischief on early Internet. Computer security wasn't a thing yet, so I had a good time reading people's files and discovering their passwords.

* * *

I had two obsessions: computers and finding a girlfriend. Like any other male nerd, I felt clueless, and like most men, I wanted I woman in my life. My interest in women's clothes never translated into an interest in men. At the time, I didn't understand that a person's sexual orientation, that is, to whom they're attracted, is separate from their gender identity, who they are.

In my second year at USC, my roommate had a connection for the hottest ticket in town, an Elton John concert. He asked his aunt, a ticket office clerk, to get us six seats up front, including two for me. I was thrilled and would have been more so with a date. I started my search. My dorm held a party a week before the concert. I spoke to Karen, a tall brunette with glasses and pretty long hair. She was a shy freshman from Youngstown, Ohio, and as a newbie, still nervous about being far from home. I liked her, partly because she tolerated my presence.

"I have tickets to see Elton John next Saturday. Would you like to go?"

"Uh, I'll think about it."

I thought we had started out well and felt disappointment when she evaded answering. At least she left it open.

She told me later she had a long discussion with her dorm mates because she thought I was kind of creepy. I didn't doubt it. Fortunately, her friends convinced her to go and I had my date.

When we got to the concert, we found our seats, one through six, were not close as we imagined, but in the back of the arena. We still had a good view of Elton John and his band, and we had an amazing time at the concert. We enjoyed hit after hit we'd heard on the radio, songs I knew not realizing he was the artist.

Karen had a good enough time that she agreed to go out with me again. As we hung out together, we discovered how compatible we were in everything from our taste in rock 'n' roll music to liking blue cheese salad dressing. We were serious about our studies and careers, and left partying to the frats and sororities.

Soon we were an item and spent all our free time together. We went out to dinner, to the movies, and to campus concerts. We flew to

Ohio to meet her parents over Christmas break. We drove to San Diego for semester break, staying in a cheap motel to visit my couch-surfing father. Being in a relationship soothed my soul. She was fun. For the first time since I could remember, I felt happy.

Meeting Karen changed my life, and it wasn't my only big change that fall. A history professor inquired at the computer science department for a bright student programmer to code reports analyzing voting patterns in colonial Massachusetts. Fortunately, one of my professors recommended me for the job.

After performing well, the history professor gave me more to do. I loved this student job. I got paid to write programs, not to change tapes and printer paper, not to flip burgers or sharpen saws, but to work in my field of study. I enjoyed the chance to be creative.

Every time the professor had a research hypothesis, he would ask for a new report. These were similar, a matter of copying the program and making a few changes. I decided it was wasteful to make a new copy for every question, and I made the reporting program more general by allowing it to compare any two variables. These programs were punched onto decks of cards and all I had to do was insert the right cards in two spots in the deck, resubmit it, and check the output. The change meant only one reporting program to support.

I felt fortunate. I cared about Karen and wanted to make her happy. I learned to be less self-centered and kinder to others. Life was on the upswing. I had a great job, computer access, and a car that worked, everything I needed and a bright future. I felt less caught up in the old ways of my life and more mature as I gained experience.

* * *

I took extra classes, summer classes, and advanced placement exams, and by fall of 1975, I was a senior on track to graduate with my BS after three years. *Yes!* Busting out of the dorm, I rented an off-campus apartment with a friend. Karen and her roommate took an apartment in the same building. We were conveniently nearby without living together.

That October, I went into a jewelry store.

"I want to propose to my girlfriend. How much is an engagement ring?"

The jeweler showed me a flashy diamond ring. "This one is $5,000." I gulped. "I'm a starving student. Do you have something under $100?"

He smiled. "I have just the thing." He rummaged under the counter. "This is a promise ring. It has a diamond chip. I can let you have it for fifty dollars."

I took it.

That Saturday, Karen and I walked along a grassy area near the student union. We sat on a bench.

"We make such a great couple," I said. "We could spend the rest of our lives together." Karen nodded. I dropped to one knee and pulled out the ring. "Let's make it official. Will you marry me?"

She nodded emphatically as her eyes turned glassy. "Yes!"

* * *

Karen and I talked about everything from our classes, to our families, to our hopes and ambitions. As an engaged couple, we dreamed of a family life together: kids, a house in the suburbs, and our careers, mine in software and hers in criminal justice.

My need to cross-dress was not as strong with Karen in my life. I felt calmer when wearing a dress or a slip, and wore one about once a month when alone. I held off telling her. That March, I decided to come out. I chose a quiet evening while sitting on a campus park bench.

"I have something to share with you. Something important," I said. I gauged her reaction, a quizzical look prompting me to go on. "Sometimes, when I'm alone, I wear women's clothes."

Her face changed to horror. "Oh, no. You can't do that. When I was in high school, I knew a guy who did that. He was weird. You have to stop."

I hoped she would take it in stride. I felt less disappointment than I thought. Instead, fear grabbed me by the throat. This was a no-brainer. She was more important to me than the clothes. I told her I would stop.

I packed up my women's clothes and threw them in the trash with the best of intentions. I stuffed that part of my soul into a box and buried it in the back of my mind. I told myself: *This compulsion isn't helping me. It isn't acceptable. I need to be like other men. Marriage will make a man of me.*

I would graduate from USC in June 1976 and invited my parents to attend. My mom agreed to come from Portland. I felt excited until I found out my dad, his girlfriend Betty, and her daughter would also come and wanted to celebrate in a big way. This created a problem. Mom didn't want Dad to know she would be present. Karen secreted Mom off in a corner where she could see the ceremony from afar and not be seen.

Years later, I found out Dad had gone to great lengths to get there. He walked away from a minimum-security jail where he had been serving time on a drunk-driving charge. Betty drove them to the graduation. Dad hadn't come to my high school graduation, and it was important to him to make it up to me. He scored points with me by coming, and even more when I found out the risk he took. He paid consequences upon his return to jail. I didn't ask for details.

Karen and I married that summer in a simple ceremony in her parents' Baptist church in Ohio. We took up married life at the University of Wisconsin. I attended as a computer science graduate student, and Karen continued her half-completed undergraduate studies in sociology. In two years I earned my master's in computer science at UW, and Karen progressed toward her BS. Winters in Madison were miserable, and when we realized it was possible to transfer to UC Berkeley for my PhD, I applied. Wisconsin was a top-fifteen program; Berkeley, top-five. When Berkeley accepted me and offered me the same teaching assistant job I had at UW, I jumped at the chance. Karen decided to resume her studies in criminal justice at San Francisco State. We sold our rusty Ford and headed west in a rented truck.

6
Berkeley

1978

Crossing the California state line near Reno, we let out a hearty cheer. Yay! We were Californians again. We drove the U-Haul truck to married student housing, a basic one-bedroom in an old navy complex a few blocks from the San Francisco Bay in Albany, outside Berkeley. Oddly, being so close to the water meant it wasn't in a good part of town. The higher elevation in the East Bay offered better views and commanded higher rent.

We unloaded our personal belongings, leaving the computer stuff from my UW office in the truck to move into my campus office the next day. We were starving and took the U-Haul truck to find somewhere to eat. Using an imperfect paper map, we turned onto an industrial street and found ourselves on a dead-end road with a police car pulling us over.

The officer strode up to the truck window. "Where are you going?" he asked.

"We're trying to find someplace to eat. My map says this street goes through," I responded, gesturing in frustration at the wall blocking our path.

"It's a dead-end," he retorted, with an unspoken "you dummy" added in between the lines. "What's in the truck?"

"We just moved here from Wisconsin. My office stuff is in the back."

"Let's take a look."

I unlocked the back, and we climbed into the cargo area with my magnetic tapes, printouts, and technical books sliding around the nearly empty truck. "I'm a computer science grad student at Berkeley. I'm taking this to my office tomorrow."

He looked through the mess, not comprehending what it was or why it was in a truck on an industrial street. He checked our IDs and called them in to check for warrants.

"Okay, you can go."

With difficulty, we turned the huge truck around on the narrow street. The same cop pulled us over again. *Argh!* I wanted to get out of there and fill my empty stomach. I struggled to hold my temper, knowing better than to get mad at a cop.

"I need to see the back of your truck again. It turns out there was computer equipment stolen."

Good grief, I thought. *This keeps getting weirder.*

I opened the back and he picked up a printout and riffled through it.

"What's this round thing?" He looked baffled by the white, twelve-inch spool of computer magnetic tape.

I opened it and unrolled a few inches of brown tape. "It's a computer mag tape. It has my programs and data recorded on it."

For the next several minutes, I listened to one side of his radio conversation with headquarters.

"Computer printouts. Magnetic tapes. No, I don't see any electronic equipment."

My patience had thinned by the time he told us we could go. We didn't wait for him to change his mind. As we turned onto the main road, we breathed a sigh of relief and soon found an eatery.

Welcome to California.

* * *

I found the University of California at Berkeley's computer science program located on the fifth floor of Evans Hall, a ten-story, gray concrete office building on the Berkeley hillside. My research professor had a west-facing office with a spectacular view of the San Francisco Bay. Six of us grad students shared the office next to hers.

Our six-person office had two desks, each with a terminal: a keyboard and monitor with a text-only cable leading to the computer in another room. We typed and the computer typed back. I thrilled to use this high-tech equipment and felt lucky because on the other end of the wire was ucbvax, a VAX UNIX system, time-shared among ten to twenty students and faculty. Grad students at Berkeley used them for classwork and research, and we loved our ability to enhance the system ourselves. We made so many improvements, other universities wanted our software, and on request we mailed out the Berkeley Software Distribution on mag tapes. I loved contributing to Berkeley UNIX, writing code hundreds of people would use.

I settled into a typical grad student work schedule. I got up at 9:00 a.m., read the paper, and arrived at school to lunch with other grad students at Top Dog, La Val's Pizza, or any of the dozen other establishments on Euclid Avenue. Then I'd cruise into an afternoon of classes or coding. As we worked into the evening, a grad student sometimes ran down the hallway yelling, "Sunset alert! Sunset alert!" We would gather in the west-facing offices to enjoy a fiery display of reds and golds, until all that remained was an orange glow over the bay. I would come home around 10:00 p.m. and turn in around midnight.

I grew a beard to meet the informal Berkeley dress code. I didn't have time or opportunity to cross-dress, so facial hair didn't matter. I had promised Karen I'd stop wearing women's clothes. Thus far, I'd been able to keep my promise. I figured the beard would prevent me from being tempted.

* * *

One grad student, Bill Joy, seemed to produce half of Berkeley's enhancements. One of his contributions was the vi (pronounced "vee-eye") text editor. He'd taken the original UNIX line-oriented editor and turned it into a full-screen editor, similar to Windows Notepad, but far more powerful. In 1979, Bill grew tired of vi and gave it to me. The enhancements I made to vi over the next four years proved crucial later in my career, helping me land two great jobs.

After a year and a half of long evenings on campus, I became envious of Bill's home terminal, as were other grad students. "What if we all went in together to buy ten terminals?" I suggested. "We could get a discount." We shopped around and settled on the Microterm MIME II terminal, a "smart terminal" at the low price of $900. I convinced my advisor to buy me a fancy 1200-baud modem. At last, I could work from home.

I would come home in time for dinner with Karen, and then work into the night. She finished her degree at SFSU and worked nine to five as an administrative assistant while I finished my doctorate. Once I graduated and we had a permanent home, she wanted to work as a probation officer.

Karen went to bed around nine. I stayed up for another three hours, working alone from a cheap desk in the living room. The feelings of being alone and wanting to cross-dress began to haunt me. Denim skirts, slips, and pantyhose appealed to me, perhaps because they were forbidden. Women's jeans and shirts were no different than men's and did not interest me. I felt strange going into a store with a beard to buy women's clothing, and discovered in Berkeley, nobody cared.

I felt more comfortable wearing my girl clothes as I coded late into the night, even with Karen sound asleep in the next room. I didn't understand why I needed them. I had to hide this part of me, and keep it a deep dark secret or I'd be in trouble. Nobody would accept it—not Karen, not my family, not the world. I felt alone in my craving. At bedtime, I reluctantly changed into men's pajamas.

* * *

I looked forward to the 1980 Usenix conference in Delaware. Usenix was the UNIX user group made up of computer techies from universities and tech companies. This would be my first professional conference, and as an impoverished grad student, I was grateful the school paid my way.

Grad students from the University of North Carolina and Duke gave a fascinating presentation about "Usenet," one of the first computerized social media networks. A person could post a message on one system and it would be copied to all the other systems. The four presenters invited others to join them and shared the software on the conference mag tape. I was all over this. I installed their software on Berkeley's ucbvax system, set up a link to a Bell Labs system, and *voilà*, we were online.

By 1981, I was the *de facto* leader of Usenet. There were so many machines on the network, we needed a map to show connections. I drew maps with the vi editor to show the connections between Usenet systems and published them on the net. Here is one of my first:

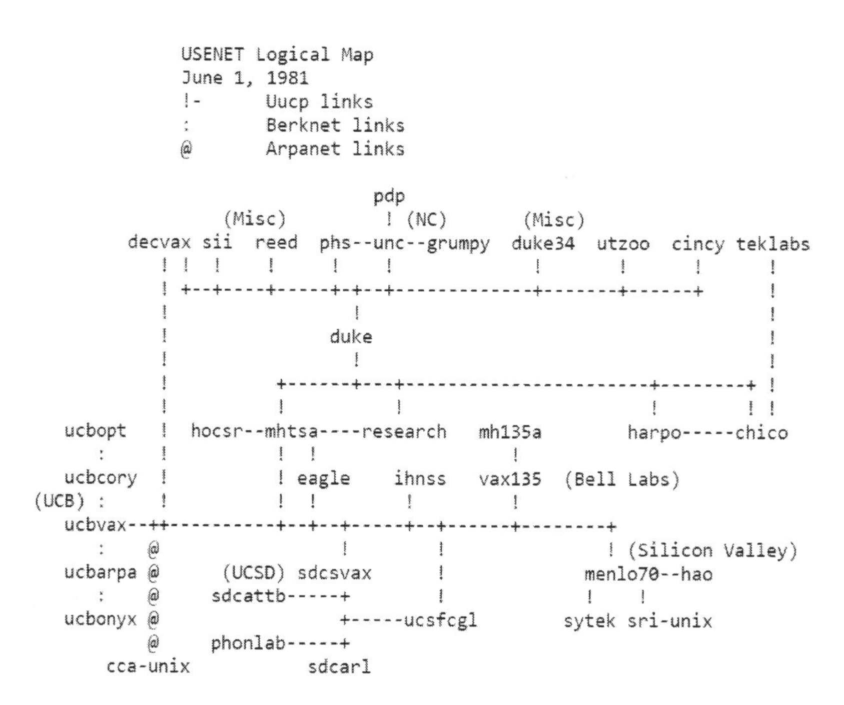

These maps turned out to be more important for email. The ARPANET (Advanced Research Projects Agency Network) used standard user@system addresses, and UNIX used system!user. If there wasn't a direct connection, the user had to give their message directions, typing system!system!user, sometimes using three or more system names. UNIX email addresses depended on the sender's location.

A University of Cincinnati professor asked, "How can I send an email to the ARPANET? I want to send to John on the cca-unix computer."

“Use the map to route it to Berkeley’s gateway, ucbvax. From cincy, go through decvax to ucbvax. Add the ARPANET address to the end. So you’d type decvax!ucbvax!john@cca-unix.”

“How does he get an email to me?”

“He’ll send it to decvax!cincy!bob@Berkeley.”

One of the best things about UNIX was its simple design. Files were generally flat text, easily edited with vi. To email a file, you had to type a command to insert a file into your message, similar to how we use copy/paste today. The recipient saved the message to a file and trimmed the extra text with vi.

Good things don’t last forever. No longer in its infancy, UNIX became more complex. People wrote programs using binary files, which couldn’t be pasted and extracted with a text editor. All the email software systems depended on email message flat files.

Working on my doctoral dissertation, I emailed other researchers and we exchanged copies of our work. A bundle of files, like a zip file, was binary and not easily emailed. I hated the hassle of sending a mag tape by postal mail.

To solve this problem, I devised two little software programs I called “uuencode” “and “uudecode.” Uuencode turned a binary file into a text file by turning three binary bytes into four printable characters, making it about 30 percent larger and easily emailed. The recipient sent the email message to uudecode, which recreated the original file. I added them to the Berkeley Software Distribution (BSD) system and went on with my life. I didn’t realize I had invented the email attachment for those binaries.

Uuencode became the standard method email systems used to send binary files. Around 1985, a popular personal computer email program called “cc: Mail” offered a paperclip button to attach a file in uuencode format. Microsoft later added the same feature to their MS Mail system. In 1992, Nathanial Borenstein cocreated a superior email encoding system called MIME, short for Multipurpose Internet Mail Extensions, which became the Internet standard. In 2017, Borenstein was interviewed about his invention of the email attachment twenty-five years earlier. The media doesn’t always get it right.

My PhD dissertation consisted of a coding editor able to work with several computer programming languages. I called it "BABEL: A Better Editing Language." Recursive acronyms were all the rage. A PhD dissertation required original research that would lead to a new discovery. While editing with text editor commands, my idea, BABEL, looked at your code and caught errors as you edited. Today, tools like Microsoft Visual Studio and Eclipse use these techniques, similar to how Microsoft Word catches spelling and grammar errors.

My BABEL software worked. It took about two minutes for each editing command, far too slow. Research doesn't have to yield a useful tool right away; it can provide something the next researcher can build on.

As I made progress with BABEL, I watched for available tech jobs. Start-up companies in Silicon Valley bloomed and thrived. Needing trained workers, they recruited grad students from Berkeley, Stanford, and other top universities. Students left for jobs before finishing their degrees. Oftentimes, once they tasted real jobs with actual salaries, there would be no going back. Many of these companies courted me. When they couldn't hire me outright, they paid me as a consultant to get vi working on their system. I could make hundreds of dollars for a day or two of work and then go back to school. The evidence was clear; I would never get my degree following in the footsteps of those who left. I resolved to finish, and then start a job. Plus, I would need a PhD if I chose academia.

I interviewed with Bell Labs, Microsoft, Tektronix, and faculty positions at Purdue and Ohio State. I felt gratified to receive their offers. After discussing it with Karen, we chose Bell Labs in Columbus, Ohio, because it was an exciting place to do UNIX work, and it was near her family in Youngstown. I knew it would be awesome to work alongside the super-geniuses within Bell Labs. I felt eager to start. My job offer was contingent on my completing my PhD, which pleased me, nixing any temptation to leave early.

* * *

In June 1981, my research professor presented me with my official PhD hood. My diploma would have to wait. A few of the faculty on my committee had minor concerns about my dissertation. It took another month to finish and get signatures from everybody.

Our apartment lease ended. Karen left with the moving van loaded with all our belongings. My friends, Kirk and Eric, offered their couch and let me stay with them for a few weeks while I finished. First, Kirk came out to me that they were a couple, a detail I hadn't noticed, in case I felt "weirded out." They were great guys and never home. We were all workaholics.

Wearing the women's clothing I had hidden in their apartment didn't feel right while they hosted me. I longed to get out in the sunlight. One morning after they had left for work, I felt compelled to give it a try. I put on my denim skirt and went for a walk. I stepped out and wandered around downtown Berkeley. I wore a yellow polo shirt, short denim skirt, and Birkenstocks. My beard, flat chest, and hairy legs were on full display.

I'd longed to feel happy and free, but fear of being spotted and ridiculed swept away the pleasure. A car passed. I cringed, hoping they wouldn't see me. *I can't chicken out now*, I thought.

A young man walked toward me on the sidewalk. My stomach tightened. *I have to pass right by him. Ugh. I don't want him to notice me.* His eyes remained ahead as we passed. The tightness moved to my shoulders, and I hunched down a bit. I tried to be invisible as I completed a circuit around the block. Each passing car brought a fresh wave of fear and each driver ignored me. In Berkeley, nobody cared.

Entering the apartment, I shuddered in relief. I felt awful. Being a man in a skirt out in public was not the way to feel happy and free. I changed into jeans and headed for school.

7
Married Life

1981

Bell Labs' parent company, American Telephone and Telegraph (AT&T), was a huge monopoly known as the Bell System. Founded by Alexander Graham Bell, AT&T employed over a million workers, and provided local and long distance telephone service. Its factory unit, Western Electric, built all the special equipment it needed. Bell Labs was its R&D subsidiary, engineering new telephone systems and specialized computers to run them, and conducting world-class research. UNIX was one of Bell Labs' research gems.

A huge Western Electric factory spread out over the equivalent of seventeen football fields comprised Bell's Columbus Works. The grounds were expansive with enormous parking lots on the east and west sides, smaller landscaped visitor lots in front, and a large area in back with softball fields. Unionized factory workers were everywhere. Their relaxed pace seemed more about taking breaks than the main purpose of the factory: building the number five crossbar telephone switch. A modern office annex housed Bell Labs workers.

Karen arrived in Columbus and found an apartment complex intended for Bell System workers with aptly named telephone-themed streets. From Belltown Boulevard you could turn onto Dial Drive or Directory Drive. Our street, Local Lane, referred to phone calls that didn't cost extra like it did for long distance. For the times, I thought they were clever. Our two-bedroom apartment had a closet for a washer-dryer hookup—a notable improvement from student housing. I didn't have to fight for parking, and best of all, I could walk across the street to work.

Karen looked for a job as a probation officer and discovered there were no jobs in her field due to government cutbacks. She took a job as an administrative assistant. I worked on-site during the day and stayed up late working from home. Running the Usenet and email networks had become my hobby at work and at home.

My need to cross-dress did not go away. Every beautiful day when I saw a woman in a summer dress, I heard the siren song of envy. Most men would want to *have* her; I wanted to *be* her. I kept a small stash of clothing. I felt soothed when wearing them in private after Karen had gone to bed, and at the same time, felt it wasn't healthy to continue hiding it from her.

One day I made a joke out of it. I found a purple print dress she never wore. I rifled through her underwear drawer and pulled out a bra and panties. Barefoot, hairy-legged, and with socks in the bra, I came out from the bedroom in her clothes.

"So, are we ready to go?"

Karen was not amused. "How dare you steal my clothes? Take those off."

Her tone of voice left nothing to misinterpret. I retreated into the bedroom and put everything back. We didn't discuss it anymore that day.

A few days later, she commented on my outfit.

"Was that a real thing for you?" she asked. "I mean, you had something stuffed in my bra."

This time she didn't sound harsh, merely curious. "Yes, it's real for me. I've been wearing women's clothes for a couple of years now."

"Why? What do you want to do with this?"

"What I'd really love is for you to be a part of it. Maybe we could go out to dinner with me dressed that way."

"Like that's ever gonna happen," she said. "Look, this is unacceptable. You need to find a counselor. You have to get cured."

I had built up energy behind my desire to be honest and share this part of my life. She stomped on my hopes, leaving me crushed with no outlet I knew of to make things better. I vowed to see someone. For the umpteenth time, I purged all my girl clothes.

The yellow pages led me to the Open Door Clinic near the Ohio State campus. In my first session, I spilled my feelings to a young lady assigned to be my counselor. She listened with her full attention and said little. When I arrived a week later for session two, I was directed to a male counselor's office. He explained, "She wasn't a good fit. I'll be working with you now."

I felt my face grow warm. She must not have been able to handle my eccentricity and asked off the case. I was sure something had to be seriously wrong with me. I loved Karen and wanted us to be happy together. I had no choice but to proceed.

"What do you want to accomplish?" he asked.

"I want to get rid of my urge to cross-dress. That's the only way to save my marriage."

"Okay, let's work on that. Do you want to be with a man?"

"God, no. I'm not gay. I don't have any interest in men. I'm very attracted to my wife."

This therapist had long hair, average-looking slacks and shirt, and I assumed he was straight. He appeared comfortable speaking with me. Over the next several weeks, he treated my issue like an addiction.

"When are you tempted to wear women's clothes?"

"When I'm home alone, or if Karen's asleep and I'm up late working."

"How do you feel then?"

"There's a temptation, and I can't resist it. It feels harmless."

"Is it harmless now?"

"No. If I don't stop, I'm afraid Karen will leave me."

"Where can you find the willpower to resist?"

"My marriage is important to me. Way more important than cross-dressing."

After several sessions and much soul-baring, I convinced myself of my inner willpower to resist. When the old thoughts crept in, I only had to remind myself how important Karen was to me.

Gay people have been subjected to similar counseling dubbed "conversion therapy" or "ex-gay ministry," often based on religion. Young men and women are trained to believe that being gay is a sin, and they must use their faith to "pray away the gay." This approach doesn't work for gay people and has been widely discredited. My therapy wasn't based on religion, as neither Karen nor I were religious. However, it suppressed my yearnings for a few years. I've since learned, like gay conversion counseling, transgender conversion therapy doesn't work in the long term.

My need came back about four years later. I am who I am, and no amount of therapy can change my true nature.

* * *

By November 1982, Karen and I had acquired the trappings of middle-class suburban life. We sold our rickety beater student car and treated ourselves to a new Honda Accord. The old vehicle wouldn't do with Karen expecting. We also decided it was time to buy a house. We saved up the required 3 percent down payment for an FHA mortgage and bought a three-bedroom ranch house in a starter neighborhood. Our cul-de-sac location made it safer to raise a child and quieter for us.

Our master bedroom was in the front of the house. We set up one of the back bedrooms for the baby, bought a used desk, and turned the other back bedroom into my home office. I learned to hang drapes and mow the grass.

Karen went through a long and difficult labor with Matt. The first is often the hardest. After twenty hours, she was close to being fully dilated. After midnight, the fetal alarm sounded. Dr. Lucas rushed in and discovered the cord was wrapped around our son's neck.

"We need to do an emergency C-section," she said.

I scrubbed for the OR and they let me hold Matt as soon as he was born. I was overcome with joy holding my living, breathing child.

Matt was born with "wet lung," a common condition for C-section babies. In this case, the baby doesn't get squeezed coming out of the birth canal, which would clear the lung fluid, and instead, stays in the lungs. My heart felt heavy listening to him cry for three days in the NICU, even though I knew it was necessary to improve his breathing. I held vigil by his incubator, wishing I could do something to help him.

In time, he became healthy and we were thrilled to bring him home, prepared for a great life. We had the house, the job, the marriage. Karen stayed home with Matt. We felt close to her family, only a few hours' drive away. It seemed perfect.

Other dads looked at me funny when I mentioned I enjoyed changing diapers. I meant it. Diaper changes were uninterrupted one-on-one time together and Matt was my world. After I got his diaper changed, I'd take the quiet time to teach him something: letters, numbers, or colors. It was great fun and we both loved it. He learned quickly.

Matt and I loved to play together as I helped him with his physical development. I could see it was great fun for him to try to stand up with my help. After a few months, he could support his weight, but he lacked balance. I'd hold my fingers out for him to grab, and he'd bounce around on his legs with both hands grasping my index fingers. At six months, he was crawling and also balancing on his legs for a few seconds. On Memorial Day, at six months and nineteen days, he took his first steps. Karen and I took him out to the backyard and let him wobble back and forth between us. After a couple of hours of this, he toddled along under his own power. The next day, I went back to work, while she was unprepared to deal with a walking baby. She complained to her relatives about him running around the house and crashing into things. Karen never let me forget it.

A few months later, I found a book called *Teach Your Baby to Read* and took it to heart. The author's idea was to use flash cards and happy times to show the baby what important words like "Mommy" and "Daddy" looked like. I created several dozen huge word cards with five-inch-tall letters, hand-colored with red and black markers on poster board. I used those diaper-changing moments for quick reading lessons. I changed his diaper, set him up on the table, and showed him a few cards.

"This says: 'Daddy,' " I proclaimed in an excited voice. "This says: 'Mommy.' This says: 'eye.' This says: 'foot.' This says: 'belly.' Yay!"

We shared a joyful time and the short duration left him wanting more. We would hug and go back to whatever we were doing. Every few days, I'd rotate in a new word and take out an old one, as recommended by the book.

Matt soaked up reading. By the time he was twenty-two months old, he could read a short book using only words on the cards. We celebrated and then…what to do next? It took too much work on my part to make the cards. We read to him from children's books and his vocabulary soared.

A related book had us teach him early math by putting red dots on poster board and telling him, "This is one. This is two." Rotating in cards with up to ninety-nine dots was easy. Contrary to the book's claims, after about twenty, neither of us had any idea how many dots were on the card. Matt grew up to be good at reading and math, and our interaction helped cement a life-long bond.

Our son, Adam, joined us in 1985. Dr. Lucas scheduled a C-section, standard practice at that time since Matt had been born that way. We held his birthday party at 8:00 a.m. on June 10th, a blessed celebration. Our traditional family had come together with all the challenges and joys. Years went by before Karen and I discovered a unique connection we shared with the doctor.

Adam had a rougher first year than Matt. Karen tended to him during the day when I was at work. I spent many nights with him, rocking him to comfort his colicky belly pain. I loved taking my turn and did so for hours, enjoying the closeness as I held him in the rocker. Karen could calm him better and she often joked her bustline was key to rocking a baby. "I've got it up front," she said. I wished I had boobs to rock him. As I rocked, I imagined having an ample bust to cuddle him. I thought about getting a bra and stuffing it, but I didn't dare.

I resolved to use the flashcards with Adam since they'd been a success with Matt. By 1985, computer technology had advanced and we had a PC in the house. Instead of handmade flashcards, I wrote a program to draw the flashcards on the screen using bright red letters for the first few words and smaller black text.

My program, Flash!, had a few other features to make it fun for the kids. They would press keys and the big letters would show up on the screen. Each keystroke made a different beep and made typing sound musical. The kids would pound on the keyboard and laugh at the gibberish they created.

I hoped to market my program and needed photos. I figured Matt, who was three, could help out.

"Matt, can you do me a favor? Sit here in front of the computer. See how Flash! says 'eye'? Point to your eye."

He pointed and looked at me.

"That's good. Keep pointing and look at the word."

He turned his head to the computer. I snapped some pictures before he moved.

"That was great, son. Thank you."

Matt moved off and six-month-old Adam crawled up to the keyboard.

Wham! Wham! Adam's wrist banged on the keyboard. Beeps and clicks later, he'd replaced the "eye" text with gibberish.

"Are you having fun, Adam?"

Distracted, he turned toward me and began to crawl. Snap! I took his picture. His expression, as if he mouthed, "Eeeeg," meaning "I'm having a terrible day," matched the computer screen. I love that photo.

I learned wonderful things from teaching my sons to read early. I learned the place we discarded our trash at Wendy's was called: "Thanks." The seatbelt latches in the back of the car had names too.

The ones on the sides were called: "Press," and the one in the middle was called: "Center." And I learned the letter "K" is pronounced "K-Mart."

* * *

Once she turned thirty, Karen grew tired of staying at home with our two toddlers and yearned for adult company. She didn't see a career path in criminal justice in Ohio, and she didn't want to work as a secretary. In 1987, medicine drew her interest and she enrolled in a class to become an emergency medical technician.

I was happy to see her find a fulfilling alternative and the money wouldn't hurt. We were always broke. Even though I had a good income, we maxed out our credit cards. Our philosophy was, "If we need it, we charge it," without regard to whether we could afford it. Not knowing any better, we accepted this way of life. We needed a second income, and Karen's training could lead there.

Once she began her studies, I felt a seismic shift in our marriage. Until then, we had expressed a steady stream of "I love you" sentiments. Weeks later, it felt like all the energy had been sucked out of our relationship. Karen studied for her EMT with a study buddy she met in class, a twenty-one-year-old woman with a butch haircut named Andi, who lived nearby with her parents. Karen and Andi became inseparable. Not only did they study together; they hung out and ate together.

"I'm going over to Andi's to study. Can you take care of the boys?"

"Sure. I love you."

"I'll be back by eleven."

My stomach panged. This was getting old. It seemed like Karen spent more time and energy with Andi than with me. I felt lousy, perhaps even jealous. I missed my loving wife.

My family was on the West Coast, and I had grown close to Karen's family. Her parents had moved to Columbus and dropped in often. I especially liked her father. I shared my lament.

"They're just good friends," he responded. "You should be more supportive of her studies."

That wasn't what I wanted to hear. I had encouraged her by giving her space for her studies and taking care of the boys in the evenings. This arrangement wasn't working for me. I was lonely, almost as if I were single again.

My feelings of aloneness rekindled my need to cross-dress. After years of drought in that regard, I bought a nylon slip and a pair of pantyhose. I couldn't let Karen see them. I put them in the corner of the closet in my home office, and covered them with ordinary items she wouldn't use, knowing she wouldn't go in there. I longed for more clothes. I wanted to experience what it felt like to dress as a woman out and about in the world. I had shaved off my beard from my grad student days, leaving a mustache.

* * *

That April, in the middle of my funk about my dissolving marriage, my department held a team-building exercise in a bar and grill to discuss communication skills. Beth, one of my coworkers, commented to the entire department, "What I can say in the workplace is different than what I can say in bars."

I hadn't noticed Beth and now she had my full attention. I imagined a conversation with her in a bar, one unsuitable for the workplace. I was more of a stay-home-with-the-kids person than a barfly, and that made my daydream seem exotic. I thought she was pretty with her long wavy red hair and a big smile, plus she rocked an autumn leaf print A-line dress. She seemed fun and I liked the way her mind worked. I considered my marriage vows and didn't act on my feelings. I wasn't a cheater, and had never been tempted. This was a new experience for me.

That May, I stopped into a discount shoe store and was delighted to discover their women's shoes went up to size 13. Twelves were too tight. I picked up a $10 pair of black high-heeled pumps. At K-Mart, I selected an inexpensive wig with medium-length curly brown hair I could stuff into my hiding place without worrying about it being messed up. Then I saw something fabulous—the cutest denim miniskirt. I had to have it. My collection had grown while my opportunities to wear them had not. When Karen wasn't home and I watched the boys, I longed to try on my new clothes.

My chance came a week later. As I arrived home from work on a Tuesday evening, I saw Karen with her keys. “I’m going over to Andi’s to study and I’m going to stay overnight. There are leftovers in the fridge. I’ll be back home before you leave for work in the morning.”

I heated up dinner for myself and the boys, went through their bedtime routine, and put them to bed. The whole evening, my thoughts kept drifting to my new wardrobe. Once the boys were asleep, I crept into my office and pulled out my stash. I donned pantyhose, a slip, my new skirt, and heels. I didn’t have a women’s top yet, so I pulled on a polo shirt. It wasn’t elegant, but it would do. Picking up my crowning glory, I carried the wig into the hall bathroom to finish up in front of the mirror. I shifted it around, trying to figure out which was the front and then adjusted it in place. I admired my new look. I hadn’t worn a wig since I was a kid. I liked having long hair. I liked the skirt. My mustache and beard shadow startled me in a new way, as did my hairy flat chest. Two up, two down, it was a start.

I jumped at a flash of light as Karen’s headlights turned into the driveway.

8

Facing the Music

June 1987

I returned home from my Phoenix conference and Karen focused on my upper lip. She frowned. "What happened to your mustache?"

"I shaved it off."

"Did you wear women's clothes in Phoenix?"

"Mmm hmm." I wouldn't lie and the truth did me no favors.

Soon Karen's family started giving me dirty looks as if my respectability stank like rotting garbage. *They all know*, I thought. I felt like crawling into a corner where I could die from embarrassment in private. I wondered what my punishment would be. Another purge? More therapy? Within a few days, Karen made her decision.

"You're a transvestite." Her words meant to shame me. "I want a divorce."

The atmosphere in the house took on a decided chill and I felt at fault. I believed there was something wrong about me. Karen named the horrible affliction. Maybe I was a sex addict or who knows what else?

Karen demanded I move out of our master bedroom. On Father's Day, I brought up a spare twin bed from the basement. I crowded it into my office and moved in my clothes. My home office was now my home, period, with my bed and large L-shaped wooden desk taking up the entire room. It was official. I was vermin.

"I've hired a lawyer. You should get one," she said. "You need to make plans to move out of the house. You can see the boys any time you like."

"Do you think we should have joint custody?"

Karen laughed. "No. I'm their mother. I'll have custody."

I was so low at that point I believed her. Speechless, I walked away with my head hung low.

I found an apartment and put down a deposit for a planned move the first of August. The lawyer could wait.

* * *

One day in late June, I invited Beth to lunch at the Bell Labs cafeteria. Beth studied computer systems for ease of use, a human factors specialist. This was a science, a field of experimental psychology. She'd earned her master's degree from Ohio State and was working on a doctorate. Maybe it was her background that put me at ease when we talked. I took a risk she'd be open to being a confidant as well. I wiped my sweaty palms across my slacks beneath the table where we lunched and leapt into the abyss.

"Karen wants a divorce because sometimes I wear women's clothes."

"Why does she have a problem with that?"

"She says it's unacceptable."

"Well, I don't see anything wrong with it."

Wow. I'd never experienced such nonchalance over my supposedly disgusting behavior. I was speechless.

"What kind of clothes do you have?" She spoke as if cross-dressing were the most normal thing in the world.

I panicked. I had once again purged my female wardrobe and the last thing I needed was to start up again. In the divorce, Karen would have a field day with it. For my safety, I resolved to resist the urge.

"Nothing. That is, I don't have any now. I threw them all away in Phoenix. I think it's better now if I don't."

"Okay, if that makes you more comfortable."

Beth listened, and my words spilled out: my marital troubles, the divorce action, the threat of losing the boys; all of it scared the hell out of me. I became consumed with the enormity. She couldn't be my therapist, she pointed out, as that wasn't her field of psychology. She suggested I see a licensed therapist. I'm sure she saw a conflict of interest. We were connecting, at least as friends, possibly more.

I took her advice. I found a therapist and opened up, knowing everything I said would be held in confidence. I dumped everything on him. I recited my history of wearing women's clothes and how Karen refused to allow it. I told him about my day in Phoenix and how I had to contend with a divorce. I was a wreck.

He didn't judge me or my cross-dressing. We discussed my anxiety and stress about cross-dressing, and how it led to the upcoming divorce. He explained how exercise could help by releasing dopamine, and with his encouragement, I tried jogging. I hated jogging, and did it anyway. It started me on a path toward greater health. This time, I found joy, if not in the exercise itself, in the benefits I received and from eating healthy foods. I developed good habits I carried forward, because my health became important to me.

My therapist also taught me how to relax. He made me a coaching audiotape with instructions on how to go through the muscles in my body, one by one, consciously relaxing them. It was like meditation, hypnosis, or prayer.

* * *

When Karen and Andi were together, they laughed like teenagers high on each other's company. They spent inordinate amounts of time together to the exclusion of all else. They often went into the master bedroom, now Karen's room. I saw the bedroom door shut and heard happy, low voices escape into the hallway. Their visits went on into the night. I suspected there was more going on between them than friendship. I followed my hunch and started listening in on their phone calls from my office extension phone. I was shocked by what I heard. My worst fears were confirmed—I'd lost my wife to Andi.

To cope, I began a daily journal and scribbled down snippets of what I'd heard.

July 16, 1987. A conversation among friends takes a sudden left turn.

Karen: *"I'm getting out this letter someone special wrote me, so I can read it again."*

Andi: *"I never get letters like that."*

Karen: *"You will now."*

(pause)

Andi: *"I love you."*
Karen: *"I love you too."*

I heard them express their love, a secret not meant for my ears. I didn't know what to make of my conflicted feelings. On the one hand, I wanted my loving wife back in my arms. We had a marriage and family, borne of our shared commitment. I didn't want to give up on those or her. I felt an incomparable hurt. On the other hand, how could we continue on when she had gone through this sea change? I didn't want to be with Karen if she had lost her attraction to me. Her new love was ten years younger with scant life experience, no job, and average looks, all of which made it hard for me to understand Andi's appeal.

My intuition about them was right. As incomprehensible as it seemed to me, I couldn't imagine anyone else buying it either. I needed proof. My confusion took a back seat. I had a task ahead.

I hightailed it to RadioShack, where I picked up a gadget to record phone calls and a cassette recorder. I set the contraption up in my closet. It automatically recorded calls on our home phone, a wired landline. Every few days, I put a new cassette tape in the recorder and took the old tape, full of evidence, to my office at work. If they found my device, I'd still have proof.

I phoned my dad in California. He and Betty were in a committed relationship and he had moved into her house. When I related the story, he asked me an unexpected question. "Do you want her back?"

His words woke me up. My thoughts fired: *Did I? I always thought I did. Now things are different.* The concept grabbed me by the scruff of my neck and shook. "No, I guess I don't."

Until then, I had believed the impending divorce was all my fault. My old patterns of behavior based on past experience told me I was the problem, and therefore, custody of the boys would go to Karen. The whole situation dripped with hypocrisy. My supposedly strait-laced wife, who could not deal with the scandal of a husband with unusual taste in clothing, was secretly lesbian. She'd made me the bad guy for being trans, while she and her lover canoodled and then some behind my back.

I considered that Karen wanted me gone so she could be with Andi. Maybe I had been set up the day she had returned home to pick up study materials and then stormed off empty-handed. I didn't know her mind; I knew mine. I loved my sons and I didn't want to give them up. I would fight for custody. From a strategic point of view, the playing field leveled off.

I didn't want Karen back, and being in my own apartment soon meant I would be single again. I saw Beth in a new light. I wanted to date her. We had lunch and I caught her up on the latest gossip. After her initial shock, she was sympathetic.

"That's terrible. She has no idea how lucky she is to have you. I don't see anything wrong with cross-dressing. It's just clothes."

Flirting was not my forte, yet somehow, I picked up a vibe. Then she made the first move.

"There's a DJ who comes to Max & Erma's on Thursdays for happy hour. He takes requests, says amusing things, and has contests. I go there all the time. Do you want to go? It's a lot of fun."

Yikes! This was tempting. Interested, yes. Ready?

"Can I take a rain check? I move out in a couple of weeks. I'd be more comfortable if I waited before getting into a relationship."

"Okay, I respect you for that."

I could see the disappointment in her eyes as a reflection of my own. We were in no hurry. We stayed friends and looked forward to August when I would live outside the marital home.

* * *

I got serious about hiring a lawyer. I found Jeff in the yellow pages. Not knowing him, I worried he would be too grossed out by my cross-dressing to represent me. We met and he gestured toward a stuffed chair.

"Have a seat and tell me what's going on."

"My wife wants a divorce and custody of our two sons. She says it's because I'm a crossdresser. Well, I found out she's in a lesbian relationship."

Jeff raised his brows as I laid it all out. It was a lot to take in, and not a typical divorce case. Other than a surprised look, I tried to discern his reaction.

"Are you comfortable representing me?"

He hesitated, searching for the right words. "Let me put it this way. I'd room with you." That set me at ease. Then he told me what I was up against. "As the law stands right now in Ohio, the courts can only award full custody to one parent. Joint custody is allowed if both parents agree to it. This is like a basketball game. The score might be 102 to 101, but no matter how close it is, only one side can win."

I wasn't much of a basketball fan, but I got the message. It was all about winning. I didn't like that choice. My sons were important to me. I wanted what I felt was best for them. The only way they wouldn't be taken away from me was to win full custody.

"How old are your kids?"

"Matt is four. Adam is two."

"Franklin county judges tend to support the 'tender years doctrine,' which says small children should be raised by their mother. Karen's attorney has no doubt assured her she'll have no trouble winning full custody. She'll tell her she'll get the house, and you'll pay for it."

I had no doubt Karen would approve of that scenario. Anything less than full custody would be devastating to her and an embarrassment to her family.

Jeff was optimistic. Knowledge of Karen's relationship with Andi would obliterate her edge. They had to stay in the closet; it was far too risky to come out.

"I think you have a good chance to win full custody. The judge will see your issue, he'll see her issue, and it will come down to who he thinks is the better parent."

Then he gave me some critical advice. "Whatever you do, don't move out. Whoever moves out, loses. Stay in the house and tough it out."

"There's a woman I'd like to ask out. Is it okay if I date?"

"It's no problem. You've got to live."

I paid his retainer and canceled my plan to move.

* * *

August arrived, and given the circumstances, Beth and I decided it was okay to start dating. I joined her at Max & Erma's and we had a great time.

Beth didn't mind if I occasionally cross-dressed. I was still in my purge and determined through sheer willpower to look and act like a man. I felt I had to be good if I stood a chance in the divorce. I stuffed it all inside, ignoring the occasional urge. Beth dressed up for me in skirts, dresses, and heels, which seemed to scratch my itch.

Beth and I planned a proper date. I put on a suit and tie, and took her out to dinner. We hit it off and love blossomed. I heard Karen's version on the phone recording I listened to later that night as she spoke to her father.

"He left here all dressed up."

"Which way?"

They both had a good laugh. I was furious at the insult, and kept it to myself.

9

Living in a Powder Keg

September 1987

Karen and I settled into an uncomfortable détente in our house. Her family was there more than they were away, as was Andi. Karen's mother was staying with us temporarily, sleeping on a spare bed in the basement.

One morning, I had an ominous feeling while I took a shower, like my room was vulnerable. Sure enough, when I dried off and checked my room, items were missing. Recorded tapes meant for my office had vanished from my briefcase. The recording equipment was gone. So were my remaining blank tapes and a RadioShack bag with my receipts. Now they knew I'd been recording their calls. I had plenty more evidence at my office. Nobody said anything to my face. It sure didn't help the oppressive atmosphere in the house.

I'd studied the Electronic Communication Privacy Act of 1986. Written by lawyers, the technical language read like bad computer code. As an example, it said it was okay for parents to listen to their teenagers on an extension phone. I interpreted that to mean it was okay to record Karen's calls. The bug was essentially an extension phone. I ran my theory by Jeff.

"No, I don't read it that way. I don't think we can use these tapes as evidence in court. We can use them to impeach testimony. We ask her a question. If she lies, we play her the tape, off the record. Then we ask her again. If she lies again, it's perjury."

I wasn't sure what to make of it. In any case, I had to keep recording. I made another trip to RadioShack, and did a better job of hiding the equipment.

A letter from the court arrived in the mail, awarding temporary custody of the boys to Karen. Until permanent custody was decided in the final divorce trial, I had them every other weekend and one night a week. It served to define who was responsible for them. This was a silly concept with both of us living in the house. I was also ordered to pay her child support, which would be withheld from my paycheck.

Ugh! The order felt like a punch in the gut. Jeff assured me it's typical for the mother to get temporary custody and we should appeal it. Other fathers found that whoever was awarded temporary custody, usually got permanent custody. I felt discouraged.

A hearing to appeal temporary custody was scheduled for October, and the final divorce trial was set for late January. Jeff prepared me for bad luck: the presiding judge was lazy and often took the easiest course. He also liked to get out of court as early as possible in the mornings and spend the afternoon at his favorite strip club. *Great.*

At the temporary custody hearing, Karen's family stood in front of the judge's bench, holding paper bags full of my telephone recording equipment, including my newest purchase. Karen's lawyer requested an order for me to vacate the house, or in other words, kick me out. The judge said he'd take it under advisement and issue an order later.

In the interim, I tried to go on living my life with a minimum of distraction. I made it a point to spend as much time with the boys as possible. Beth and I grew more serious.

In November, for my birthday, I asked Beth to teach me how to cook my favorite dish—fried chicken. She found a Betty Crocker cookbook and showed me how to follow the recipe. We treated the boys to a delicious chicken dinner that night.

* * *

Friday, December 4th, was the coldest day of 1987. Jeff called me at work.

"I received the judge's decision today." I felt unnerved by his subdued voice. "I'm afraid I have bad news." I braced myself as he summarized it. "Temporary custody to mother. Order to vacate is granted. I'm afraid this means you'll have to move out."

Damn. This was the worst possible news. My heart ached and my throat closed. "How long do I have?" I managed to ask.

"I don't know. Two weeks would be reasonable."

"I guess I need to look for an apartment. This is my weekend with the boys, so it will have to be next week."

"I'm sorry, man."

His remark hit the floor along with my hopes for my family's future. After work, I went to the house. It was four degrees outside. My key wouldn't turn in the knob.

Karen opened the door. She blocked my way and taunted me with a haughty expression. "You don't live here anymore."

Before I could comprehended what was happening, Karen and Andi started handing over paper bags filled with my belongings. I was too stunned to protest. I took as much as I could fit into my car. As I pulled out of the driveway, I saw Andi's car in the garage, parked in my space. Karen's plan came into focus. Andi would replace me and I would foot the bill.

I found myself cold, alone, and homeless. Thank God for Beth. Not having access to a phone, I showed up on her doorstep. She invited me in, and we commiserated about my bad fortune.

That weekend I found a furnished apartment. The boys noticed the address, 104, nailed next to the front door. They began to refer to my apartment as "104" and the house where Karen and Andi now lived as "2843." I went along. It sounded better than "Daddy's apartment."

* * *

Jeff suggested bringing in expert testimony about who made a better parent. Both lawyers agreed to hire a group called the Custody Evaluation Team. Karen and I would see each of them separately and with the boys, and then they would make their recommendation. The team consisted of the leader, Dick Fetter, a social worker; Jerome Meers, a psychologist; and James Christopher, a psychiatrist. Between them, they had more letters after their names than I'd ever seen. Jeff called them a "blue-ribbon panel."

I met with Fetter in November. He sat at his desktop computer, speed typing with two fingers. It was hard to imagine how he could be listening to me and typing so much. Something about him rubbed me the wrong way.

"Tell me what this case is about?"

"I like women's clothes. My wife is a lesbian."

He didn't react to this news and kept typing. "Uh-huh."

"I think she could handle the gayness a lot better than she does. She says they're just friends, but she puts her girlfriend ahead of the boys."

Clickity, clackity. "Go on."

"I recorded their phone calls. I have the whole thing on tape."

He perked up. "You have tapes?"

After I offered to make him a combined tape of all the highlights from her phone calls, he got back to basics. "Tell me about your mother."

Oh, crap.

I had a better impression of Dr. Meers. The fish tank in his office contained a huge puffer fish. It seemed curious about my presence and wanted to interact. The receptionist said the fish was named ET, because his eyes resembled the movie alien. Like his office environment, Meers seemed warm and friendly.

"My role is to administer psychological tests." He showed me Rorschach inkblots, and then had me fill out the Minnesota Multiphasic Personality Inventory (MMPI) test. "The MMPI is the standardized psychometric test for adults, checking for everything from masculinity to paranoia," he explained.

As I completed the test in the waiting room, I noticed several questions asking if I agreed with statements about people plotting against me. One question simply said, "I hear voices." I chuckled as I heard the office receptionist chatting with another client, but I checked "no" on the paper.

Meers shared the results when they came in. "You're in the normal range on most of these scales. On the M/F scale, you're in the middle of the scale between masculine and feminine. You're also *very* introverted."

Dr. Christopher had a different approach. "I want to see the boys with you and Beth, to see how you are as a family unit. I'll also interview Karen and Andi with them."

When the four of us came, most of his questions were directed at me, and Beth wound up distracting the boys from his rather personal questions about my sex life. After about an hour, he had Beth take the boys to the waiting room and interviewed me in depth. He never spoke directly to the boys.

* * *

In December, a friend from my group at work invited me to his church. Other than my wedding, I hadn't been to church since I was six. Karen's parents had their pastor baptize Matt and Adam in their house in Youngstown. I considered myself agnostic. I didn't know if there was a God or not, and I didn't think about it much.

I'd been baptized Lutheran as a baby, and attended a Lutheran kindergarten. Then we stopped going. My dad explained. "The pastor told us we had to give money to the church, ten percent of my income. There was no way we could afford it. I asked if we could work at the church instead. He said no, and that was the end of that."

I thought a visit to a church might help with my mood, what with the divorce slowly grinding my soul into dust. I accepted my friend's invitation and began to attend the Pataskala Church of the Nazarene.

I didn't remember anything about the Lutheran teachings to compare it with the conservative doctrine I heard there. The Nazarene *Manual* spelled out extra "thou shalt nots" that weren't in the Bible: no dancing, no drinking, no movies, and certainly no homosexuality. Though not mentioned, I figured they wouldn't take kindly to cross-dressing. I wasn't joining the church, I merely attended, which made the rules seem less onerous. The pastor was nice, and the church services seemed okay. I thought it would be good for the boys to be exposed to religion.

I felt soothed when I prayed. And pray I did, whenever I felt stressed or I wasn't sure what to do. I found myself having inner conversations with God. I would ask Him questions in my head. Often, I got answers.

Me: *Am I evil for wearing women's clothes?*

God: *It's fine. You're not hurting anybody.*

Me: *The pastor wants me to give money to the church. Should I?*

God: *Read Malachi.*

I found this passage in Malachi 3:10: "Bring the whole tithe into the storehouse...Test me in this and see if I will not throw open the floodgates of heaven and pour out so much blessing."

Me: *How much should I give?*

God: *Figure out how much you've gained in the year and give ten percent of that.*

Ten percent of the increase in my net worth wasn't much at the time and easy to accommodate. I tried it. Over the years, He's asked me to give more and more. He coached me to give, not only to my church, but also to charities where I could make the greatest difference. God rewarded me. The more I gave, the richer I became.

* * *

At Christmastime, the boys made ornaments at school. Matt adorned his blue and gold spray painted macaroni wreath with a sprinkling of red and green glitter, which he had pasted onto a small paper plate. In Sunday school, Adam made an angel of white felt with a cotton ball glued to gold paper wings. Their names and the year were written on the back. I hung these heartwarming mementos on my tiny Christmas tree, along with a smattering of store-bought generic ornaments. I treasured these handmade ornaments. They have brought me joy every Christmas, and today my tree overflows with special and sentimental ornaments.

On Christmas Day, the temporary order allowed me four hours with the boys. After we opened presents, Adam wasn't feeling well. I kissed his feverish forehead, gave him a Tylenol, and let him rest in bed. In the living room, Matt and I sat on the floor and played Candy Land, the boys' favorite board game.

"Daddy, why do you live at 104?" Matt asked.

"Mommy and I are playing another game. I call it the Divorce game."

"Who is winning?" he asked.

My answer used the familiar squares of the board game. "Mommy is ahead, up around the Lollypop, and Daddy is back around the Plum. I have a feeling I'll draw the Snowflake card soon and win." The player who drew the Snowflake jumped close to the finish and usually won the game.

Matt put his hand on mind. "Here, I'm giving you the Snowflake."

I felt so happy I started to cry. "What a special gift." I hugged him with all my love.

* * *

A week later, I went to Jeff's office to prepare for trial and anxious about the custody report. I sat in his waiting room. My heart pounded, I had a headache, and my nervous stomach did flip-flops. I lay on the waiting room couch and prayed. Soon I calmed down and the headache abated. After about five minutes, I opened my eyes and I felt okay. A few minutes later, Jeff led me into his conference room. He excused himself to take a phone call.

He had left a sheet of paper on the table, filled with scribbled notes. In big letters at the top, I read: "FATHER GETS FULL CUSTODY." I was incredibly relieved. I spent a moment thanking God.

Jeff returned and translated the cryptic notes. The team recommended full custody of the boys to me and no restrictions on visitation for Karen. They suggested that if the issues of cross-dressing or lesbianism were to come up with the boys, I could be more open, honest, and fair, so I should be the one to explain it to them.

The written report spelled everything out, detailing my cross-dressing and Karen's lesbian relationship. We were both fine parents. The decisive difference came down to my open and honest approach to my "non-dangerous peccadillo" whereas Karen's "statements to us were not honest." This report was evidence to be read by the trial judge.

The final divorce trial that would decide custody was postponed until April, and again to June. Matt, now five, took it the hardest and I was a wreck. Adam was too little to be affected as much. I did my best to assure them this wasn't their fault, that I loved them, and wanted them to live with me. For their sake, I tried to set a good example during the wait.

Our divorce trial began on a Thursday morning in late June. The case had been reassigned to a conservative retired judge who had stepped in to help clear a backlog. Both attorneys went into the judge's office for pretrial, leaving Karen and me to make small talk. I was amazed Karen wore a skirt because I hadn't seen her in one for years. I wore a suit and tie.

When they came back out, Jeff didn't look happy.

"The judge just now read the report," he explained. "He read the first paragraph, saw 'cross-dressing' and 'lesbian,' and his reaction was, 'Maybe we should refer this to Juvenile and take custody away from both of them. Are there any relatives in town that can take them?' " Jeff continued. "Both of us urged him to read the rest of the report. He calmed down, saying maybe joint custody was a good idea. He said the report was one piece of evidence, an important one. Karen's attorney would have to overcome it or show it's wrong."

It took a minute for my heart to start going again. "Can this judge give us a fair trial?" I asked.

"Sure, he'll be fine. I still think we'll win."

I wanted to know for sure. There was nothing to do but proceed with the trial.

I had painstakingly indexed the original tapes. I listed every juicy sound bite, date, time, who spoke, which tape, and where it was on the tape. I brought in my oversized boom box and a box of cassette tapes.

"I'll do the questioning," Jeff said. "You play the tape when I tell you."

After hours of boring testimony, we got to them. Karen was on the stand. Jeff cross-examined.

"You indicated you had a gay lover. Her name is Andrea. Is that correct?"

"I had a female lover. Her name is Andrea."

"Did you tell the custody evaluation team that the lesbian relationship was over?"

"I said I was not currently sexually involved with her."

I fumed beneath my starched collar. *The nerve*. Admitting to the relationship, but claiming it was over. Unbelievable.

"Do you remember telling Andi on July 23rd 'I love you'?"

"No, I do not."

"Would listening to the phone conversation help refresh your memory?"

"Objection," Karen's lawyer said.

"Your Honor, at this time I would like to play a tape recording of a conversation from July 23rd. I understand the court's position and I would like to proffer it for the court reporter."

"Okay," the judge said. "I'm going to step aside." He left the room.

Jeff looked at me. "Play the clip."

I pressed the button on my boom box. We all heard Karen's voice say "I love you," and Andi's "I love you too," response.

Jeff signaled for the judge to return and resumed his cross examination.

"Did you recognize the voice?" Jeff asked.

"I think it was my voice."

"Do you remember saying to Andi 'I love you' during that particular time?"

"No, I don't."

After three clips, I felt this tactic was getting old. "Jeff, you're not going to do this for every 'I love you,' are you?"

The judge got the message and Jeff moved on.

After three days of testimony, the attorneys wrapped up the case. The judge took it under advisement and left the courtroom.

I felt stunned, as if my body stopped. I had expected a decision at this point. Jeff told me the judge never ruled from the bench, not wanting to face an angry loser. He said the judge was going on vacation in a few weeks, and he hoped we'd have a decision issued by then. *Three weeks!* I was devastated and had more waiting ahead.

* * *

Jeff called that Friday. "Mark, this is Jeff. Are you sitting down?"

His voice was full of enthusiasm. This had to be the good news phone call. I sat down with the boys playing nearby.

"We won!"

At the top of my lungs, I yelled, "All right, Daddy got the Snowflake!"

I called the boys over to hug them. I gave Matt a strong hug and told him again, "Daddy got the Snowflake. You guys get to live with Daddy!"

I hugged them so hard they didn't know what to think. I couldn't remember the last time I'd been so excited. We celebrated with a delectable picnic lunch, eaten with a large measure of joy on the banks of a restful creek.

Three months later, Karen and Andi moved out of the house, and handed the keys over to me. What a supreme pleasure to be back home with the boys.

A year later, Jeff passed along some gossip. "Your case was the talk of the courthouse. The crossdresser against the lesbian."

"Did they at least learn something?"

"Oh, yeah. It was already established that you couldn't play the 'gay card' in court. Now you can't play the 'transgender card.' The court looks at who is the better parent, not whether they're gay or trans."

10
Finding Myself

January 1988

After my trip to Phoenix, I buried my feminine yearnings deep inside myself. The divorce, the boys, and Beth took priority. All this changed dramatically in January 1988.

"Beth, I need to tell you something," I said. "You know those feelings I told you I had about needing to cross-dress? They're starting to come back."

Beth didn't say a word. She walked into her bedroom and emerged with a manila envelope and handed it to me. "I saw a Phil Donohue TV show about crossdressers. I wrote to the address they gave for more information. I kept the envelope in case you might want it."

I was overcome by this loving act and by her tact in waiting until I was ready. She knew what to do, and she meant the world to me.

The envelope was from a national crossdressers group called the Society for the Second Self, or "Tri-Ess." The group described itself as a sorority with chapters in many cities. They welcomed heterosexual crossdressers and their partners, spouses, and families. They explicitly ruled out transsexuals and gay men. I identified as a crossdresser, so I qualified.

Their closest chapter was in Cleveland, a two-hour drive from Columbus. Going with the sorority theme, each chapter had a Greek letter name. The Cleveland chapter was called Alpha Omega, a biblical reference I appreciated because it told me there were Christians involved with the chapter.

I phoned Alpha Omega and spoke with Jane.

"I'm a crossdresser," Jane said, "and the outreach contact for the chapter. I live as a man, but sometimes I experience life as a woman.

Tri-Ess is a social group for heterosexual crossdressers." Jane interviewed me over the phone. "Groups like Tri-Ess attract gay and bisexual men looking for dates, and the group takes pains to keep those men away. Our group is a great place to meet friends; this is not a place to find a date." That had never occurred to me. Only heterosexual crossdressers and their female partners were welcome.

"Alpha Omega has monthly meetings in Cleveland. We are a safe space to wear women's clothing and socialize with other crossdressers. We'd like to encourage you to fully present as female. We can help you with that if you like.

"One of Tri-Ess's main purposes is to welcome the wives of crossdressers. Beth would be welcome to come with you to a meeting. Many crossdressers want their wives to be okay with them cross-dressing from time to time." That idea resonated with me. "Some wives are afraid their husbands could be transsexual, wanting to be female permanently, or gay, wanting to date men. Our rule accepting only heterosexual crossdressers is meant to help wives be more comfortable."

Beth didn't need convincing that cross-dressing was okay. She had stated her attitude early on, "It's just clothes." She helped me shop, steering me toward clothes appropriate for my age and away from the short skirts and high heels my inner adolescent girl had been drawn to.

A week later, Beth treated me to a special gift: a makeover by Michael, a drag queen friend of her hairdresser's. Michael spent over an hour at the beauty salon painting my face. He explained every step in detail, while Beth took copious notes. I used those notes to do my makeup until I memorized it.

Even though Michael was a drag queen, he understood I wanted an everyday look. Drag queens were usually gay men who dressed in over-the-top women's attire and garish makeup, and performed onstage in gay bars, often collecting cash tips for charity. I wanted to blend in, not stand out. "Drag queens have to master normal makeup before they can exaggerate it for drag." He knew the tricks that worked on the male face.

The most important trick was to cover the beard. Even with a close shave, beard shadow showed through normal foundation. He used Pan Stik, a more convenient form of Pan-Cake makeup that covers everything, provided I had a close shave. "Use a hand razor, not an electric. You'll get a closer shave."

Michael followed up with powder, blush, eyeliner (heavier on the outside), eye shadow, mascara, and lipstick. He chose colors that worked well for me. When he was done, I looked in the mirror. My reflection soon showed a self-satisfied smile; I thought I looked good. He gave us a shopping list for the corner drugstore. After the makeover, Beth and I went out to dinner. Being out as a woman with Beth felt wonderful and liberating, and I loved being able to share this part of myself in public with her by my side.

* * *

One Saturday in February, we drove up to Cleveland for a Tri-Ess meeting. I put on a dress and makeup before leaving Columbus. Beth coached me on all things female as we went: how to walk, talk, check my makeup in case it needed to be fixed, and to never touch my face. We parked at a freeway rest stop. I shook off my fear and went in to the ladies' room, trying to blend in and use the stall like everyone else. I was relieved when everyone ignored me.

Jane and her wife warmly welcomed us to the meeting held in the home of an Alpha Omega member. Jane was surprised I had come "dressed," presenting as a woman. It took a lot of courage to walk through a new door in a dress, not knowing what awaited inside, but I had my superpower; Beth had come with me. She approved of me, protected me, and reassured me I looked okay, so I felt safe. I was so thankful to have her in my life. Jane showed me a back room where members could change and put on their makeup. Others arrived in pants, dressed *en femme*, that is, as a woman, for the meeting, and changed back for the trip home.

The living room filled with crossdressers, who chatted in small groups like at any other house party. Snacks and beverages sat on a table, and a small donation was requested to cover expenses. I paid my membership dues and officially became a Tri-Ess member.

I learned the important distinction between "male/female," that is, referring to our physical body, and "men/women," referring to the gender being presented. The founder of Tri-Ess, Virginia Prince, wrote a book explaining it, *How to be a Woman though Male*.

During the meeting we discussed "passing" and wives. Passing, meaning people you met believed you were female, was the Holy Grail to crossdressers. It was hard to pull off. Everyone put a tremendous amount of work into it. I listened and took mental notes as topics came up discussing makeup, wigs, how to hide leg hair, using a feminine walk and voice. Experienced women gave tips to newcomers like me.

Wives and girlfriends were welcome, yet only a few wives were present. Most of the crossdressers had come alone, and the majority with partners didn't tell them about the meeting. Some had wives who knew and were hostile. Others went to great lengths to hide it.

Most Tri-Ess members had a post office box to get their newsletters and magazines, as did Alpha Omega and Tri-Ess National. One attendee shared how she had built a secret compartment in the back of a closet at her home to store her girl clothing and accessories. I wished I'd had a place like that to hide my feminine clothing in my earlier houses.

There was no such thing as being "out of the closet" in the Tri-Ess world. I had never heard the term. As my understanding increased, I realized the depth of those dark closets. Tri-Ess meetings were our chance to take a tiny step out.

I didn't need the contrast of my past negative experience with Karen to appreciate the luxury of sharing my experience with Beth. I felt more fortunate than most crossdressers, and it warmed my heart. I never considered telling anyone else. I could not tell the kids, and I couldn't let Karen find out, not with the trial pending. I couldn't tell anyone at work or at church. I would never have to feel alone with Beth by my side, and my anxiety lessened with the addition of my new friends at Tri-Ess.

These monthly meetings in Cleveland were my big chance to spend time *en femme* as Mary Ann, and I looked forward to them. The long drive and preparation time strained our weekends. They were held on Saturday evenings, so Beth and I stayed overnight in a motel and drove back Sunday. I missed the meetings on the weekends I had the boys.

* * *

At an Alpha Omega meeting early in 1989, Kelly, a crossdresser from Athens, introduced herself. Like most attendees, Kelly drove alone. “My wife knows about Kelly and chooses not to see me dressed,” she said. Kelly mentioned her three-hour drive, and that she and friends in Columbus had discussed starting a group there. That sounded like a great idea to me and Beth.

Kelly knew some crossdressers and transsexual women in Columbus, and in turn, that group knew others. They put out the word. Beth and I hosted the initial meeting in our home on a March weekend when the boys were with Karen.

I took my usual two hours to get dolled up, and Beth made an impressive array of hors d’oeuvres. She put too much vegetable waste down the garbage disposal and the sink clogged. She called for help, and in my dress and heels, I climbed under the sink, took apart the plumbing, and cleared the clog.

Thirteen of us met that evening, twelve crossdressers and transsexuals, and Beth. Our group was excited about starting a local chapter. We debated whether it should be an exclusive group for crossdressers, like Tri-Ess, or for transsexuals who wanted full-time lives as women, or both. We decided to have an open group that would welcome all transgender people, crossdressers and transsexuals.

As it turned out, some of the crossdressers at that meeting eventually determined they were transsexuals and transitioned. We were all male-to-female (MTF) trans women, born male and presenting as women. There were no female-to-male (FTM) trans men, born female and presenting as men, and no drag queens or drag kings among us, so we focused on crossdressers and transsexuals.

Some in the group felt it would be a bad idea to host the group in someone’s home, as the trans women coming and going might get the neighbors talking. Darkness came early in winter and worrying about the neighbors had not occurred to me. Soon that would change and we needed a different place to meet. Kelly and I volunteered to find a suitable room at a hotel. We all agreed a meeting fee could be charged to each attendee to cover room expenses and snacks.

Our group needed a name. Many great ideas were proposed, and we decided to call our group the Crystal Club because the name sounded feminine without drawing attention. We felt a need to stay under the radar, and would adhere to strict confidentiality of our membership. Members could not afford for their families, friends, or employers to find out how they spent their evenings; they could be ruined.

Kelly and I looked at hotel rooms dressed as men. The manager at the Knights Inn, a middle-aged man, showed us their two meeting rooms. We toured a small room, essentially a basic hotel room equipped with a large table and chairs, and a larger room twice the size with tables, chairs, and couches.

The transgender community was unknown to the public in 1989, and we didn't count on people to be cooperative. I wanted to make sure the hotel management would be okay with renting a room to our group. I didn't beat around the bush.

"We're a group of crossdressers and transsexuals. We'd be coming here dressed as women. Would that be okay with you?"

Kelly about had a heart attack. He couldn't believe I would ask a blunt question like that. He shrank back, expecting an angry reaction from the manager.

"Sure."

The manager replied as if it weren't a special request. He wanted our money. I guessed he had seen stranger things running that hotel. His attitude welcomed us in and the Crystal Club met in that hotel's large conference room for many years.

Several of the Crystal Club founders got the activities going. One organized the meetings. Another wrote a chatty newsletter. I used my UNIX tools to format it and make copies. One person designed the Crystal Club logo we posted on all our newsletters, and a different member answered letters and phone calls inquiring about membership.

Our monthly meetings felt like the Alpha Omega meetings. The difference was about half the members were transsexual on their journey toward permanently living as women. We had a few wives and partners there, and everyone got along.

Some of the conversation centered on the steps transsexuals undertook in their transition process. A local doctor well-versed in transgender medicine presented a great session on hormones. At another, people raved about Meral Crane, a Columbus therapist who counseled transsexuals from Ohio and beyond. She led a group where people going in either direction—male to female or female to male—could discuss their journey and compare notes about hormones, surgeons, legal steps, and other areas of concern.

I thrived at these monthly Crystal Club meetings. Being Mary Ann soothed my soul. The meetings were fun, like going to a party. I could spend an evening as Mary Ann, and the rest of the weekend was open. I was happy spending one or two nights a month *en femme,* and didn't feel a need to take more permanent steps.

* * *

I was more open than most in that I was able to go out in public as Mary Ann from time to time, whereas for some, our Crystal Club meetings provided their sole outlet. I learned about Harry Benjamin, a doctor who had studied transgender people decades ago. Gay and lesbian people were assessed on the Kinsey Scale from 0 to 6, a number that corresponded to their level of gayness.

Gender identity is sometimes confused with sexual orientation. The two are different. Sexual orientation is who you love, who you are sexually attracted to. Gender identity is who you are inside your head, not the appearance of your body. I was attracted to women, especially to Beth. I had no interest in men, and therefore, was heterosexual.

In his book, *The Transsexual Phenomenon*, Benjamin described a similar scale to measure transgender qualities.

0: Not transgender at all.

1: Cross-dressing once or twice, for example, a Halloween costume, and enjoying it.

2: Crossdressers who occasionally cross-dress partially, such as wearing ladies' clothing underneath men's or sleeping in a nightgown.

3: Crossdressers who occasionally cross-dress completely. They might go to a monthly support group like the Crystal Club.

4: Significant complete cross-dressing. They have friends in both roles. Benjamin considered these people to be transsexuals.

5: Transsexuals who have transitioned to full-time living in the gender not assigned at birth. There may be some medical intervention, but no bottom surgery.

6: Transsexuals who have transitioned full time with surgery being a goal.

Most of my friends in the Crystal Club were either at 3 or 6 on this scale. I realized I had gradually progressed, from 2 as a child, to 3 in 1987, to 4. I wondered if I would continue to 5 and 6. For now I was comfortable with my dual life. I discovered the term "bi-gender" in an online transgender glossary, meaning someone who has a life as a man and also as a woman, and felt it fit me well. I had a secret identity. Nobody knew Wonder Woman was secretly Clark Kent.

* * *

In July of 1989, Nova University in Ft. Lauderdale invited me to give a technical presentation about Usenet. They flew me in and put me up in a nice hotel on the beach. Late that evening, I decided to take a walk on the beach, and I longed to do it as Mary Ann. I pictured myself on the beach in a skirt with the breeze ruffling the fabric around my legs, and found the idea alluring.

To avoid obvious detection, I waited until after dark. Many crossdressers feel safer outdoors at night where dim lighting escalates the prospect of passing. Any cis woman (born into the gender in which you identify, non-transgender) will tell you this can be dangerous, but mothers don't teach this basic rule of female safety to their sons. I wore the one-piece women's swimsuit I'd brought and a sarong. I combed my shaggy hair out in a semi-feminine style. I didn't want to hassle with makeup or a wig for a nighttime beach walk.

I rode down the elevator holding my room key card, slipped out the rear hotel door and onto the beach unseen. It was a lovely night with enough moonlight to see my way. As I strolled along the beach, I put my feet in the warm Atlantic. As I imagined, a gentle breeze caressed my sarong against my hairy legs. *Ah! Pure heaven.*

After a half-hour walk, I washed the sand off my feet and came back into the hotel. As I waited for the elevator, two hotel managers saw my hairy legs and six-foot frame, and glanced at each other as if concerned an undesirable character had come into their hotel. One began to speak. "Excuse me, um…," Before he could get out half a sentence, I fidgeted with my room key so they could see it in my hands. That changed everything and their shoulders relaxed. "Enjoy your stay at the hotel."

11

Be All You Can Be

1991

On a fine Thursday in June, I drove my Honda Accord hatchback along the interstate with the back compartment packed so high with dresses, shoes, and makeup, I couldn't see out the rear window. My cross-dressing friend, Adrianne, from the Crystal Club and I headed to Cleveland to spend a long girls's weekend with two hundred new friends. Yesterday, we'd been working as men, all to be forgotten for a few precious days.

Be All You Can Be was 1991's largest transgender conference in the Midwest. A yearly circuit of these conferences happened around the country: First Event in Boston, Paradise in the Poconos in Pennsylvania, and the grandmama of them all, Southern Comfort in Atlanta. These treasured events gave crossdressers and transsexuals a safe place to spend a few days living as women, learning important skills, and networking with each other, vendors, and medical experts.

Be All rotated among five Midwestern cities, and this year it landed at the Marriott in Cleveland, an easy two-hour drive from Columbus. Several of us from the Crystal Club would be there. Adrianne and I thought it would be fun to ride together. Driving up *en femme* seemed like a perfect way to begin the trip. Adrianne wore a gorgeous green dress suitable for rubbing elbows with high society. I'd done my makeup and nails, and donned a wig and blue jeans, figuring I'd change when I got there.

We cruised along an orange-barrel section of I-71 about forty miles short of Cleveland chatting about all things feminine when I heard a noise and felt a vibration from the front of the car. *Dang.* A flat tire. I was furious at the timing.

Pulling the tiny spare tire out of the back took a lot of effort with a hundred pounds of dainty clothes covering it. As I pondered the jack, a truck whizzed by an inch from the car and blasted us with its air horn. *Hmmph*—so much for chivalry. I pulled the car farther off the road. The construction made for a tight space to do the job. As I jacked up the car, I wondered where all the guys were that were supposed to help. I chipped a nail and my hands took on road grime.

I had the spare in place and started on the lug nuts when a trucker pulled off the road ahead of us. As he walked back, my emotions were a mixture of worry over whether we'd pass, anger at the tire, and consternation over what took him so long. Seeing the newly mounted tire, he said, "It looks like you have the situation pretty well in hand."

"We sure could have used you ten minutes ago," I replied in my best feminine voice. He walked back to his truck and took off.

I picked up the ruined tire and nicked my thumb. *Great.* I was dirty, had chipped two nails, and my thumb was bleeding. I should have let the trucker finish the job. We got back in the car and headed up the road. A quarter mile down the road, the construction ended and opened to a wide shoulder where it taunted me. *Too late.*

* * *

A *Gone with the Wind* themed dinner presented an apt opportunity to show off hoop skirts and Southern belle outfits the attendees couldn't wear elsewhere. I didn't own anything along those lines, nor did many others, and I felt fine in regular street and evening clothes. Perhaps a dozen ladies entered the costume contest, easily won by a trans lady sporting a frilly, red Southern belle hoop dress and matching parasol.

After dinner, I don't think the hotel bar patrons knew what hit them. Dozens of large women, many in hoop skirts, arrived on the scene. Adrianne and I joined others at a table. A gentleman came up, introduced himself, and offered to buy us all a drink. He wanted to know what this was all about and guessed it was a Southern belle convention. We explained we were crossdressers, and his jaw hit the floor. We educated him about ourselves, and he listened, all the while squirming to get away. Half an hour later, he reappeared with a drink for each of us. He was a man of his word.

I wandered to the far side of the bar. I was greeted by a friendly woman who had been chatting with two others.

"My friends and I wanted to know who all these Southern belles were."

"We're crossdressers. There's a transgender conference here at the hotel."

"I had no idea you were a crossdresser. I had noticed you're very tall."

With three-inch heels, I towered at six feet, two inches. One of the women stood up from her barstool and I found myself looking up at her. In flats, she was three inches taller than me. The conversation turned to shopping, and where to find shoes and pantyhose that fit.

I signed up for a series of workshops about female presentation. I'd only been cross-dressing for a couple of years and I wanted to pass. The series was presented by a trio of accomplished crossdressers from Renaissance, the Philadelphia transgender group.

We began with a morning workshop about makeup. I was comfortable doing my own makeup ever since Michael first made me over. Nonetheless, from the speaker's lecture and her book, I learned why Michael had me put tan powder in certain places and blush in others, and got several tips to fix my "raccoon eyes" and look less garish. I took several pages of notes.

Next, another Renaissance expert led a seminar on deportment, an area where I needed a lot of help. I knew I looked masculine when I sat and stood. I learned how to correct my awkward movements. Then it came time for the walk. Mine resembled Frankenstein's monster's clomp. She showed several things to do at once: walk from the hips, sway the shoulders, lead with your breasts. I admired her easy-going flow.

We all lined up to have our walks critiqued. The leader complimented some of us; others received constructive criticism. When my turn came, I tried doing everything at once for the first time. Then I heard my critique: "I don't mean to be cruel, but if you lived in a zoo, they'd lock you up and feed you bananas." I was crushed and couldn't argue. She was right. I looked and felt clumsy.

She stayed after to work with me and another lady. I struggled and with more tries, I got the hips and breasts parts down. My shoulders misbehaved, and like a kid throwing a tantrum, if I ignored them, I stayed out of trouble and could concentrate on the hips.

At lunch, Adrianne and I sat with a man and his wife. He was a leader in the female-to-male transsexual community and a bearded post-op himself. *What a man*, I thought. He gave me a bit of insight into what FTMs faced and gave me his card so FTMs in the Crystal Club could call him for advice. I could not imagine him as female.

A professor from Cleveland State University led the "Should We Tell the Children?" session. We heard both sides of the issue. He pointed out that children are pretty smart and may already know. If they found out later their parents kept a secret, they could be upset. In his view, telling them early may be the best thing to do, if they can be trusted to keep the secret.

As for the negatives, each child would probably confide in one close friend. It could damage the child's relationships with friends. Teenagers go through other problems, and dealing with a cross-dressing father could complicate a tense father/child relationship. A need to know should be more important than the risks.

During a break, I went shopping. The conference organizers had arranged for a vast array of vendors in the hotel. They offered regular outfits, sexy clothing, wigs, cosmetics, eyeglasses, accessories, and photography.

After browsing, I found a delightful room run by a New York store catering to crossdressers. In addition to makeovers and cosmetics, they offered wigs, jewelry, and clothes. Clip earrings stretched as far as the eye could see, as did expanding bracelets large enough to go over huge hands. I found big earrings to match the lavender dress I had worn that morning. I had to have them.

Then I saw the *pièce de résistance*: a wig with a French braid, lavender bow, and tapered fringes along the sides. The saleswoman helped me try it on. I looked much improved and younger. The wig did wonders to frame my face and soften the hard edges of my chin. I looked and felt pretty. My self-confidence soared and I could feel the femininity I radiated. Of course I bought that too.

* * *

I dreaded driving back to Columbus on the small spare tire. I decided Mary Ann would buy a set of tires. Adrianne mentioned a Goodyear store she had seen a couple of blocks away from the hotel. First, I called around to shop for price, my male telephone voice proving useful. As it turned out, Goodyear had a sale on 45,000-mile tires with the best price around town.

I drove to the Goodyear store, which looked like a converted gas station and did not inspire confidence. However, I felt new confidence from the conference and proceeded as Mary Ann, the Empowered.

"May I help you?" the manager said.

"I hope so. I need a new set of tires."

He showed me a fancy set of wide tires at a high price.

"What's the warranty?"

"These tires don't have a mileage warranty."

Sheesh, the things they try to pull on women, I thought. "I'm not interested in those. What about the 45,000-mile tires you have on sale?"

"Sure, I can fix you up with those."

I filled out the paperwork with my femme name and told him I was staying at the Marriott. I asked for a ride back to the hotel, and he called out for one of the employees to "give her a ride." The "her" pronoun validated my identity; it felt pleasing and proper to be accepted as a woman.

When the car was ready, I decided to walk the half-mile down a busy city street. I'd been practicing my walk and wanted to strut my stuff. I stepped out of the safe bubble the hotel provided and headed for the store with a steady stream of traffic to my right. A male truck driver smiled and waved as he drove by. I flashed him a smile in return. The driver of the truck behind him whistled. I was passing, and it felt great. It never occurred to me such uninvited attention might be demeaning.

After I paid, I went to the car to check it out. The jack compartment was empty, and something was jammed in under the spare. I didn't want to get grimy moving stuff around. Right then, the manager came out to see if I needed help. I let him put everything back where it belonged and thanked him. I liked this: having men do the dirty work for me. No more chipped nails.

* * *

After dinner, I hung around for the talent show. I expected a hokey camp-style arrangement with a few skits and lip-syncs to a pocket tape player. A stage with professional equipment opened next to the banquet room. What I saw next captivated me for hours.

A crossdresser I met at Alpha Omega emceed the show. In addition to introducing the performers, she interspersed recordings of congratulatory phone calls from many living and dead celebrities. The voices of George Bush, John Wayne, and Elvis Presley greeted us and extolled the wonders of the Be All. Many of them told cross-dressing jokes. Whoever did the impersonations was amazing.

The show began with a few ladies who felt great about themselves, strutting around on the stage to their favorite tune. Then the serious talent came on. Many of the numbers were top-quality lip-syncs. A Renaissance member donned a revealing Cher disguise and danced around a statue-like naval officer. The mustachioed man, hidden behind sunglasses, stood at attention with a sword by his side. I had no idea who her partner was until after the show when he took off his hat and sunglasses, and I recognized the male alter ego of one of the Renaissance presenters.

The emcee performed a hilarious Ginsu knife commercial parody, showing a full range of transgender power tools, such as a belt sander to deal with troublesome beard growth. Two trans women did a skit as old biddies discussing a recently deceased "funny" relative. The highlight of the show was the emcee's lip-sync to "When you Wish Upon a Star," accompanied by a slide show from her past. In her presentation, I watched her transform from an unhappy child, to grow, blossom, and become a glowing, vibrant, happy woman. The audience gave her a well-deserved standing ovation at the end of her number. I would have paid extra to see this show.

The next day, I looked forward to the "Speaking as a Woman" class and hoped to pick up a few tips to lighten my baritone voice, which caused me trouble in public. I sat with three friends at the front of the room. A few people had it easy because of their regional accent—a cultured New England voice worked beautifully, as did an Oklahoma drawl.

My technique had been simple: raise my pitch. I tightened up my throat when I went *en femme* and left it there. The leader called this "elevating my larynx."

She presented several techniques. "Use feminine words and sentence structure. 'Rose' or 'crimson' instead of 'red.' 'Lovely' instead of 'good looking.' Vary your intonation instead of speaking in a monotone as men do."

We practiced with the others in the workshop and offered feedback. The lady sitting next to me thought my pitch was okay. I was amazed to discover my voice had gotten better from constant use. Modulating my pitch felt like jumping hurdles when I needed to find an easy gait. I had to think about it, which didn't feel natural. Much like a voice actor, I learned to rehearse my line in advance, as in, "Table for two, please."

Two presenters discussed going out in public. Their workshop began with a couple of important observations. First, while we may think our goal is to pass, we should strive to be accepted instead. After all, we don't know if we passed or were read and ignored. But we do know if everything worked out okay for us. Second, everyone gets read sometimes. These accomplished leaders appeared as guests on a talk show in Philadelphia and passed at the studio before introducing themselves to the staff. Later the same day, they were read by a random passerby. You can't fool all the people all the time, so it's better not to set yourself up expecting to always pass.

I realized the wisdom in their words. If they didn't pass all the time, I knew I wouldn't. Acceptance is a more realistic goal, plus it's what matters.

Next up was the seminar I had dreaded from the start—the video critique. I brought in a blank videotape to record my session and volunteered to go first. The walking expert smiled and asked me if I had "gotten those shoes fixed yet." After being called a gorilla, I expected the worst.

I wore a simple black dress with a white belt, large multicolored flashy earrings I'd bought at the boutique, and my favorite slings with a three-inch heel. I stood at one end of the room and walked toward the camera, sat down, and introduced myself.

The panel took turns giving feedback. The walking expert liked my walk and wanted more shoulder movement. She thought my deportment looked good. Another liked my makeup and made suggestions about a more balanced jewelry image; the flashy earrings worked better with bigger, flashier jewelry elsewhere, such as bracelets. She suggested a larger watch and a lower neckline. The speech expert had good things to say about my voice and smile. She pointed out a few words and phrases, such as "lovely" and "time of my life," that I could benefit from by working them more often into my vocabulary. No bananas this time; this girl looked good. I brought home the videotape as a prized memento.

Before the prom, I did a little more shopping to find the right earrings and a red hair bow to complement my formal dress. And what a dress! A Jim Bridges creation, the "Rainbow Sparkle," made of black velvet with an above the knee hemline and extra-long sleeves to fit the male body. Sparkles covering the dress caught the light and dispersed a rainbow of color, as if a fairy godmother had waved her wand in Disney-esque fashion. I still get compliments on that dress.

After four days in heels, my feet were killing me, and I sat at every chance. Everyone was nice, which helped me get through the evening. I missed Beth, and I felt like a part of me was missing without her at the prom. Not wanting to rub my sore feet in the ballroom, I called it a night, went up to my room, and called her.

On our final morning, it was the Be All tradition for everyone to come to a late breakfast dressed *en homme* in their usual male attire. Many of the participants expressed having a hard time changing back after four days *en femme*. I understood. For me, having on my guy clothes didn't take away from the enjoyment of the past few days. I felt great and resolved to carry those positive feelings forward into my male life.

By 9:00 a.m., Adrianne and I had the car loaded, the new tires shining in the morning light. As I checked out, I ran into a new friend. She gave me a puzzled look and was shocked when I told her I was Mary Ann. At breakfast, I ran into the FTM and his wife. She recognized me, saying she could tell by my eyes. He looked up, shrugged his shoulders, said he had no idea, and went back to the food line. *Men*, I thought, rolling my eyes.

When I got back home, I was on a post-conference high. I felt like my feet didn't touch the ground again for days.

12

Dual Boot

1992

"Mark and Beth, I now pronounce you man and wife."

My pastor officiated from the Nazarene church. Matt and Adam grinned from the first pew and a few close friends sat nearby. I wore my best suit and tie and beamed at Beth, who glowed with loving radiance. We spent a fabulous week honeymooning in St. Maarten.

Karen and I had been in court about the boys' schedule from the day the divorce was final until 1992. We ended up with joint custody and a fifty-fifty schedule. Matt and Adam spent Mondays and Tuesdays with me and Beth, Wednesdays and Thursdays with Karen and Andi, and we alternated long weekends.

Beth and I lived in the same house I'd owned with Karen, and the specter of the past didn't give Beth a warm fuzzy feeling. We decided to buy a new place together. We liked the city of Bexley, a suburb in the middle of Columbus. It offered a yuppie vibe, a friendly upscale community, and most important, excellent schools.

House after house sold before we could make an offer. We toured an amazing house on Sherwood Road, newly remodeled with high-quality materials and workmanship. The seller was a big-name developer who had divorced and remarried. His new wife didn't like his house, so he kept improving it. He finished the attic into a huge master bedroom, a library with amazing built-in bookshelves, and a master bath with a generous spa tub, shower, skylights, and a second-floor laundry. She finally told him, "You know, no matter how much you fix it up, it's still *her* house." He cut his losses, and Beth and I moved into the showplace on our block.

Over time, I had more difficulty relating to the conservative teachings at Nazarene. Christ Lutheran Church was behind our new house. We gave it a try. I'd been baptized Lutheran and it felt like coming home. Once we joined, I could walk out of our house and across the alley to the church's back door.

* * *

Brian McNaught, a gay rights educator, presented an "LGBT in the Workplace" workshop to our department at Bell Labs. Gay and lesbian issues were touchy, and people groused about mandatory attendance. Our department head relented and made it optional.

I asked one of the "good old boys" if he would be going. He elbowed me cheerfully. "You bet! I want to see who sits in the front row." I sat in the middle of the room.

Afterward, I chatted with Brian. "You had wonderful LGB content, but there wasn't any 'T'."

"Let's get lunch," he suggested. "I'd like to learn more."

Brian was gracious. I shared my story and told him of transexuals who had good and bad experiences where they worked. The next time I saw him at an LGBT conference, his content was inclusive and helpful.

Our Black History Month diversity workshop had a warmer reception. Reggie, one of two Black workers, was well liked. He shared his experience. "When something bad happens to me, I have to stop and think. Did that happen because I'm Black? Or did that happen because I'm Reggie?"

I wondered the same thing when I got reactions that for one reason or another didn't fit what I might have expected in the moment. For example, one time I'd shopped *en femme* at a department store and when I didn't find a particular skirt in my size, I asked a passing clerk if they had it in a size 16. "I'll be with you in a minute, sir," she replied. I cringed at the insulting pronoun and feeling indignant asked, "Do I look like a sir?" The clerk made eye contact and looked startled. "Oh, I'm so sorry, ma'am. I heard your voice and just reacted. I'm helping another customer, and then I'll be right with you."

Reggie's wise words resonated with me over the years. After atypical encounters, my first instinct was to assume it was because I was trans. Thanks to Reggie's wisdom, I learned to look deeper. I often discovered the unexpected behavior had nothing to do with me, and everything to do with something else happening in the person's life. I learned not to jump to a transphobic conclusion. My attitude improved as my confidence grew. I got along better with colleagues and found they appreciated me.

* * *

I admired Bell Lab's POST email system. POST used a directory from HR to combine email with people's names, departments, and locations, allowing R&D folks to send email to a name, for example, "Mark.Horton," or to general groups, such as "everyone in department 45264," or to "all supervisors in Columbus." A team of eight in New Jersey kept the directory working and supported the UNIX command-line email program. Unfortunately, it only worked inside Bell Labs and could not integrate with the Internet.

I found a way to combine Internet email and POST into a best-of-both system that allowed Internet email to be addressed by a person's name. I put mark.r.horton@att.com on my business card. My system looked for matching names in the employee directory, and if it found exactly one, it turned it into an email address like mark@cbosgd.att.com and delivered the email to me. I would have used m.horton@att.com, but there was more than one match.

This system turned out to be so useful Bell Labs decided to make it our standard email system. We formed a new group for email support with John Bagley as the supervisor, me as technical lead, and a half-dozen skilled staff.

John and the rest of the group were in the Chicago area, working in Bell's Indian Hill campus in suburban Naperville. I was the only group member in Columbus. John didn't mind me working from home. I went into the office each Friday to have face-to-face people contact.

* * *

Now that the boys spent half their time at Karen's, I had the freedom to be Mary Ann when working from home. I felt more like me on days when I put on a dress and makeup, made the mental adjustment, elevated my larynx, and did my job. I spent two, three, or even four days a week in what I called "girl mode," going by Mary Ann Harris, borrowing the surname from my ninth-grade friend. I was still in the closet, but I felt safe behind my femme name.

I tired of wearing wigs. They were hot to wear, and high maintenance to clean and style. Beth said, "Let your hair grow, if you want; lots of men have long hair." I grew it out in 1995 and was delighted the day I could tie my first ponytail.

Beth's hairstylist, Ken, cut my hair so I could wear it as a man or a woman. The trick was to have bangs. Mark combed his hair straight back and put it in a low ponytail. Mary Ann brushed down her bangs to hide her masculine brow, and either brushed out her hair on all sides or put it in a high ponytail with a scrunchie.

I loved the freedom of not having to wear a wig. Beth liked my long hair. She was fine with cosmetic changes that could be undone from one day to the next. Permanent changes to my body were out: no shaved legs or pierced ears. I wore opaque tights or resorted to the drag queen trick of donning several pairs of pantyhose, and had to use clip earrings that hurt. Beth would accept Mary Ann if she got to spend time with an un-feminized Mark. I didn't care for the limitations. I obliged to keep her happy at the expense of nice nails and bare legs.

Beth had an impressive career. She designed user interfaces for Lucent products, ensuring they would be easy to use. I liked that we were peers, equals at work and at home.

She chaired an international committee writing standards for human/machine interfaces. That summer, she flew to Geneva for one of her committee meetings. The boys were with Karen for her two summer weeks. I had ten days alone. I could work from home and decided to enjoy my time by making the most of it.

I had Ken wax my upper lip. When he ripped off the linen strip, I thought he had taken half my face with it. *Yowch!* Ken repeatedly apologized, even as he did what I had asked him to do. It felt like torture. Next, I had a set of fake nails put on—long tips, bright red nail polish, the works.

At home, I shaved my legs, which I had done during the winter when pants would cover them. I'd documented how long it took the hair to grow back and wrote it up for the *Crystal Chronicle* newsletter.

It took two months to grow to one inch, but after only a month, the half-inch stubble looked too dense for anyone to notice. I was bold and shaved them, even though it was shorts weather.

And enjoy, I did. I went about my routine, appreciative of not having to go back to guy mode. I had no quick changes to attend to. Life was simpler when I could stay in my favorite gender for over a week. It gave me a pleasant taste of living full time as a woman. Our cat noticed my long nails and became my best friend.

I had Ken take off the nails the day Beth returned. It didn't take her long to notice the other change.

"You shaved your legs?"

"I did. While you were gone, I spent the whole time as Mary Ann. Ken waxed my face and I wore fake nails."

Beth was not happy. "Why didn't you tell me you were doing this?"

"I guess it's easier to ask for forgiveness."

After the initial awkwardness, she took it in stride. Nobody noticed Mark's legs, so I got to keep them shaved all year.

I liked to compare having a dual life with a dual boot PC. When you turned on the PC, it could boot up either in Windows 95 or Windows NT, popular at the time. The systems were similar with subtle and important differences. They both had access to the same personal files. As Mary Ann, my appearance was different, my voice was higher, my body language was different, but I had the same memories and skills. I could work on a computer program one day as Mark and then pick up the next day as Mary Ann.

* * *

Some of the Crystal Club crossdressers planned a fall weekend getaway. We booked a cabin at Deer Creek State Park and spent an entire weekend *en femme*—quite a treat. Beth's interest had waned in my cross-dressing excursions and she stayed home.

We awakened to a crisp October morning. The leaves were turning their signature crimson and gold. The scenery was gorgeous, alive with color, and the air smelled of the season's change. I felt good being out in nature *en femme* with my long hair brushing along my shoulders. One crossdresser said she was jealous. "When you wake up, you have hair." Everyone else wore a wig.

We spent hours of light-hearted fun hanging out in the cabin amid girl talk and clothing changes. Our fashion sense had yet to mature. We were middle-aged women enjoying a second adolescence, donning short skirts, hose, and high heels, outfits better suited for teenagers. I wore a short tank dress to the Saturday night dinner at the main lodge. Adrianne's wife, the only cisgender woman with us that weekend, questioned my choice. She sighed at my resistance, and said, "You will be cold." She was right.

I excused myself to go to the ladies' room, something I always did whether on my own or with Beth. I didn't realize how our group of crossdressers with their varying abilities to pass, might change what I had been used to. Our large group attracted attention. Sunday, after Adrianne checked out at the main desk, management informed her of a complaint they had received about us using the restroom. In the future, they asked us to use the cabin bathroom. I felt terrible because I had caused the problem and everyone else would have to pay for it. The rest of the group didn't seem to mind. They didn't feel comfortable using a public ladies' room and had planned to hold it in during dinner.

* * *

Beth was an avid baseball fan and missed watching the Oakland A's from her time as a Cal State Hayward student in the Bay Area. I followed the local minor-league Clippers team, and went to an occasional game. Discovering our common interest, we went to games, first as a couple, then with the boys as a family. We purchased Clippers season tickets located in the fourth row near home plate. Games were convenient and inexpensive, and they became a frequent family outing. Foul balls made nice souvenirs. One popped back and fell into no-man's-land behind home plate in the narrow space between the front row railing and the net. I couldn't reach low enough and I had an idea.

"Hey, Adam, do you want that foul ball?"

"Yeah!"

"Okay, here's what we'll do."

I picked him up by his ankles and hung him upside-down over the railing. I positioned him over the ball and lowered him into place.

"Grab the ball!"

I brought him back up and once his feet hit the ground, he grinned and held up his new trophy for all to see.

* * *

In 1996, Adam came home from Bexley Middle School and looked distraught. Karen had dropped him off that morning and one of Adam's schoolmates saw the rainbow bumper sticker on her car. The kid taunted him on the way into class: "Your mother's a lesbian. Your mother's a lesbian."

In his angriest voice, Adam told me what happened and punched his fists near his sides for emphasis. "I was sooo mad. I followed him into the classroom and I went up to the teacher, and I very politely…asked the teacher for permission…to *kill* him."

Middle school is a tough place, even in a great school like Bexley. Kids can make your life miserable if they learn something can be used as ammunition against you, for example, your parents are gay or transgender.

I had discussed parenting with my trans women friends about whether it was okay for the kids to know their dad had a feminine side. Some wives went ballistic, demanding the kids never see their father as a woman. Some divorced and had cut off contact. Other transsexuals had been through the experience and discovered their children did fine when exposed to their dad as a woman. Mental health professionals advised parents to tell the kids together and make it a positive experience.

I couldn't turn to Karen for help. She and Andi, the same-sex couple, used a nasty tone when saying: "Your father wears dresses." I had no such worries with Beth. We were on the same page from the get-go. We called a family meeting where Beth and I presented a united front.

"Yes, I wear dresses, and more," I told the boys. "I spend some days as Mark and some as Mary Ann."

Beth added, "We want you to know about it because you might see your dad as Mary Ann. It's okay. There's nothing wrong. It's a positive."

Adam's face lit up in astonished excitement. "I think it will be cool to meet Mary Ann."

Matt had a more practical response. "It's fine, except you remember what happened with Mom's bumper sticker; you can't come to school as Mary Ann. We won't go through that again."

Adam agreed. "And you can't come to church as Mary Ann. Half of our classmates go to our church and word would get out."

These restrictions made sense and I assured them I would abide by their rules.

Matt raised his hand. "What do we call you?"

Hmmm. I pondered. "Well, Dad won't do. And you have a mom. I'm not trying to take her place." The term "Aunt So-and-so" worked for some when their father was in girl mode, which would make me Aunt Mary Ann. I didn't like it. "Why don't you just call me Mary Ann?"

The boys nodded. I felt relief. I had taken a big step with Beth's support and we got through it without drama. Taking up Adam on his offer, I said, "How about if Mary Ann is here tomorrow when you come home from school?"

The next morning, after the boys left, I showered and dressed. I wore my royal blue dress, full makeup, and chunky high heels. As the time grew near for them to come home, I felt a change in my body, adrenaline notching up each hour: heart going a little faster, sweaty palms, tension where before I had none. I trusted my kids and put faith in their assurances from the previous day.

When Adam came home and saw me, a huge grin spread across his face. "Wow. You really are Mary Ann." He examined my shoes in amazement. "How can you walk in those things?"

I grinned, too, and felt my heart expand. I stood up and took a few elegant steps. Satisfied by my transformation, the four of us, Adam, Matt, Beth and I, went on to have a perfectly ordinary evening.

From that day on, as both Mark and Mary Ann, I had no reason to be nervous in front of the boys.

13

EQUAL!

1997

As I walked down the hallway at work, a flyer caught my eye promoting a group called EQUAL!, a Lucent Technologies employee group for gay, lesbian, bisexual, and transgender workers. *Whoa!* I had never seen the word "transgender" at work. I worked up my nerve and decided to go.

At the appointed time, I walked into a room full of friendly faces. To my delight, I recognized a coworker. I thought he was a good guy. I never thought about him as being gay and now it was obvious. I felt a shared vulnerability that we knew each other's secrets. He and everyone else gushed welcoming support. I had never felt so much at home outside of a trans setting.

LEAGUE, an acronym at AT&T for Lesbian and Gay United Employees, held its place as the mother organization for more than ten years. The Columbus chapter was one of several local chapters of the national organization. When Lucent spun off from AT&T, their lesbian, gay, and bisexual groups were forced to separate. Rather than call the Lucent group LEAGUE at Lucent, they chose a name about equality. The inside joke was that EQUAL! stood for Every Queer at Lucent.

Both groups had recently added the "T" to their diversity mission statements and I happened to show up as the first. No one there had a clear idea of what it meant to be transgender, and it fell to me to educate everybody. I was glad to have a seat at the table. Over the next several years, I would educate the members of EQUAL! and many others about transgender people.

We spent a large part of that first meeting planning for an upcoming national yearly conference. The HR department gave their full support to LEAGUE and EQUAL! as a part of overall diversity. The 1997 conference would be held in April in Denver, and the Columbus chapter would send several people, each with their management's support. It had never occurred to me that trans-related behavior would be allowed, even encouraged, by my employer. What an eye opener. On top of that, travel expenses to the EQUAL! conference were no different than any other technical conference, and would be paid in full by the company. Truly mind-boggling.

The Columbus chapter held convenient lunchtime monthly meetings. I worked from home most days and that made it easy to slip away. I decided to go to a meeting as Mary Ann, partly to educate others about what it meant to be transgender, and partly to test the waters. This would be another bold step in my journey to perform everyday tasks as a woman.

On the meeting day, I spent the morning working from home as Mary Ann, and left for the lunch meeting. Every new familiar experience I undertook *en femme* was like adding another badge to my transgender sash. These moments felt satisfying, another mountain to climb and conquer. I had climbed so many, going to the lunch seemed like just another one—until I drove to work. *What if someone recognizes me?* I thought. *Will they tell everyone else? Will I get fired?*

Usually, I'd park in the west lot close to my office near the western end of the first floor. The EQUAL! meetings were in a conference room on the fourth floor, a penthouse hosting the centrally located executive offices. I had never been to the fourth floor. To ease my anxiety, I decided to park in the east lot and go up the stairs on that side.

I came in through the building's east gate and walked toward the middle of the complex. The fourth floor was smaller than the lower floors and centered above them in such a way that the eastern staircases wouldn't reach the top floor. I had to go down a long familiar hallway to reach the correct staircase, possibly passing someone I knew. My pulse quickened. This is what I had tried to avoid. *Argh.* I walked in circles, hunting for the elusive staircase. I began to perspire. I hated to admit I was lost in the building I had worked in for nearly twenty years. It seemed foreign. Nothing was where it should have been. Panic seeped in. I had lost track of north and didn't know where to go. Finally, I found a wall map of the building, worked my way in the right direction and located the staircase. Mentally exhausted, I climbed to the fourth floor.

I thought I was in the clear, except now I couldn't find the conference room. When I found the door, I realized I was in no condition to go in. I was sweaty and scared out of my wits. My makeup had run, and my feet, clad in three-inch pumps, hurt. I found a ladies' room—empty, *thank you, Jesus*—and fixed my makeup. Once I entered the meeting room, I was okay. I took a few minutes to calm down, and shared my story about getting lost to a bevy of sympathetic listeners.

* * *

I had not come out to my boss, John, and with nervous trepidation, asked him for permission to attend the EQUAL! conference in Denver. I was astounded when he gave me the green light. Attending a conference about LGBT issues at the company's expense was wonderful and unexpected, and what I saw there changed my world forever.

I asked the conference registration team to make two name tags for me: one for Mary Ann and one for Mark. I figured the best way to make a point of being bi-gendered was for them to see both sides of me. The conference organizers were happy to oblige. I packed clothes for both Mark and Mary Ann. Dressed as Mark, I picked up my registration materials and name tags, where I was advised, "Someone named Sandy might be here. You should meet them." Mystified, I made a mental note.

I discovered I was the first transgender person there, and the first to have contacted anyone at EQUAL!. The attendees looked to me for education. By now, I was used to being the token, and plunged right in.

EQUAL! had added the "T" to their LGB mission statement; other groups had done so and it was topical. The EQUAL! leadership team made it a point to talk to me, one or two at a time. They didn't know what the "T" meant and were eager to learn. When I became the visible face at Lucent of what it means to be transgender, people assumed all trans people were like me: male to female crossdressers. I was new at activism and didn't correct them. In later years, other trans activists resented me for leaving them with that impression. I learned to emphasize that every journey is different and mine was atypical.

On the second day of the conference, I dressed as Mary Ann, pleased to have a matching name tag. A man approached me. His name tag told me this was Sandy, the person I had been advised to meet. He introduced himself as another transgender employee. Seeing me there dressed as Mary Ann gave him confidence. After lunch, Sandy came back dressed *en femme.* I was glad to have inspired her to be herself and grateful to have a trans friend at the conference.

Everyone came to the introductory session. The male and female conference co-chairs welcomed the attendees. The female, a popular lesbian, stepped from behind the podium to surprise the audience with her chic, skirted suit.

In the past, EQUAL! had focused on gay and lesbian issues. They were proud of LEAGUE, from whence they had all come, for having added "sexual orientation" to AT&T's nondiscrimination policy.

"When I started at AT&T years ago, I had to hide who I was," the male co-chair said. "I couldn't put my boyfriend's picture on my desk. On Monday morning, my office mate would ask how my weekend was, and I would have to make up a story. I couldn't tell him about my date. I could have been fired if I'd told the truth. Now I have the freedom to be out in the workplace. This is so important. I no longer have to expend energy hiding part of myself, worrying I might be discovered. I'm more productive at work because I can focus on my job."

The woman spoke about EQUAL!'s next goal. "People automatically get health insurance for their spouses. We can't marry, even if we've been together for years. My partner can't be on my health benefits. She has to buy her own insurance, which means I'm being paid less than my straight coworkers for doing the same job. We want Lucent to provide domestic partner benefits to make our compensation fairer."

I felt moved by their stories. These perks didn't apply in my situation, and as I became more aware of the consequences others faced, I resolved to keep an open mind and learn more.

I went to EQUAL!'s first workshop about transgender people. Gay men and lesbians packed the room. I sat front and center, proud to be there. A well-known local transgender activist gave a presentation on how being transgender was a workplace issue, and I didn't want to miss a word.

She began by discussing what makes a person intersex and did not skip on detail. She explained how some intersex children are born with a microphallus, too small to be a penis and too large to be a clitoris. Parents would expect to hear: "It's a boy" or "It's a girl," and if neither were apparent, the freaked-out doctors had panicked consultations with everyone, except the parents, and would decide to "normalize" the infant's genitalia through surgery. "It's easier to make a hole than a pole," they would say, and declare the surgically reduced child a baby girl.

She segued into her main topic: transgender. She had us fold our arms as we always do. Then she switched it up. "Now fold them the other way. Get up and walk around with your arms folded backward and see how comfortable you feel." When I tried it, I got so wrapped up, I kicked over the can of soda I'd parked at my feet.

"It doesn't feel right, does it?" she said. "That's how it is for people who feel they are one gender and are forced to go through life presenting the other gender."

At lunch, I sat at the table where the activist held court. "Transsexuals go to great lengths to be presentable in the workplace, to look and act the part. I had a person come to me for help who worked in a restaurant. She was bald and wouldn't wear a wig. She looked ridiculous."

I thought I looked presentable, even if I didn't pass.

"Being an activist means being visible. I've had my picture printed in the Denver newspaper. You'd better be prepared for that if you're going to make a difference." She figured a crossdresser would want to remain closeted.

"I'm already plenty visible," I said.

This was good preparation for me. I set my expectations to be visible. I learned about the internal controversies in the trans community that pitted transsexuals against crossdressers. I began to develop a thick skin—I'd need it.

At another workshop, a lesbian executive at Bell Labs in Denver told us that to get things done, opportunities arose where activists would need to ask the powers that be for big things like changes to policy, changes to the law, or for money, all prospects that could prove to be nerve-racking for the unprepared. She taught us to "do an ask," that is, how to ask a powerful person for an important consideration.

Her process stuck with me and gave me the courage to do many asks over the next several years. In her view, the most important part of the process resided in my own head. Once I presented my case and asked the decision maker for what I wanted, I was to shut up and listen. At that moment, I had succeeded because I "did the ask." No matter the response, I had succeeded. That's an empowering mindset.

At the conference closing plenary, the leadership summed up their goals: being out in the workplace, and expanding education and domestic partner benefits. Afterward, I reflected on the message from the gay and lesbian leadership, and their focus on gay and lesbian issues. Instead of spending energy hiding part of one's self, employees were happier and more productive when they were out and supported. I liked the sound of that; however, as a "T", my difference wasn't about protections and benefits based on who I loved; it was about who I was.

14
The Activist

1997

“I want to go to today’s Clippers game.” I was in girl mode that day.

Beth didn’t look up from her book. “So change and go.”

“I don’t want to change. I want to go as Mary Ann.”

Then she looked up. “That’s one of the few things we have together that isn’t about being trans, where we can just relax.”

I felt deflated. I needed Mary Ann to be part of everything in my life.

“I’m wearing jeans. I’ll be inconspicuous.” I watched her eyes roll. “If I sit in another section?”

“Tom sees us and wipes our seats for us. Frieda knows the beer you drink.”

I sulked. She was right in that I couldn’t be inconspicuous—not there. I went to the game as Mark.

Afterward, I stopped by a favorite spot, the Union Café. Sundays could be a slow bar night, so to encourage participation, they displayed show tunes on their TV screens. A VJ played from his extensive collection and took requests. The place was packed. To get a prime spot where I could see the big screen, I had to arrive at six when it began.

Show tunes were cathartic to my soul. I could sit immersed in them for hours. Most people went there to socialize. I felt entranced, and didn’t make good company, though Beth would come, too, on occasion. I could go as Mary Ann and I’d be welcomed there.

The VJ threw in an *Animaniacs* cartoon, Yakko’s “Nations of the World.” Yakko danced and pointed to a map, naming off all the countries on the planet. I loved educational stuff, especially for my sons. I thought about the boys and had a wonderful time singing along to the video.

I got up to use the men's room. A young gay man standing next to me at the urinal started a conversation.

"My friends and I saw you were having a great time watching that cartoon," he said.

"Yeah, it makes me think of my kids."

He was astonished. "*Yooou* have kids?"

"Yes, I have two sons."

"Do they know you're gay?"

"Well, actually, I'm trans."

His eyes widened. "*Yooou* used to be a *girl*?"

After I cracked up, I came out to him as a crossdresser. When I returned to my table, my heart was happy.

* * *

A handful of members at the Crystal Club heard about a transgender activist in Maryland who started a group called "It's Time, America!," to lobby for transgender civil rights. My friend, Sarah, had an idea to form an Ohio chapter, and those of us who found the idea exciting, met at the Grapevine to plan it. Every Tuesday, the Crystal Club held Ladies' Night Out at this gay and lesbian friendly restaurant in downtown Columbus, conveniently and coincidentally located on Gay Street. We listed the Grapevine on the Crystal Club's "Pink List" of welcoming establishments, where transgender people could go dressed as they chose, knowing they would not be asked to leave.

We soon realized some of us were more serious about activism than others. Sarah and I assumed leadership roles. We formed "It's Time, Ohio!." Each of us volunteered to be president at one time or another.

GenderPAC, based in Washington, D.C., was America's largest transgender rights organization in 1997. They launched an appeal for transgender people to come to Washington to lobby Congress for transgender employment protections amid huge controversy. A bill before Congress would have made discrimination based on sexual orientation illegal. As written, the bill would protect GLB employees, but not transgender workers. Over time, gay and lesbian groups included "bisexual" in their mission statements, while "transgender" struggled to gain a foothold.

GenderPAC sent the clarion call for trans people from each state to ask their senators and representatives to support an inclusive bill that would protect all GLBT people. I drove with Sarah and another woman from It's Time, Ohio! to join the effort. We drove together to Washington, D.C. for the lobby day and shared a cheap motel room.

In the hotel room, our friend said, "Transsexuals need workplace protection, but crossdressers don't." She and Sarah were proud transsexuals, having transitioned to living full-time as women. Most crossdressers were closeted, but a transsexual transitioning at work was visible. Activist transsexuals didn't think crossdressers should be seen in the workplace and advocated only for transsexual workplace rights. I was the rare crossdresser who wasn't afraid to come out.

I defended the community. "I'm a crossdresser, and we need rights too. A grocery store chain fired a truck driver for cross-dressing on his own time."

"You're not a crossdresser, Mary Ann; you're a transsexual."

"Am not."

"Are too."

"Am not."

"Are too."

Our verbal slap fight ended when I touched my sore ear.

"Mary Ann, you're bleeding."

"I see." I went in the bathroom to clean up. "It's these clip earrings. I wish I could pierce my ears, but Beth, you know...,"

* * *

The next morning, we dressed in our best women's suits to look as professional as possible. We assembled in a hotel conference room on Monday morning for a briefing and training. GenderPAC had prearranged appointments with many of our legislators and gave us our talking points.

Two Congressional bills had been introduced to protect the GLB community. The Employment Non-Discrimination Act (ENDA) would prohibit discrimination in employment based on sexual orientation. The Hate Crimes Prevention Act would add sexual orientation to the list of reasons why a crime would be considered a federal hate crime. Neither bill included the word “transgender.” No language, no protection.

ENDA had been going nowhere since 1994. None of us thought these bills would pass any time soon, but whether sooner or later, we all believed they would become law. Our mission was to gain inclusion in these bills so when the day came, we would also be protected. I worked hard to gain “T” inclusion in GLB wherever I could.

Stories were everywhere of transgender people being fired as soon as they came out. At the time, it was almost expected that when a man transitioned to become a woman, she would quit her job as a professional, move to another city, and take a new job as a secretary. In many cases, the newly unemployed woman couldn’t get a job in her new identity. Desperate trans women, especially those facing additional discrimination because of color, felt they had no choice but to turn to prostitution. This line of work could be dangerous and degrading; however, there was quite a demand on the streets for women with something extra between their legs.

On the train to the Capitol, the GenderPAC director stood near me in her skirted power suit, her short haircut standing out from the long hair worn by most trans women. She could see I was nervous and took pity on me. She chuckled and confided in my ear, “What nobody knows is, underneath all this, I’m wearing women’s underwear.”

When we arrived at the Capitol, Mariette Pathy Allen, the trans community's loyal photographer, took our photo on the Capitol steps. That's me in the cranberry suit on the left holding the tote bag.

Photo by Marriette Pathy Allen

Columbus was politically red. Our Central Ohio representatives were Republicans John Kasich and Deborah Pryce; our senators were also GOP. GenderPAC secured appointments with staffers in Kasich's and Pryce's offices. We proudly marched into Pryce's office in our skirt suits and heels and were introduced to her legislative assistant (LA).

"The representative is unavailable. I can hear your concerns." Pryce's LA listened as we made our case. "Representative Pryce is totally supportive of ENDA."

We were astonished. Imagine, a Republican in 1997 supporting a gay rights bill. He said lobbyists from the Human Rights Campaign (HRC) had been there, and told them to support the bills as written, without added support for transgender people. Now we were shocked in a new, unpleasant way. Our meeting with Pryce's office ignited a huge controversy.

HRC, an enormous gay and lesbian activist organization headquartered in Washington, D.C., was not immune from controversy among the trans community. They held yearly fundraisers in larger cities considered to be *the* social event among gays and lesbians where they could get dressed up and support a good cause. HRC put on a nice face for the trans community, and yet many trans people didn't trust them. Now I understood why.

The lobby day leadership met later and compared notes. They found at least seven representatives and senators had been lobbied by HRC, asking for support of a GLB-only ENDA and opposing trans inclusion. HRC denied it. There were witnesses. We were furious.

Several radical trans activists launched a full-out war on HRC. They formed an activist group called the TransFlakes, later called the National Transgender Advocacy Coalition. I heard about infighting in that group, so I decided to avoid them and put my energy into more productive outlets.

While lobbying, I met a trans woman who reminded me of first-time crossdressers from the Crystal Club. Penni Ashe Matz wore an obvious wig, had a male-sounding voice, and to me, came across as the most visible trans member of our group. Most of the lobbyists were transsexuals passable to different degrees. I identified as a crossdresser and wasn't contemplating another step. I thought Penni might be more like me and I started up a conversation. We hung out that evening and shared our stories.

"I live full-time as Penni. I legally changed my name. I have some medical issues, so I can't have sex reassignment surgery—it could kill me."

She was the leader of It's Time, Massachusetts! and a well-known trans activist in the state. What she said next changed my life.

"I made a conscious decision not to pass as female. Transsexuals who pass are not helping the cause. Nobody knew they were trans. I choose not to pass on a day-to-day basis, and that way everyone I interact with knows they met a transsexual."

"You educate the world one person at a time."

"I make an effort to be nice to people. I feel I'm an ambassador for the transgender community and by making a good impression, people will have a positive impression of the one transsexual they remember meeting."

"I really admire you, Penni. The more people who know a trans person, the harder it will be for anti-trans activists to paint us as child molesters."

I mulled over Penni's perspective. I'd spent a great deal of energy trying to acquire passing skills, and it hadn't worked. Despite my best efforts, I sounded male. I'd never been threatened, and wasn't worried about my safety. Going out *en femme* didn't change my six-foot stature or the confidence I projected. I decided Penni's idea was right for me as well. I could stop worrying about passing and focus on education.

I made a good friend that day. Penni and I stayed in touch, and I visited her in Boston when I was there for training. I have missed her since she passed away in 2001.

To this day, I don't try to pass. I live my life in comfort as my true self. My voice sounds a lot like Mark's. People who know me as Mary Ann say the higher girl voice sounds faked. It's far more authentic to use the voice God gave me, and I feel I do more good for the world by not passing. I try to be kind and helpful to people I meet. For the next several years, I became the face of the transgender community in central Ohio.

15
Lucent's Historic Policy

1997

Gays and lesbians at EQUAL! emphasized the importance of being out, and to be safely out, a company needed a nondiscrimination policy. Otherwise, you could be fired for coming out. This policy was a significant accomplishment at AT&T and at Lucent, and it made a healthy difference in the lives of the GLB people who worked there. I thought this was a wonderful message.

I wanted to come out as transgender, and have this comfort and safety too. Lucent's Equal Employment Opportunity (EEO) policy in 1997 forbade "discrimination or harassment because of race, color, creed, religion, national origin, citizenship, sex, marital status, age, etc., and sexual orientation." As written, it protected gays, lesbians, and bisexuals, not transgender persons. Since I was the first trans person to join EQUAL!, and EQUAL! had recently added "transgender" to its mission statement, this was a new opportunity.

I felt ready to "do the ask." I called the EQUAL! vice president with connections to the HR department. "Would it be possible to include transgender people in the EEO policy?"

"I'll ask," he said. "I have to go through channels."

Weeks later, a response came back through those mysterious channels. "If we were to add transgender people to the EEO policy, what language should we use to be as inclusive as possible?"

Wow! What a great question. I needed a great answer, and to get one, I asked lobby day activists. They connected me with a transgender attorney in Washington, D.C., who had written the proposed language for a trans-inclusive ENDA.

She recommended: "gender identity, sex and gender characteristics, or gender expression." What a mouthful. What did it all mean?

- Gender identity: A person's strongly held internal sense of self. Do you feel yourself to be a man, a woman, or a non-binary alternative? This language would protect transsexuals.
- Sex characteristics: Hidden medical conditions that blur whether you are biologically male or female: chromosome combinations other than XX or XY, such as XXY, XXXY, or XYY; chromosome mosaicism, where one part of the body might be XX and another part XY; full or partial androgen insensitivity syndrome; hypospadias; and true or pseudohermaphroditism. These conditions made a person's biological sex separate from the XX/XY binary. This language would protect intersex people.
- Gender characteristics: Visible biological cues about whether a person is a man or woman, such as height, voice pitch, body hair, facial hair, hand and foot size, breasts, and hips. This language would also protect intersex people with both masculine and feminine characteristics, like breasts and body hair.
- Gender expression: Social gender constructs, including hair length and style, makeup, clothing choices, body language, interest in dolls or trucks, in nursing or construction work. This language would protect almost anyone who isn't Barbie or Bubba, especially feminists, gays and lesbians, and crossdressers.

HR frowned on the language. They didn't want "sex characteristics" in the policy. One person reportedly asked, "Does this mean it's okay to drop your pants?"

I suggested a simplification. We could protect "gender identity, characteristics, or expression." We would define "gender characteristics" to include both the hidden and visible medical intersex properties. Gender identity and expression stayed the same. A long period passed where I heard nothing. On October 28, 1997, Lucent's CEO, Rich McGinn, signed the new EEO policy. The co-president of EQUAL! informed me via email with an attachment of the new, trans-inclusive EEO policy. I took a moment to appreciate how this latest accomplishment had been delivered using my uuencode attachment method.

LUCENT TECHNOLOGIES EQUAL OPPORTUNITY POLICY STATEMENT

Diversity and the equal opportunity it affords is strategically important to Lucent. It makes Lucent more competitive in the marketplace. It has been Lucent's long standing tradition, as well as our corporate policy, to treat each individual with dignity and respect. This is both a question of equity and of market success. To guarantee this, we will effectively utilize all of our human resource talent and continue to pursue this effort.

Lucent's policy is to:

- comply with both the letter and the spirit of all applicable laws and regulations governing employment;
- provide equal opportunity to all employees and to all applicants for employment;
- take appropriate affirmative action to make equal opportunity a reality;
- prohibit unlawful discrimination or harassment because of race, color, creed, religion, national origin, citizenship, sex, marital status, age, physical or mental disability, one's status as a special disabled veteran or veteran of the Vietnam era, or because of a person's sexual orientation, gender identity characteristics or expression, in any employment decision or in the administration of any personnel policy;
- make reasonable accommodations to the physical and/or mental limitations of qualified employees or applicants with disabilities;
- ensure that maximum opportunity is afforded to all minority and women-owned business to participate as suppliers, contractors, and subcontractors of goods and services to Lucent Technologies; and comply with regulatory agency requirements and with federal, state, and local procurement regulations and programs;
- advise employees of their rights to refer violations of this policy to their supervision, or to the appropriate Lucent Technologies organization charged with the administration of the Equal Opportunity/Affirmative Action policy, without intimidation or retaliation of any form for exercising such rights.

I want to reaffirm Lucent's commitment of providing equal opportunity to all employees and applicants for employment in accordance with all applicable laws, directives, and regulations of federal, state, and local governing bodies and agencies thereof.

I expect all managers throughout Lucent Technologies to comply fully with all aspects of this policy, and to conduct themselves in accordance with the principles of equal opportunity.

Demonstrated commitment to equal opportunity is an investment in our people and our future growth. Consequently, a company that attracts, selects, develops, and retains the best will remain the industry leader. Lucent's ongoing efforts in this direction will provide us with a critical, competitive advantage in the marketplace.

Richard A. McGinn

Richard A. McGinn
Chief Executive Officer & President

October 1997

I wrote the announcement for our activist group, "It's Time, Ohio!."

LUCENT TECHNOLOGIES PROTECTS TRANSGENDER EMPLOYEES

Columbus, Ohio. December 19, 1997.

It's Time, Ohio! is pleased to announce that Lucent Technologies, the leading producer of telecommunications products, has adopted an Equal Employment Opportunity policy statement that includes protection for transgender and intersex employees.

In the EEO policy statement, Rich McGinn, president and CEO of Lucent Technologies, said, "Demonstrated commitment to equal opportunity is an investment in our people and our future growth. Consequently, a company that attracts, selects, develops, and retains the best will remain the industry leader. Lucent's ongoing efforts in this direction will provide us with a critical, competitive advantage in the marketplace."

Lucent is leading the way in the creation of an open workplace. Lucent's new EEO policy contains specific language to prohibit discrimination based on "gender identity," "characteristics," or "expression." Lucent's wording creates a separate, but equal status for transgender employees, next to the protection for "sexual orientation." To our knowledge, Lucent Technologies is the first large company to provide specific language in its EEO policy to protect transgender employees.

Lucent's wording protects transsexuals ("gender identity"), intersex ("gender characteristics") and crossdressers ("gender expression"). The wording goes beyond these three narrow categories, protecting people whose gender presentation is nontraditional, including masculine women and feminine men.

Lucent's wording goes beyond a promise not to hire, fire, or promote based on gender issues or sexual orientation. Lucent also prohibits any discrimination or harassment of our employees.

Lucent's policy is to: prohibit unlawful discrimination or harassment because of race, color, creed, religion, national origin, citizenship, sex, marital status, age, physical or mental disability, one's status as a special disabled veteran or veteran of the Vietnam era, or because of a person's sexual orientation, gender identity characteristics or expression, in any employment decision or in the administration of any personnel policy.

It's Time, Ohio! would like to encourage other organizations and companies to follow Lucent's example, and add specific transgender language to their policy statements.

It's Time, Ohio! is the Ohio chapter of It's Time, America!, a transgender lobbying organization.

We'd made history—Lucent was a safe place to come out as transgender. If you've ever wondered if one person can change the world, stop wondering. It happens.

* * *

Now that I was safe, at least on paper, it was time to come out at work. I felt it would be appropriate to begin with my boss, John, who worked in Naperville. I traveled there often to meet with the rest of the email support group. I wanted to come out face to face, and waited until my next business trip.

I scheduled a half-hour meeting without telling him the topic in advance. I had never revealed such a personal thing about myself to anyone at work. The transgender community had stories galore of high-performing workers who were fired or harassed out of their jobs. I felt frozen with fear. I had no idea how John would react, and brought a copy of Lucent's new policy with me—just in case. We met in his private office. I shut the door.

"I have something personal and important to share with you," I said. "This is difficult, so bear with me. Lucent has a great history of supporting minorities and has groups for women, blacks, and GLBT people." John nodded as my anxiety level tripled. I continued, my voice shaking with vibrato. "I've been active with EQUAL!, the GLBT employee group." I studied his face for clues. He gazed at me with concern. "John, I'm transgender." There, I said it.

"Oh. What does that mean?"

"I'm a crossdresser. I spend some of my life as Mark and some as Mary Ann. I need to tell you this because there may be a time when I come into work as Mary Ann." My body trembled along with my voice.

John's face relaxed into a compassionate expression. "That's fine," he said, "as long as you get the job done."

My relief came in a flood of emotion and I cried. John pushed a box of tissues across his desk toward me. I took one and dabbed my eyes. I figured I had better say everything on my mind while I had the moment.

"While working at home, I'm often in Mary Ann mode. I do my

job as usual, and nobody knows how I look through email or over the phone. However, I spend a lot of unnecessary energy hiding this part of myself. I want to be more productive by removing the worry about who knows."

"I have no problem with your productivity," he responded.

"I need to tell the others in our group."

"Okay. I'll put you on the agenda for our meeting this afternoon. I'm also interested in knowing more about what it means to be transgender."

At the group meeting, I was much calmer. With John's backing, I felt confident everything would be okay. When my turn came, I came out to the group, and though I was still nervous, I had crossed the hardest threshold and emerged on the other side, this time without crying.

The group accepted the news without showing emotion. I couldn't shake the feeling the guys were in denial and held in their reactions. The one woman in our group had a practical question. She looked at my tight ponytail that showed off my sharp, masculine hairline. "How do you fix your hair?" she asked. I took out a photo of me as Mary Ann and passed it around. "Oh, bangs. I couldn't picture how your hair would work as a woman."

The photo seemed a good way to make an introductory gesture. I wanted them to experience me as Mary Ann, so it wouldn't be a mystery. I thought again about Penni's good advice. People who had met a trans person relaxed more than those who hadn't and based their impression on scary stereotypes of fangs and fishnets.

"I'd like to come to work tomorrow as Mary Ann. Is that okay?"

Heads nodded around the table. "Sure, that's fine," John said. "My wife needs my car. Can you give me a ride to work?"

The next morning, I took time with my makeup, selected a long blue dress, and styled my hair down with bangs—my standard Mary Ann look. I was ten minutes late picking up John. He was standing on his front porch and pointed at his watch.

"Sorry I'm late."

"I've been reading online about this transgender thing. I keep seeing pictures of people with penises and breasts."

Great. I cringed, imagining him seeing pictures of transgender porn stars. "Those people are out there. I guess there's a demand for transgender prostitutes. But that's not what I'm about. I'm just another woman, doing her job."

My coworkers were fine interacting with me as Mary Ann. My nervousness abated and I felt perky, happy to dig into our work while being authentic. They made a point to get my name right, and my pronouns, too, most of the time. I felt grateful they made an effort, and let an occasional slip-up pass without comment, though each "he" stung a bit. It was 1998, and changing up pronouns wasn't on my radar yet.

We held a planning meeting to design our next small project. We all took on follow-up tasks and I was thrilled to see my work had been assigned to Mary Ann rather than Mark. I luxuriated in the feeling of acceptance by my peers.

When I returned to Columbus, I began my tasks as Mark. This created confusion when a job involved interacting with a coworker in New Jersey. More than once, an activist told me, "A business cannot deal with a crossdresser flip-flopping at work. You should pick a gender and stick with it." For the most part, they were wrong. I flip-flopped, and the business dealt with it fine.

Names and pronouns were different. As a rule, transsexuals insisted everyone get their new names and pronouns right and gently corrected anyone who slipped a pronoun. Anyone looking at me would know which gender I was presenting and could use the appropriate name. People often got it wrong on the phone or in email where they couldn't see me working in a dress and heels. I couldn't blame the innocent person on the phone, nor did it feel right to correct them. I had to deal with it—the price I had to pay for coming to work sometimes as Mary Ann. In time, I settled on a standard response. "My name is Mark. Mary Ann is my nickname. You can call me either one. If you want to be especially supportive, you can call me by the name matching how I'm dressed that day." My coworkers would nod, relax, and stop worrying.

A week after my business trip, I started the coming out process in Columbus. I invited Chuck, my office mate to lunch. He looked worried as I picked my bread into little pieces with my long nails coated in clear polish. Gathering up my courage, I said I had been working with EQUAL!, and was transgender.

He took a deep breath and his face relaxed. "Geez, I thought you were going to tell me you had some terrible disease and were dying." He took another noticeable breath. "Now I see it. You've grown out your hair; you have long fingernails. Hey, be you. It's cool."

Each time, I got better at coming out. At first, it felt like a leap of faith, jumping, and then hoping I would land safely on the other side of the abyss. I was relieved to discover most people accepted my news. The few who were uncomfortable with the concept were polite to my face.

I no longer needed to hide my identity behind the "Harris" pseudonym. I changed my email to "Mary Ann Horton" and introduced myself that way in person. I still used separate personal email addresses for Mark and for Mary Ann, now with my legal surname.

EQUAL! at the national level issued a challenge. They offered an award to the first person to come out to fifty people. Two months later, I claimed the award. Beth, and I as Mary Ann, celebrated the achievement with a nice dinner at a favorite restaurant.

16

A New Frontier at Work

I'd worked at home as Mary Ann. I'd gone into the Naperville office with my group, and I'd ventured into Columbus for an EQUAL! meeting. None of those were the same as coming into my own office to work face-to-face with people who knew me, and doing my regular job. I longed to bridge this new frontier.

Company policy said I was safe to work as Mary Ann. I worried about potential backlash from a disgruntled employee. Local chapter leaders told me they had received anonymous voicemails with death threats. Sometimes EQUAL! posters were torn down or defaced. I needed to get my ducks in a row.

I considered a business justification for Mary Ann's first appearance in my workplace. The opportunity presented itself in October 1998. National Coming Out Day, celebrated in mid-October, commemorated the 1987 National March on Washington. Local GLBT groups held events that month to encourage people to come out. EQUAL! in Columbus invited a local gay couple to give a talk: a male executive with a local pizza chain and his partner who opened a downtown Columbus GLB-themed restaurant. They had the interior decorated with impressive gay and lesbian memorabilia, including a tennis racket donated by Billie Jean King, a Speedo from Greg Louganis, and an over-the-top outfit Elton John had worn on stage. It seemed appropriate for a visibly GLBT person to introduce the speakers. Mark looked like a straight man, and many knew I was married to Beth. If Mary Ann made the introduction, I'd have my business justification. I was delighted to volunteer for this lunchtime talk. It made sense for me to work all day as Mary Ann. EQUAL! approved, as did John.

I was set to make the introduction on Friday, October 9, 1998. On the preceding Monday, I got a disturbing call from EQUAL! National.

When I had come out to so many people, someone had anonymously reported me to corporate security. This individual expressed concern, God forbid, Mary Ann might use the women's restroom at work. If I did, they would file a complaint against me. I would be accused of creating a hostile workplace environment. Some bigot had found a way to stick it to EQUAL!

Transgender use of restrooms is controversial today, and even riskier then. The penalty for using the "wrong" public restroom was an M-1 misdemeanor, punishable by six months in jail. A company on private property, such as Bell Labs, could set their policy, as opposed to a park located on public property, but they had little guidance. Everyone assumed your driver's license dictated which restroom you used. EQUAL! scheduled an emergency meeting with one of their co-presidents from National present, along with my boss John, HR, corporate security, and the Bell Labs medical department. The topic: which restroom would I use? One stakeholder was missing: me.

The national co-president called me to relay their intense discussion. Everyone agreed I couldn't use the men's room. It would trigger a complaint if I used the women's room, and HR didn't want to defend a hostile workplace complaint. Their solution was for me to use the women's restroom in the medical department, a single occupancy restroom. I was crushed.

Photos by Chuck Bryant

Nonetheless, I had to make a choice. I was so happy to be allowed to go to work as Mary Ann that I accepted their decision.

That Friday, I arrived at work wearing a royal blue, two-piece skirt set, nylons, and pumps. I walked in and said hello to Chuck. He kindly snapped a picture of me at my desk.

For the lunch meeting, I signed our guests in at the front desk and escorted them to the Capital room, where we found an audience of about thirty people. As I introduced the speakers, it felt good to be myself. During my introduction, I came out as transgender. The audience spontaneously broke out in applause. The presentation by the speakers was marvelous and well received.

After lunch, I needed a restroom break. Medical was about a quarter-mile walk from my office, and I wore heels. The first time I walked up there, I was struck by the route I had to take. The only path went through busy, well-lit hallways. I could have encountered someone I knew who didn't know I was trans. On the way, I passed an internal customer I hadn't told. He didn't give me a second look.

I entered the tiny, single-occupancy restroom in medical. The cramped room had a toilet, sink, mirror, and a hard plastic chair covered with junk and dust. It was functional, though the dim light was inadequate to redo my makeup.

On the way back, I passed a coworker I wasn't out to yet. Perking up with recognition, he turned around and exclaimed, "Mark?"

I shook his hand. "Hi, I'm Mary Ann."

He laughed uncontrollably.

"I'm transgender. I spend some of my time as Mary Ann."

"Well, whatever works."

I'd made myself vulnerable, and the result was laughter. I felt icky. Comedians had taught the world that men dressed as women were hilarious, and he reacted accordingly. Salvaging my self-respect, I decided to take heart I'd brought joy into his day.

About 4:00 p.m., my phone rang. Instead of my usual baritone "Mark Horton," I answered, "Hello." An EQUAL! friend from New Jersey asked about my first day. I appreciated the support call. She made me promise to send out a report.

About 5:00 p.m., my office mate was on his speakerphone with my boss and two others. An emergency had arisen: an email wasn't working right, and people's expense vouchers were not getting through. My office mate said, "Well, Mary Ann's right here," and I joined in the call.

Before I knew it, the folks on the other end had conferenced in the customer. I'd worked with her before as Mark. My boss introduced the three of them, and after an awkward silence said, "There are two other people on the call." My office mate introduced himself and looked at me. Paralyzed by fear, I introduced myself as Mark, but I stayed in Mary Ann's persona and girl voice. We soon found the solution to her email problem and she profusely thanked us with our boss still on the call. One crisis averted.

My Lucent ID badge bore Mark's name and photo. Company policy required me to wear it at work. This was fine in boy mode, where I could inconspicuously clip it to my belt. This felt wrong as Mary Ann, and HR would not issue me a second badge.

I found a creative solution. I noticed sometimes people's badges flipped around backward, and nobody cared. I printed a full-sized copy of a Lucent badge that had my *femme* name and featured a photo of me in girl mode, and taped it to the back of my official badge. If I came to work as Mary Ann, I flipped it around backward so the unofficial picture would be visible. It was a bit badass, but it worked.

On occasion over the next few years, I came to work as Mary Ann. I put up with the restroom issue in Columbus. I needed fifteen minutes to walk there, do my thing, and walk back, which irked me. When I traveled, I used the restroom matching my presenting gender. I advocated for this, and in 2000, Lucent agreed and made this company policy.

* * *

Matt turned sixteen and needed a car. I passed along my thirteen-year-old Honda Accord to him, and bought a new top-of-the-line Camry. What a treat to sell stock and pay cash for the car.

I felt great about working for Lucent and contributing to Bell Labs. I'd bought Lucent stock each month through the employee purchase plan, and the share price soared. In addition, we had a groundbreaking EEO policy. In fact, I was so happy with Lucent that I chose LUCENT 1 for my new license plate. Lucent was number one with its shareholders, and number one in the trans community. A motorist honked at me, gestured to my plate, and gave me a thumbs-up — no doubt another satisfied Lucent shareowner.

* * *

All good organizations need hard workers. As the only out transgender person at Lucent, I was called on to work with the Columbus chapter and at the national level of EQUAL!.

We all pitched in to plan the 1998 EQUAL! conference in Columbus. One of the items I pushed for was transgender visibility. I wanted a top-name transgender speaker to give a plenary speech everyone at the conference would see. The planning committee asked me to find a speaker. I thought of Jamison Green, whom I'd never met. His reputation as the best-known trans man in the activist community was superb.

"He'll educate them by his presence," one activist told me.

I arranged for EQUAL! to fly Jamison from San Francisco to Columbus for the conference. When I met him, he spoke with a deep voice, had a thick beard, and a strong manly presence. It was impossible to imagine him ever having been female. He was also an accomplished public speaker.

I introduced Jamison, who received a warm welcome. He began his speech with a memorable anecdote.

"A few years ago, my young daughter was trying to figure out what it meant for me to be transgender. We were eating at Jack in the Box, and in a loud voice she asked, 'Daddy, do you have a penis yet?' My response was, 'Of course I do, sweetheart,' which reassured everyone who was listening in the dead silence that followed her question."

He paused and made eye contact with the audience. "Well, I have one *now*."

Jamison's presence cemented the trans presence in EQUAL! at Lucent. Finally, I felt our issues met the mark.

* * *

Coming into the GLBT political space as a transgender woman, I learned about the notable tension between gay men and lesbians in the 1990s. The women felt ignored by the men and had to be assertive and persistent to be heard. This was an issue in the straight community, too, with the difference being lesbians had no interest in being charming merely to assuage male egos. Gay men outnumbered lesbians four to one at GLBT events, which stacked the odds against the women.

EQUAL! addressed this issue in their bylaws. Leadership positions had to have equal numbers of men and women. Local chapters had two co-presidents, one male and one female. Nationally, there were male and female presidents, and three male and three female vice presidents.

My presence disturbed the balance. Everyone wanted me involved and working, but the women didn't want me taking up one of their hard-earned slots. I was different from the cis lesbians, and neither they, nor I, felt I could adequately represent lesbian concerns. EQUAL!'s female president was skeptical of transgender inclusion. "It distracts from our core mission of sexual orientation," she said. She was good about including me, but I had to work extra hard to earn her respect.

EQUAL's leadership invited me to a strategic planning meeting. We created new positions for up to three transgender vice presidents for the national organization and appointed me to one of the slots. This eliminated the tension and brought me on board.

17

The Spirit Calls

1998

Spending half of my time in girl mode, I felt driven to experience more areas of my life as Mary Ann. I sensed a strong calling to go to church. Even though I'd prayed often about my gender, it seemed wrong to hide this part of me from God's house. I promised the boys I wouldn't go to my home church *en femme* because their friends would see me. I needed to find a suitable church.

Stonewall Columbus, the local GLB community center, published a list of welcoming businesses and it included a few Lutheran churches. I tried Redeemer Lutheran. It wasn't far and wasn't in Bexley, so it seemed a safe choice.

On Easter Sunday, I dressed up in my brightest outfit—a cranberry skirted suit with a bright yellow floral top under the jacket. As I pulled into Redeemer's parking lot, I felt a flash of panic. I was about to walk into a church in a skirt. Would I be welcomed or laughed at? I summoned my courage and walked in the door.

The greeter, an older woman in a pastel Easter dress, welcomed me and wished me a happy Easter. Entering the foyer, I met several gay and lesbian members who were glad I was there. As always, I was the only trans person.

I started a conversation with Katheryn, who introduced me to her partner and invited me to sit with them. She was a balloon artist and had created a festive Easter cross sculpture. Katheryn and I formed a warm friendship, and she remains my best friend today.

I met a gay member of the church council, which was like a board of directors for the congregation. I asked him, "What's Redeemer's policy for welcoming GLBT people?"

"We welcome all people regardless of sexual orientation."

"Does that include transgender people?"

"Well, no, not officially."

"Would you consider adding transgender people to your welcoming statement?"

"I'll ask the church council."

A month passed. The council had met and discussed it, and the answer was no. What a disappointment.

"But," he continued, "that doesn't mean a final no. Council needs to go through a process, become educated, discuss it, and deliberate."

It sounded like a lot of work. I wondered how they could become educated about transgender people. I asked Meral if she would do a panel at Redeemer.

I'd known Meral Crane since she presented to the Crystal Club. She was a social worker, a loving mother figure who guided transsexuals through the transition process. She also presented transgender education workshops, bringing one or two passable male-to-female (MTF) transsexuals and one or two masculine FTMs to tell their stories. I'd seen her workshops, and they were excellent. Everyone was post-op and wowed the audience with their personal stories.

She agreed and then surprised me. "Would you be on the panel?" Here I was, not transitioned, not planning to, and not passable. I was delighted to be included.

We gave the presentation after a Sunday service. Meral spoke for twenty minutes about what it meant to be transgender, including transsexuals going in both directions, crossdressers, and intersex people. The panel then told their personal stories.

The first trans woman on the panel was a gorgeous blonde, tall and slender. She wore a cute dress that showed off her great legs. Next, a trans man with handsome features and a trimmed beard spoke. In a deep voice, he told the story of his transition from a female. I told my story, beginning with my childhood interest in my mother's clothing, my marriage to Karen, attempts to be "cured," our divorce and child custody battle, and how Beth loved and accepted me.

Seeing actual transgender people and hearing their stories, helped the church members understand. We heard only positive comments after the talk. Meral knew what she was doing. This presentation did a wonderful job of educating people whose only exposure had been to media stereotypes. A month later, the Redeemer council voted to officially welcome gay, lesbian, bisexual, and transgender people. I rejoiced in the knowledge we were welcome.

Meral invited me to be a regular on her panels as she gave these talks over the next few years. We presented the panel many times to churches, LGB activist organizations and workplaces, including one at my Lucent workplace. When I met the three post-op transsexuals at the lobby to help them sign in, the security guard checked their IDs. One of the trans women needed to use the restroom; the guard directed her to the ladies' room. I asked him why she got to use that restroom and I didn't.

"Her paperwork is a little more in order," he apologetically replied.

He meant she had an F on her drivers' license, but mine still read M. I hated that it mattered.

A motherly woman at Redeemer told me about a group called Lutherans Concerned. "I'm straight," the woman said, "but my son is gay. I got involved as an advocate for him. He's grown and moved on, and here I am, still involved with the group. Would you like to come to our next meeting?"

I felt welcomed at the Lutherans Concerned/Central Ohio (LC/CO) meeting, an activist group populated with a dozen gay and lesbian adults from Redeemer and a handful from other GLB friendly Lutheran churches. Activists working in LC/CO had two concerns facing the church: could gay or lesbian pastors in committed relationships be called to lead a congregation, and could a Lutheran pastor perform same-sex commitment ceremonies?

Gay and lesbian pastors had been called to congregations in Berkeley and Minneapolis. The national Lutheran body, the Evangelical Lutheran Church in America (ELCA), was threatening to kick them out. Strong statements of conscience arose from pastors, their church councils, and allies, who believed their continued service to the church was like an act of civil disobedience. Similar drama followed straight pastors who had openly performed the forbidden "wedding" ceremonies. My heart went out to these steadfast activists. I thought it was terrible they were being persecuted for who they loved.

ELCA pastors were expected to live by a Visions and Expectations code, which required them to be faithful if married or chaste if not. Only straight couples could marry, which ruled out gay and lesbian pastors in committed relationships. Ironically, single gay pastors seemed to be fine until they wanted to commit to a partner, and then they were in trouble. The ELCA had no formal edict forbidding a pastor from performing a "marriage" ceremony for a same-sex couple, and many Lutheran pastors performed them on the QT. Those visible about it found themselves in trouble with their bishop.

Several members of LC/CO and I went to Minneapolis to attend Jubilee, a national GLBT conference hosted by LC/NA (Lutherans Concerned/North America). Both LC/NA and the ELCA were based in that city. As usual, out of a hundred or so attendees, I was the only transgender person there.

Janet, a lesbian co-chair, greeted me and expressed interest in learning about me. I spent time getting to know her and the other females in leadership roles. At one point, Janet took me aside. "I thought you'd hang out with the men, and here you are, hanging out with us." She had never met a transgender person before and I didn't fit her narrative.

"Oh, no," I said. "I definitely prefer to hang out with women. And now that I'm familiar with LC/NA, would it be possible to include transgender people in their mission statement?" I asked.

"We've already done that."

I repeated what had happened at Redeemer, hoping a national action would mean trans people would be welcomed at the local level. The response wasn't as positive as I hoped.

"LC/NA sponsors a 'Reconciling in Christ' (RIC) program, where a congregation, or an entire synod, can declare they welcome people regardless of their sexual orientation. They go through an extensive educational process to understand sexual orientation. RIC congregations have learned what it means and then decided to welcome gay, lesbian, and bisexual people.

"We love the idea of adding 'gender identity' language. The problem is the existing RIC congregations. If the language were suddenly updated in the central LC/NA documents, those congregations would be unaware. They wouldn't know to welcome transgender people."

I had personally experienced that at Redeemer. I didn't like the idea that another trans person could go to a RIC congregation who welcomed all sexual orientations, and then be rejected for their gender identity. I knew how much courage it took to walk into a church in a dress.

I returned to Lutherans Concerned meetings in Columbus, mostly to hang out with the many friends I'd made there. When the 2000 national conference was held in Columbus, I helped organize it. I worshiped at the three RIC congregations in Columbus and felt welcomed by all. I knew we'd eventually be officially included because the leadership knew me and understood that transgender was different from drag.

Soon I wasn't alone. Over the next decade, trans women in other cities came to local LC meetings and worshipped in friendly Lutheran churches. Young trans students called to seminary were coming out to their classmates. The Lutheran movement for inclusion eventually became LGBT in both spirit and reality.

In 2009, after many attempts at previous church-wide assemblies, the national Evangelical Lutheran Church in America resolved the two sexual orientation issues in our favor. LC/NA rebranded as Reconciling Works, an organization to support LGBT people in the Lutheran church. They amended the RIC policy to "welcome people of all sexual orientations and gender identities." A sister organization, Extraordinary Lutheran Ministries, spun off to provide professional support for LGBT Lutheran pastors.

18

L, G, B, and T!

1998

After Lucent added transgender language to its EEO policy, I decided to seize the momentum. I trumpeted the new policy everywhere I thought it could be useful. After the It's Time, Ohio! press release, I spread the news to transgender email lists.

Many companies had employee groups like EQUAL!. They were set up in different ways and collectively called Employee Resource Groups (ERGs). For example, Lucent had ERGs for women, Asians, Latinx, African Americans, GLBTs, Indigenous peoples, and disabled workers. They all worked with HR to further the needs of the minority group.

Lots of other companies had gay and lesbian ERGs, and by 1998, most of them included "bisexual" in their missions. Only a few included "transgender." I knew of trans-inclusive ERGs at AT&T, Lucent, Apple, Chase, Boeing, and Sprint. I made myself as visible as possible by sharing the good news about Lucent with other GLB organizations, and suggested they use Lucent's inclusive EEO language for their missions and policies.

A trans woman from Apple's ERG reached out to me in the spring of 1998. She was in the process of transitioning on the job with the full support of Apple. She wanted to know how we got the nondiscrimination policy added at Lucent. We connected our respective HR directors to work out the details. That fall, Apple released their new EEO policy, using Lucent's "gender identity, characteristics, or expression" language. I felt like we were on a roll.

When Lucent split into three companies—Lucent, Avaya, and Agere—in 2000, all three kept the policy. I worked with Xerox in 2000, and then with American Airlines, who made the news for a pilot transitioning on the job. Both signed on and both simplified the language to "gender identity."

I felt as if I had pushed a snowball along, making it bigger and better as it gathered size and momentum. I networked with representatives from Kodak, NCR, and JPMorgan Chase. The ball began to roll on its own, its path sloping more downhill, needing little push from me.

In 2001, a gay activist published a scorecard for corporate America, which he called the Gay and Lesbian Values Index, or GLV. This ten-point index included a point for a trans-inclusive nondiscrimination policy. He passed it to the Human Rights Campaign in 2002, who renamed it the Corporate Equality Index (CEI) and converted it to a 100-percent scale. I had not been a fan of HRC since I learned of their stand at lobby day, but I felt the CEI had the potential to make a difference. When the first HRC Corporate Equality Index came out in 2002, thirteen companies were listed with a 100 percent score, which required a nondiscrimination policy protecting "gender identity" or "gender expression." The snowball finally rolled on its own.

* * *

At first, the so-called gay rights movement focused primarily on gay White men. It changed to gay and lesbian, and by the early 1990s, it had become gay, lesbian, and bisexual, in some circles: LesBiGay. In 1995, progressive organizations added "transgender" to their mission statements. One important part of the Columbus community lagged behind.

We held an It's Time, Ohio! evening meeting in the spring of 1998 at Stonewall Columbus. The last staffer asked us to lock up when we went home. As we packed up, we took a long look at all the Pride decorations.

Stonewall had chosen a "LesBiGay Holiday" theme for the 1998 Pride event. The lobby was covered in glittery LesBiGay decorations. Our exclusion did not add to the merriment.

"What day is it supposed to be for transgender people—Monday?" Sarah said. We wanted to be included in the theme. Something had to change.

Sarah had a devious idea. "Let's change it to LesBiGaTr, like you say 'alligator.' " We marked up printer paper to hang a huge, colorful banner from the ceiling proclaiming, "LesBiGaTr Holiday." We locked up and left.

Stonewall was not amused. They were offended we had dared to question their Pride theme. Stonewall's mission statement included lesbian, gay, and bisexual only, not transgender. They were clear we were welcome at their events and community center, though we were not part of their mission.

We were not about to meekly accept their putdown. Enter the activists! It's Time, Ohio! officially asked Stonewall how to go about updating their mission. We hoped to establish a dialogue and work toward trans inclusion. At first, we were told to address their board meeting. Then we needed to write a letter. Our phone calls were not returned. The formal rejection letter from Stonewall contained misinformed statements like: "We believe our language 'gay, lesbian, and bisexual' already includes you," and "There aren't enough of you."

We didn't take no for an answer. We asked. We cajoled. Sarah designed a colorful T-shirt with a smiling rainbow alligator labeled "LesBiGaTr." We pointed out how Stonewall listed transgender groups and events, and encouraged us to use their meeting facilities.

Graphic by Sarah Fox

At Sarah's urging, *Outlook*, Columbus's leading gay newspaper, ran a story. They were outraged Stonewall said no, and wanted to do an exposé. *Outlook* ran a cover story in our defense with a positive tone. We got phone calls and letters of support.

And what do you know? Stonewall took a new interest in us. We met with the executive director. He listened and they had a change in tone. Stonewall asked us to participate in Pride month events. I sensed a careful decision process would result in transgender education for Stonewall and constructive dialogue. Sarah and I applied for seats on Stonewall's board.

As Sarah and I staffed the It's Time! booth at Pride, unknown to us, another miracle occurred. Up the street, dozens of progressive students from Antioch College in western Ohio marched in the parade, carrying banners protesting Stonewall's refusal to include us. We discovered this happy news in Cleveland's *Gay People's Chronicle*, complete with a photo. We sent a heartfelt thank-you to Antioch College's student newspaper.

Pride that year was a busy weekend, and I found myself double booked. In addition to the It's Time, Ohio! booth, Adam's piano recital was at 2:00 p.m., a half-hour drive north. He'd been working hard, and he wanted his dad and Beth to hear him perform.

I wore a tie-dyed tank dress to Pride with scant makeup. Sarah and I set up the table, offering "virtual sex changes" as a fundraiser. For twenty dollars, we took a photo of an interested male passer-by, used a makeup program to add a woman's hairstyle, eye makeup, and lipstick, and presented an image of the person as a woman. It was a fun way to boost transgender awareness. I was grateful when Sue, from It's Time! in Cleveland, stopped by and pitched in.

At 1:30 p.m., I excused myself. I changed into slacks and a shirt in a Porta Potty, used my car mirror to brush my hair back into a ponytail, and rushed to the recital.

Beth and Adam were there when I arrived. The piano teacher arranged the performers from beginners to advanced, so the show got better as it progressed. Adam played second to last. His challenging piece drew enthusiastic applause from the parents.

After we congratulated him on his flawless performance, Beth took him home. I headed back to Pride. At a traffic light, I took off my ponytail and brushed out my hair and bangs. It was good to feel like Mary Ann again.

On the freeway, Beth's car passed me on the left. Adam spotted me from the passenger window. His mouth gaped. I smiled and waved.

Back at Pride, I put my dress back on and rejoined my group. Sue worked on the computer, transforming a topless butch woman into a long-haired femme. I exhaled and took a moment to decompress.

When I got home, Adam rushed over.

"Wow! I couldn't believe you could change into Mary Ann so fast. You were Dad just a few minutes before."

I had only changed my hairstyle. As long as I had foundation to cover my beard shadow, my hair was the first gender cue people noticed.

Dialogue continued with Stonewall, and in 2000, they offered Sarah a seat on their board for a three-year term. Sarah plunged into her board membership with zeal. At her urging, the mission statement of Stonewall Columbus was updated to include gay, lesbian, bisexual, and transgender.

Perhaps Sarah was too zealous. After a year, she decided to step down from the board. Her bold, controversial ideas didn't click with the other GLB board members. The board president reached out to me in her stead. I felt it was important to have a trans presence, and I accepted. I was a good match with the other board members and with the work, which spanned all the letters of the mission statement: keeping the website working, raising money, and planning for Pride.

* * *

Out & Equal, a new GLBT activist group focused on workplace rights, formed in 1998. I heard about them in time to attend their annual conference in October 1998 in Rochester. Out & Equal became one of the most important groups of my activist career.

Traveling to Rochester was a treat. Usually, I had to pack my bags for Mark and Mary Ann. This time, traveling as Mary Ann, my bag was smaller. My Thursday night flight was uneventful, and I checked in for the Friday through Sunday conference.

I spoke with the new executive director at Out & Equal. She was friendly, energetic, and fully committed to trans inclusion. She took great interest in my report as I shared the successful outcomes at Lucent and Apple.

Best of all, this was a bigger version of EQUAL!. The attendees were a Who's Who of Fortune 500 companies. Banks, conglomerate product manufacturers, technology companies, health care, transportation, and other sectors were represented by their Employee Resource Groups and HR directors. I wasn't the only trans person there, though I may have been the most outspoken. ERG leaders were happy to hear about Lucent's new EEO policy and felt fired up to do the same for their companies.

When it came time to leave on Sunday, I was tired and happy. I had that "first conference" feeling, where my feet wouldn't touch the ground for days. I felt so good I decided to wear a floral skirt on the plane home, although jeans would have been more appropriate.

My euphoria lasted until my connection in Newark, New Jersey. I had an America West Airlines ticket with a flight from Newark to Columbus on People Express Airlines. I grabbed a light dinner at the Newark airport and waited at the gate for my connection. A thunderstorm boomed outside, and the gate staff announced a delay of the incoming flight due to the storm. As the storm dragged on, there were more delays, and the passengers grew restless. I had my book to read, my euphoria, and my skirt, so I didn't mind the wait.

After two hours, the gate crew decided to placate the restless passengers and brought out cases of warm canned soda. Our plane circled overhead and would land as soon as the weather cleared. I took it in stride. At 9:30 p.m., we heard an announcement: the plane was required to return to its origin because it had grown low on fuel. We would all have to rebook our flights for the next day. Now I began to worry.

My checked bag held my shaver and makeup. I had shaved that morning, and my full face of makeup had lost most of its effect. By morning, it would be a lost cause. My boy clothes were all at home, so changing back to Mark wasn't an option.

An angry mob of passengers converged on the gate desk to rebook their flights. I thought I would be clever and go to the America West customer service center down the concourse. They had a line, too, but shorter. Two customer service representatives, a man and a woman, worked their way through the waiting customers. I hoped my turn would be with the female. My ticket was in Mark's name and I looked female. I expected the man would be less comfortable and perhaps give me a hard time.

As I waited, the crowd became agitated. People walked away from the desk, seething and yelling about how the airline treated them. The male agent announced, "I want you to know, if a problem is caused by weather, we don't give out a hotel room." *Crap.* I hadn't thought about the hotel. I would have to find a room and pay for it. None of the people in line had seen any relief and loud, angry voices didn't help their case.

My worry quotient rose higher. When my turn came, the male agent called me up. *Gulp.* I showed him my ticket and told him my problem. He called down to the gate to no avail. All the staff had left for the night. This made him mad. I had an America West ticket, good for a People Express flight, and in his opinion, the People Express gate agents hadn't treated me right. "They should have taken care of you at the gate."

After several minutes on the phone without satisfaction, he started writing me vouchers. A voucher for a hotel room. A voucher for dinner. A voucher for breakfast. I was shocked and relieved. Furious at the airline workers, the agent apologized for the poor treatment I'd received. He told me where to pick up my bag. I boarded a shuttle, grateful to have my bag with my makeup. I would sleep well.

Monday morning I shaved in my hotel bathroom mirror and did my makeup. I boarded the rebooked flight to Columbus, my belly full from the free breakfast, and went home to Beth, my love. It was going to be a good day after all.

19
The Federation

The National Gay and Lesbian Task Force (NGLTF), one of the biggest national level activist organizations, had a fully LGBT-inclusive mission. Their annual Creating Change conferences were packed with thousands of young, inspired activists. The Task Force was the first group I saw to consistently order the letters as LGBT instead of GLB or GLBT.

In addition to national level activism, the Task Force decided it was important to work for LGBT equality at the state level. In 1997, they created the Federation of LGBT Statewide Political Organizations. Nobody could say that name more than once, so we shortened it to the Federation. I made the obligatory Star Trek joke to myself.

The NGLTF invited statewide organizations to join the Federation. Ohio didn't have a statewide LGBT organization at the time. We did have a statewide transgender organization, It's Time, Ohio!. The leadership of ITOH agreed I should be their representative.

My first Federation meeting in November 1998 was part of Creating Change and held in Pittsburgh. I attended both the conference and the Federation meeting. At the conference, a trans friend noticed my dark whiskers and gave me a tip. "If you ever want to do electrolysis, you'd be a good candidate for laser hair removal." That would entail a permanent change, but I remembered her advice.

At the Federation meeting, I felt cheered not to be the only trans person; others there represented It's Time, Illinois! and a Pennsylvania LGBT group.

The Federation decided to hold a nationwide protest in March 1999 called Equality Begins at Home. Each state would decide on their particular events that would occur in the same week across the nation. These events were intended to kick off a grassroots effort to build a coalition of LGBT activists in each state for serious work statewide. I wound up responsible for Ohio by default.

Back in Ohio, Sarah and I put a great deal of effort into planning. We picked a rally event on the steps of the Ohio Statehouse, the state capitol building. We worked our networks, gathered a long list of interested people, and coordinated a sign language interpreter, a first-aid station, flags, speeches, and fundraising.

I had to be in New Jersey for Lucent the week prior. I flew back to Columbus on Saturday morning to find Sarah had done an amazing job with last minute preparations. I also found the weather hadn't cooperated. A blustery forty degree chill would make for a brisk outdoor rally.

A sizeable vocal crowd assembled on the Statehouse lawn. We gave our speeches and as soon as it was over, we retreated to our cars in the underground parking garage to get out of the wind. As I had learned from Lucent, we succeeded because we asked everyone to get involved. We raised about $1,000 for Ohio statewide LGBT activism, and I became its custodian. I squirreled it away in an unused bank account, anticipating the formation of a viable statewide LGBT group.

* * *

The Columbus Quest was our beloved women's pro basketball team until the league folded in 1998. Five of their superstar players and the coach went to the new WNBA Minnesota Lynx. The Lynx had a home game the same weekend as the Federation meeting. I packed my souvenir Quest basketball jersey, hoping to wear it to the game. As the only Ohioan at the meeting, I figured I'd be going to the game alone.

Of the Federation attendees, about half were gay men, the rest were lesbians and one me. It felt like a setback. I'd been the token trans woman before, sighed, and pressed on.

There was quite a buzz among the women about the game. I hadn't realized lesbians were dedicated women's basketball fans, not only in Columbus but everywhere. A large group planned to go to the game. I was stoked.

Halfway through the first day, we met the new University of Minnesota Gay and Lesbian Student Services group leader.

Introducing herself, she announced, "I am a professional lesbian." She said they were hosting a fancy reception for the activists that evening, and they wanted us to all be there. "To show you how important this is, I have season tickets to the Lynx game tonight and I'm going to the reception." One of the boisterous butches in the room called out, "Can I have your tickets?" The room convulsed in laughter.

The reception could not be moved to the other night, nor could the game. Professional women's basketball teams sprang up in a limited number of cities and we didn't want to miss this rare opportunity. Most of the women, including me, decided to go to the game instead of the reception. Two dozen of us mobbed the Target Center. I wore my Quest jersey and got a great group photo at the entrance.

Katie Smith, the biggest name in Ohio women's basketball, played for the Lynx. As she warmed up, she spotted me in the arena. Seeing my Quest jersey, she called attention to the Lynx logo on her jersey to let me know she appreciated my support.

After the game, the group decided to find a women's bar to go dancing. I was taller than everyone, and I felt a bit out of place as the only trans woman in the group. Bars for women are almost as rare as women's basketball teams. We scoured the gay district in Minneapolis without finding one. Someone referred us to a bar in St. Paul that turned out to be mixed. We hesitated and went in.

Once inside, we drank, ate, and partied. The women joked about dirty dancing, grinding out on the dance floor. When I piped up, everyone quieted, and when I tried to cut a move on the dance floor, the woman next to me backed away as if I had cooties. Nobody knew my surgical status, so I guessed I carried an ick factor. I wanted to be included, and it hurt that inclusion only went so far.

* * *

There were several attempts to start up statewide groups in Ohio. Most were unpopular and criticized as A-list groups run by gay men uninterested in the full LGBT community. I showed up to their forming meetings and I didn't get the vibe they would succeed. These groups didn't last long.

It wasn't until 2005 when Ohio finally formed an inclusive group dubbed Equality Ohio. The group stuck around, and I felt welcome as a trans woman. I handed their executive director a check from the Equality Begins at Home proceeds. Though modest in size, it felt good to contribute to a great cause.

* * *

One day, a professor from Ohio State called me. "I'm teaching a class on human sexuality," she said. "We have a session on LGBT issues next month. Would you like to be a panelist?"

"It sounds interesting. Tell me more."

"We'll be in a classroom with about fifty students. There's a stage at one end where I lecture and room for a panel of eight. We'll have a straight man, a straight woman, a gay man, a lesbian, a bisexual man, and a bisexual woman. I want to include a transgender woman and a transgender man."

"It sounds like fun, but before I agree, to really get the idea across, I think I need to show them both sides of myself. Is there any place I can change clothes part way through the session?"

"Our restrooms are safe. Ohio State has fully inclusive policies."

"Okay, I'll be there."

I arrived in Mary Ann mode at the classroom ten minutes before the class. I carried a large duffel bag. Mark was in there; or at least his clothes were. I set it on the floor next to my purse.

The professor returned her students' homework and segued into our presence. "I have invited several panelists. For the next hour, they're going to answer two questions: When did you first realize your sexual orientation? And when did you first realize your gender identity?"

The gay man told a tender coming out story. The bisexual woman went next with her tale, followed by the straight man.

"Um, I never thought about it," he said. "I always liked girls."

"What about your gender identity? When did you first realize that?" the professor asked.

"I don't know. I always knew I was male."

I spoke next. "I had no idea until I was nine. Then I noticed skirts, and I thought they were cool. You could twirl." I told my story.

As the presenters continued, I inconspicuously picked up my bags and left for the ladies' room to do a quick change. Removing makeup went fast. Once I had my dress and bra off, I felt awkward in the restroom. I put on a pair of khakis and a polo shirt. I replaced my flats with socks and tennis shoes, combed my hair back into a masculine ponytail, and stuffed Mary Ann's items into the duffel bag. I slipped back into the classroom and watched the remaining presenters.

The lesbian told her heartrending coming out story and how her family rejected her. The straight woman apologized for always knowing she was a woman and liking guys.

The instructor opened the room for Q&A.

A young woman in the back raised her hand. Looking at me, she asked, "Who are you?"

I introduced myself as Mark, and borrowing a joke, explained I was Mary Ann's evil twin.

Another student raised her hand. "I don't get it. If your ex-wife is a lesbian, and you're a woman, why did she have a problem with you?"

I didn't have a good answer for that. "I think the only person who can answer that is Karen, and she's not here."

A young man hit me with a difficult question.

"When you're home in your boxers, who are you?"

I shuddered in revulsion. "*Eww.* I can't imagine wearing boxers. I prefer panties," I replied.

Years later, I understood his real question. I'd never heard the phrase "in your boxers." He meant "alone and not talking to anyone." He'd asked a profound question. When I presented differently, I became whoever I needed to be for the situation. Many women did this every day, changing from "working woman" to "mom" and then to "wife" after the kids were in bed. This wasn't a part of my experience and I'd never thought about it. Who was I? I was me. Attaching a name and a gender was external. By myself, I didn't think of genders. I thought of actions, comfort, and what was next on my things to do. I was comfortable alone, being myself, just being.

20

Permanent Changes

Once in my twenties, Dad asked, "Do you still wear dresses?"

"No," I muttered. At the time, I wished my desire would go away.

"Good." He dropped the subject.

Almost twenty years later, Dad asked me again.

"Mary Ann is not a big part of my life," I wrote in an honest, heartfelt letter. "The relaxation, joy, and insight it brings me are important. I don't need to dress often, perhaps once a month. I know you may be uncomfortable with this aspect of my personality. It's not something that will go away, and I only ask for your understanding. It's not harmful. Accept me for the person I am. Someday I hope you can meet Mary Ann in person."

On a 1998 phone call with Betty, I gave her an update. "I'm a transgender activist now. I'm working for equal rights."

"Well, you can't come to our house as Mary Ann. Your Dad's greatest fear is you'd show up on the six o'clock news. We'd be so embarrassed."

I took a solo trip to San Diego in April 1999. I stayed in a hotel when visiting, and planned a couple of Mary Ann days where I would enjoy San Diego by myself. This time, Betty surprised me by saying she was willing to meet me as Mary Ann, and offered to take me to lunch. I about dropped the phone. Upon arrival, I rented a car and bought a bouquet of fresh daffodils, tulips, and roses for my hotel room.

I looked presentable in a comfortable knit cotton dress and white sandals. From my large collection of cheap jewelry, I chose baseball earrings in keeping with the opening season. Betty picked me up at the hotel and took me to an upscale club. The luncheon went well. I felt she had accepted me.

As she dropped me off in my hotel room, I flashed on my new one-piece swimsuit with a built-in skirt and pockets for the silicone breast forms. "I want to show you my swimsuit. Would you wait a minute while I change?"

When I came out of the hotel bathroom, Betty mumbled something, and headed for the door. "Don't come to the house as Mary Ann. And don't wear those baseball earrings with your pretty dress; wear some nice earrings."

Ow. I didn't like her comment or her tone. I reframed her comments as parenting advice, meaning she was beginning to see me as a daughter.

I planned to visit their house the next day as Mark. I had a nice visit with Dad, Betty, and their two friends. We decided on Chinese for dinner. I drove us all in my rental car.

After dinner, I picked up the check. They protested and I insisted, saying I had done well money-wise. I was oblivious to the fact I had offended them. Then I made a much bigger mistake.

Driving back home, I drove down a hill toward a light that changed to yellow. Thinking I couldn't stop in time, I kept going. I didn't make it before the light turned red.

Betty tore into me from the back seat. "How dare you run a red light. Don't drive like that."

Rather than accept her criticism and apologize, I doubled down. I pulled the car over, turned to face Betty and snapped back. "Do you want to drive?"

"Well, no."

"Then let me drive."

We passed the remainder of the trip in uncomfortable silence. I thought about what had transpired. I was driving an unfamiliar car made heavier with five people. I hadn't expected the traffic light, and I had been going too fast to stop the car in time. I parked in front of their house. Their friends said their goodbyes and went to their car.

Dad said, "We're going to call it a night. You take your leftovers you paid for with 'all your money.' And here, take this for our share. Good night." He pushed a few bills into my hand, and stormed into the house.

I was left standing by my car with two Styrofoam boxes of leftovers and their unwanted money in my hand. I felt angry. I had no use for leftovers with my return flight the next afternoon. I left the boxes and the bills on the curb and returned to my hotel. Looking for sympathy, I called Beth from my room.

"Well, what did you expect? You should never have done that."

I was dumbfounded. I didn't understand what I'd done wrong.

"Look, it's midnight here. I'll see you when you get home."

I'd forgotten about the three-hour time difference. I sat and stewed in my own juices that evening. My pretty flowers mocked me, doing nothing to cheer me up.

The next morning, I had calmed down though I still felt confused. I realized I owed Betty an apology and called from the room.

"Betty, I'm sorry about last night. I shouldn't have said that to you."

"An apology? It's not enough," she huffed and hung up.

Her reaction didn't help me understand what she wanted or what I should do. I guessed she needed more time. I didn't realize I had permanently damaged my relationship with them. I would not get another opportunity to make up with Betty.

* * *

I held the phone to my ear as my mom yammered on.

"Those homosexuals are out to victimize women. They marry us and then go out and mess around. And they all want special rights. They're a cult."

I hated phone calls with my mom. She would talk my ear off about whomever she hated at the moment. She received mail from anti-gay groups, and she soaked up their vitriol. Listening was like a replay of my childhood when she'd tower over me, screaming in my face. The old parent/child dynamic remained unbroken. Even in my forties, my mother still scared me. I found it impossible to break in when she was on one of her diatribes. I wanted to get away.

This time, she had a new idea. "I want to stay in touch with you, but these phone calls are too much for me. I want to email you once a week. If something happens to me, you'll know because you won't get an email."

Emails with my mom? Really?

I loved email. I could read it any time I wanted. I could reply at my convenience. And I wouldn't be stuck listening to a screaming fit.

"That's a great idea, Mom. You send me an email each week, and I'll send you a reply."

For the rest of her life, Mom and I exchanged newsy emails each week. My blood pressure dropped. There was no reason to be afraid of an email.

* * *

After years of enduring pinched and bloody earlobes, I broke down and decided to get them pierced. I entered a Claire's jewelry store in boy mode, and the teenager behind the counter was happy to pierce them, no questions asked. It was common for men to get one ear pierced, sometimes both. I had to keep the small studs in place for several weeks.

I was scheduled to lead a training session in Denver about the Bell Labs email system I'd created and my upcoming trip was in the middle of my keep-your-studs-in period. This session would be videotaped for future staff. I didn't want my earrings to show; it seemed unprofessional.

I discovered I could take out the studs for a couple of hours. An eight-hour day should be fine, right? I took off the studs that morning in my hotel room. I gave the training, ate dinner, and came back to my room. The first thing I did was put the studs back in. One went in fine. The other...*uh oh.* I tried soaping it. No luck. I tried fiddling around with two mirrors so I could see it. Nope. I looked for the slipperiest substance I had in my room and settled on hair conditioner. I was able to get the stud back in. All that poking made my ear sore. *Damn.* It hurt to be beautiful.

"The doctor says my ear is infected, I said to Beth. "I have to clean it with peroxide and leave the stud in another four weeks."

"I don't like you making permanent changes to your body."

"Why not?" I'd hoped for sympathy, not this.

"I fell in love with Mark. I'll support you being Mary Ann, but I see more and more of Mary Ann and less and less of Mark."

She was right. Now that I'd come out to pretty much everybody, I spent half my life in girl mode. Her remarks left a bruise on my feelings. As much as I wished she could share in my enthusiasm for my developing womanhood, her husband was disappearing and she didn't like it.

21

Leadership Development

1999

I'd been working toward a management promotion for years. When my boss recommended me to a program for high potential staff, my prospects improved.

Lucent's version of this program offered an opportunity for a wonderful growth experience. I was honored to be accepted into the 1999–2000 Lucent Information Technology Leadership Development Program (Lucent IT-LDP). They sent two dozen of us to Babson College near Boston for a "mini-MBA," consisting of four week-long sessions in October, January, March, and June. We would spend seven days on campus and work remotely on projects the rest of the time while performing our regular jobs.

I wanted to be Mary Ann, at least some of the time. Blocking Mary Ann from any part of my life felt like a barrier, one I had to bust down to be fully out.

I'd made arrangements to attend NGLTF's Creating Change conference in Oakland, Thursday through Sunday. The IT-LDP started at 4:00 p.m. Sunday at Babson. To cross the country in time, I would need to take a red-eye flight, leaving Saturday at 6:00 p.m. and missing the Creating Change dinner event. I would attend Creating Change as Mary Ann, and did not want to change genders on an airplane. I felt annoyed with the awkward schedule. I phoned our IT-LDP contact.

"I'm transgender," I said. "I go to work some days as Mark, and other days, I'm Mary Ann. Would it be all right if I came the first day or two as Mary Ann?" I didn't mention Lucent's nondiscrimination policy. When I spoke in a matter-of-fact manner, instead of defending myself, I'd found most people were accepting.

"Well, it's okay with me. Let me talk with Elaine."

An hour later, I got my approval. "What name would you like on your nametag and table tent?"

I nearly cried at her warm acceptance. Not one to be shy, I asked for what I wanted. "Could you make me two sets? One for Mark and one for Mary Ann?"

"Sure."

These two women were wonderful, and we became good friends.

* * *

Creating Change was an exhilarating conference. I had work to do, and I also listened to informative, inspirational talks.

Mel White of Soulforce, an LGBT nondenominational religious advocacy group, talked about his time working for religious conservative Jerry Falwell. Mel went on to work for LGBT rights. His catchphrase was: "Love your enemy. Relentlessly." When conservatives expressed disgust at what he and his partner did in bed, he'd reply: "What do you think we do? We're old. We sleep."

A group of eight intersex activists, led by the Intersex Society of North America founder, Cheryl Chase, presented a panel on intersex issues. She told her personal story. At birth, her external organ was too small for a boy and too small for a girl. The doctors were confounded and assigned her as female, but her parents named her Brian. At eighteen months, doctors surgically altered her external organs to appear female, and removed her internal organs. Her family renamed her Cheryl and raised her as a girl. She went through many secret medical visits and felt severe shame about her body. The others on the panel told similar stories.

I had fought for intersex inclusive language in Lucent's EEO policy. Some companies proposed using "gender identity and expression" language without "characteristics," and I wanted to know how the intersex community felt.

After the panel, I asked about the "gender characteristics" language. The group looked at each other with puzzled expressions. Workplace rights weren't on their radar; for the most part, they were concerned about the unwanted surgeries forced on them as infants.

Cheryl said, "There's one intersex activist you should talk to. He had a workplace issue."

When I tracked him down, he said the way he understood things, transgender workplace protections would include intersex people, and "gender identity and expression" was fine.

I stopped pushing for the "characteristics" language and went with the flow. "Gender identity or expression" language began to appear in nondiscrimination policies.

At one workshop, we went around our circle and introduced ourselves. I went first. I gave my name and a brief recitation about who I was and what I did. The last man, who sat to my left, introduced himself as the leader of an anti-gay organization. He went to LGBT events and took notes to report on what happened there.

I glanced at his notepad and was horrified to see he had written down my name, crossdresser, and my city. My skin prickled. I feared this man would publish snarling comments about me, calling me out as an example of how the trans community was some kind of sick cult. The last thing I needed was to have the far right attacking my family and me. None of the other attendees objected to his presence, and I wondered why. I felt I had to watch my back, alert for attacks from the haters.

I slept in fits and starts on the plane, and managed to squeeze in the bathroom with my ditty bag to wash my face, shave, and redo my makeup. I was grateful I didn't have to change clothes in the tiny space.

* * *

Babson College was a private business school with a beautiful, treed campus in a Boston suburb. The Center for Executive Education building offered a hotel, classroom, and dining room. We stayed inside all week.

I found the roomy state-of-the-art classroom all set up. Three tiered rows of desks allowed each student to see the instructor. My place had a Mary Ann Horton table tent, which meant the world to me. I plopped down in a padded office chair, admiring my work space. I had eight feet of desk space in which to spread out my books and notepad. Power and network jacks awaited my laptop. I could keep up on my day job during breaks.

I didn't know any of the other students except an IT guy from the Philippines with whom I'd shared conference calls as Mark. We went around the room to make introductions, and I came out as trans. Though my heart rate jumped, judging by their reactions, it wasn't a big deal.

PJ Guinan, a business professor at Babson, chaired the program. "This is a mini-MBA program," she explained. "We'll bring in expert business professors to teach key topics. This program will earn you academic credit equivalent to one-third of an MBA."

Sunday evening after dinner, we were treated to a reception with an open bar so we could get to know each other. I hung out with Elaine and her colleague.

"I was concerned you wanted to make a splash," Elaine explained.

"Make a splash?"

"Like, um, boas."

Sigh. She'd expected a drag queen. I gestured at my outfit, the same blue skirt set I'd worn to introduce the speakers in Columbus. I always wanted to look professional on the first day.

"I'm just me. I want to fit in."

She dropped her shoulders and took a relaxed breath.

Monday morning, I enjoyed myself so much I stayed in girl mode. Tuesday morning, I switched back to boy mode. Before class I was greeted with a "Good morning, M—"

I turned around to greet Kai, a sweet student from Illinois. "Oh, you're Mark today."

I smiled and said, "Hi." It was that simple.

Friday and Saturday, a guest speaker came in to speak about people skills, not my best subject.

He gave us a twenty-four-question self-assessment that charted each personality into one of four quadrants. A person might be a Controller, who wants everything their way; a Persuader, the life of the party; an Analyzer, who loves facts and numbers; or a Stabilizer, wanting everyone to get along. We were sorted into one of these four styles based on how we achieved results and processed emotions.

Taking the test Friday as Mark, I was an Analyzer, no surprise—I was a computer nerd. I bordered near Stabilizer. On Saturday, I retook the test as Mary Ann. This time it said I was a Stabilizer, not far over the line from the Analyzer category. It made sense. Mark did all the computer techie stuff. Mary Ann tried to find balance and harmony, especially for transgender inclusion and equality.

I ducked out at lunchtime to buy a Babson shirt. On the way back to class, I got lost. As I searched campus, my heart raced and I couldn't focus. I arrived at the center fifteen minutes late drenched in sweat. I couldn't go to class disheveled, so I took a quick shower. The long denim skirt and sweater I'd worn were gross, and because this was my last day of the trip, I didn't have any clean clothes. I decided to wear a knit dress I usually slept in. I picked up odd reactions when I arrived at class forty-five minutes late, even though I apologized profusely.

There was time set aside at 4:00 p.m. for goodbye hugs. A female student from Sweden motioned to my dress. "This morning you were wearing denim," she said.

"I had to change at lunch, and this was all I had left." My explanation had no effect on her cold attitude. I felt confused.

I rode with the people skills instructor to the airport, and I asked for insight on the denim comment.

"That's a persuader dress," he said, meaning my outfit was too sexy for a classroom versus the ankle-length denim skirt.

He reiterated a point he'd made in class. We each have a natural personality style. We can function in either of the styles in the adjacent quadrants for some time, but it's more stressful. He looked at my Mark chart and said it was almost an overbalance, meaning too close to the center. He told me an overbalance can lead to illness, injury, or death. He meant Mark's personality tried to do too much with too many different personality characteristics, stressing me out. Being Mark was trying to be someone I'm not, and could affect my health. No wonder I was happier as Mary Ann.

The class taught me an important lesson I applied for the rest of my career. Instead of arguing with a coworker about a decision, or worrying about my personal wants or the goals of my group or project, it's best to appeal to the needs of the company as a whole. It's a winning argument every time, and it usually leads to the right decision.

* * *

During our second segment at Babson, Elaine asked us to give a ten-minute talk to the class about our cultural background as a way to learn about each other and our various cultures. Students from Sweden, Poland, and the Philippines told fascinating stories of their countries. Our two African American students copresented an inspiring talk about what it's like to grow up Black in America. The White American guys were stumped and resorted to drawing pie charts, depicting their European ancestry.

I gave an abbreviated version of my personal story from Meral's panel. It fell flat; even the jokes didn't work. I wondered why. When I had given the same talk to other audiences, there was tremendous interest and empathy.

Kai explained it to me later. "It's not like we don't already know you."

The novelty of being trans had worn off.

PJ divided us into teams for our class projects. Each group had instructions to do a business analysis of Lucent on a topic of our choice. We would work until June and present our results the final week at Babson.

Our team of five was inspired by the Just In Time (JIT) model of manufacturing. By employing JIT, businesses avoided the need for large, expensive inventories. We called ourselves the JITRBUGS, pronounced like the dance. We made good use of the months between classes to work on our project.

* * *

To gain international experience, Elaine had Lucent's facility in Hilversum, Netherlands host our March meeting.

Flying overseas is a long time to be cooped up in an airplane, and I was more comfortable traveling as Mary Ann. Domestic airline security was lax before 9/11, whereas international travel required stops at immigration and customs where my passport would be checked. I worried that my female face would be deemed a mismatch from my female appearance. Friends told me I'd be fine. I wasn't as sure. The singer, Boy George, had been stopped because of his makeup and long hair. As I waited in line, I felt a lump in my throat as I approached immigration.

I did my best to stay calm as I handed my passport and ticket to the agent. He checked that the names matched. He looked at my passport photo, which I'd recently updated with an androgynous look. Glancing up at me, he seemed bored.

"What's the purpose of your visit?"

"Business. I'm here for training in Hilversum."

He stamped my passport. "Have a pleasant visit."

I learned that bureaucrats just want to do their job. You could be a trans person or a Martian. Unless there's a problem for them to check off their boxes, they go on to the next traveler.

* * *

Our class read marketing case studies on Walmart and Cisco. The finance professor taught us how to read a corporation's annual report and noted which metrics concerned the shareholders. I was all about numbers and loved this part. The rest of the class glazed over.

To improve revenue per employee (total company income divided by the number of employees), Lucent considered outsourcing. They had outsourced IT to IBM, which I thought was a terrible mistake. Lucent lost flexibility, and IT staff morale went into the dumper. We heard rumors they would also outsource Western Electric, their manufacturing arm.

The JITRBUGS decided to study this potential decision to outsource Western. We thought it may be better to spin it off into a separate company. We surveyed Lexmark, Agilent, and Trilogy to see how their spin-offs went. We talked to contract manufacturers Celestica, Solectron, and Jabil about outsourcing. We studied people issues, financials, and security. One of our team had a connection to Lucent executives and we planned to present our findings.

* * *

Elaine gave us one afternoon off to take us to Amsterdam's famous Red Light District. The streets were calm on this pleasant sunny afternoon, and no surprise, we heard there was a lot more going on at night. We were amazed to look into the window of a shop and see dozens of healthy, legal marijuana plants growing inside at a time when it was illegal in all fifty states and most of Europe.

I spent that day as Mary Ann to better enjoy Amsterdam. As I walked with the group in jeans and a sweater, Kai asked. "Do you ever wear skirts?"

I'd worn jeans most of the time at Babson. The question cracked me up. Originally, dresses and skirts had been the whole point.

Later, one of my male classmates took me aside.

"Some guys in the Red Light District were looking at you in a way we didn't like. We were concerned they might give you trouble."

"Oh! I didn't even see them. Was I in danger?"

"Don't worry. We'd protect you."

I relaxed, knowing my teammates had my back. They were awesome.

* * *

Our team assembled a term paper and a PowerPoint presentation. We had the numbers to back up why a spin-off made a better approach. We presented to two high-level people from Lucent's leadership. The executives heard us out and complemented our good points. They intimated Lucent might be going in a different direction.

A few weeks later, Lucent announced it would spin off two companies, one for business telephone systems called Avaya, another for microchips called Agere. The Western manufacturing unit would be outsourced to Celestica. As I listened in on the phone call along with most of Lucent, I made a quick update to our email configurations so email to user@avaya.com and user@agere.com would work.

Our email support group of eight was expected to contribute one person to Avaya and none to Agere. John assigned our Microsoft guy to Avaya. I was glad to be staying with Lucent—that's where Bell Labs would be.

* * *

Our final week of IT LDP was held at Babson in June. A year of hard work culminated in presentations of our projects to the Babson faculty, followed by a graduation ceremony. I felt this was a Mark event, disappointing several in the class who asked the whereabouts of Mary Ann.

The JITRBUGS gave our presentation as a team PowerPoint talk. I would cover financials. When my turn came, I said, "This is the part of the talk where everybody goes to sleep, and the finance professor perks up." When we finished, the staff had high praise for us, as if we had been students in their MBA program. We learned the material and did the work, and came away with our mini-MBA status.

While I was still at Babson, my boss called. There had been a last-minute shuffle of staff assignments. I was in Columbus, and with the rest of the email team in Chicago, they decided to assign me to Avaya.

What? I was stunned.

Avaya was the former business communications systems unit. They made office telephone PBX systems. There was no Bell Labs in Avaya and a tiny UNIX R&D community. I loved Bell Labs. My career was built around UNIX. I didn't want to leave. However, it presented an opportunity. I'd wanted a promotion to management, and the Avaya team would need a leader. I decided to go for it.

I told my Babson classmates I was going to Avaya. Like me, many of them were on track for supervisory positions. Some had gotten their promotions and had left for their new jobs.

We graduated in a beautiful lawn ceremony at Babson. PJ and Elaine presented us with our certificates. I returned to Columbus to move on to the next chapter of my career.

22
Mall Cop

From time to time I phoned Dad. I often got their answering machine. "This is Betty. Leave a message at the beep."

"Happy birthday, Dad. Hope you're having a great day! Give me a call sometime."

I heard from him once. He called to say he was setting up a small house for Betty in Hemet, in Southern California, as if he needed to inform me of a non-emotional business arrangement. I didn't know what to make of it and that was the last time we ever spoke.

* * *

In 2000, it was generally accepted that employer medical benefit plans excluded help for people transitioning. They contained specific language stating there was no coverage for anything related to a sex change. Transsexuals had to use their own money for hormones and save up for a surgery costing as much as a new car. The few surgeons who performed trans-related surgeries knew insurance wouldn't cover their work and demanded to be paid in cash before surgery. The cash expense and inconvenience constituted a hardship for many. Changing this inequity was high on the wish lists of activists.

The trans community networked to find workarounds. Psychological counseling could be covered without much trouble. Other times, the counselor had to code a reason other then trans counseling for the sessions. Anxiety and depression weren't unusual and could be addressed.

As for needed medications, trans women were often prescribed the same estrogen and progesterone cis women used when going through menopause, and could combine them with a blood pressure medication that suppressed testosterone. Efforts by trans women to slip these prescriptions through the system met with mixed results. Men weren't "supposed" to take female hormones. Trans men needed testosterone injections, which were more out of the ordinary. This didn't affect me because I hadn't transitioned. I hadn't gone to counseling for gender dysphoria and hadn't sought hormones. The activist in me wanted to change the unfair system.

A transgender Lucent employee in California contacted EQUAL! for help and they referred her to me. Saving for her surgery had been a burden. She hoped Lucent's trans-friendly/non-discrimination policy would allow for the surgery to be covered. I asked through the requisite channels if HR would be willing to remove the exclusion.

HR's Director of Diversity had been our champion. I wasn't allowed to talk to her directly, but the co-presidents of EQUAL! could, and they did. Changes to benefits take a long time, and HR was afraid armies of transsexuals would bust the budget. Surgeries for trans men could cost up to fifty thousand dollars, and the media implied this figure was typical. My request dragged on.

In the meantime, my friend's surgery date came around. She went to Thailand, where two excellent surgeons performed male-to-female surgery at about half the price of American surgeons. She paid her Thai surgeon $7,500 in cash.

I bugged HR through my contacts and one day, an answer came back. "We've always covered it." *Yes!* I was surprised and happy to hear the good news.

Since she had paid for her surgery, I put her in touch with HR to be reimbursed. A month later, she let me peek at the check they sent for the full amount of her surgery. I was happy for her and ecstatic Lucent covered trans surgeries.

* * *

The Saturday before Easter 2000, I was in a great mood. I decided to shop for a new Easter outfit for church. I didn't put a lot of energy into getting all prettied up, and wore basic makeup, a green turtleneck top, and matching velour pants.

I started at the Eastland Mall food court for lunch. While awaiting my food, I made a quick stop in the nearby ladies' room, which was empty. I picked up my sandwich and scouted for an open table. Before I could sit, a mall security guard approached from the hallway by the restrooms.

"Excuse me, ma'am, do you have a driver's license?" he asked.

I knew I was in trouble. I carried an ID card from the Crystal Club showing both names and pictures, which I offered to the guard. His smile faded.

"No, show me your driver's license."

I tried to evade him. "I don't need a driver's license to come to the mall."

"You'll come with me now."

I had no choice. He led me to a nondescript office down the hall.

"It's my sixth day on the job," he shared. "Now show me your driver's license."

I complied. It showed my name as Mark Horton and my sex as M.

"You are trespassing in the women's restroom. I can have you arrested by the Columbus police."

Through my activism, I knew on private property, it was up to the property owner to decide restroom policy and most had not addressed it. Social mores dictated using the restroom that matched the sex on your driver's license.

"What is the mall's restroom policy?"

"I don't have to show you a policy. I decide what the policy is here," he said.

Great, I thought. *I'm facing a green, self-important mall cop with an attitude.*

My annoyance turned to fear. Trans women had been charged with an M-1 misdemeanor and up to 6 months jail time for using a public women's room. Going to jail would be a nightmare. I'd be put in with male inmates and probably harassed, beaten, or raped. I decided to play it cool and get out of there at my first opportunity.

"Where do you work?" he asked.

"Lucent Technologies."

"Do they let you dress like that at work?"

"Yes, they do. What policy have I violated?"

"Stop being argumentative."

There was a designated family restroom intended for diaper changes. I thought perhaps he'd want me to use that one. "Am I allowed to use the family restroom?"

"No, you are not."

He wrote a lengthy report while I sat there. Then he picked up the phone and called the police.

By the time the Columbus police officer arrived, I had sweat circles under my arms. The mall cop handed him my driver's license and told him I had been caught using the ladies' room. The officer called in my license number and was told there were no arrest warrants, tickets, or other blemishes on my record. He said there was no reason to arrest me.

The officer offered to escort me off the property, and the mall cop agreed.

I asked the mall cop, "What should I do about restroom use in the future?"

"There will be no future problem in terms of restroom use. I am banning you from Eastland Mall."

"May I have a copy of the report you wrote?"

"No."

The officer led me out of the office and to my car in the mall lot. "I'll follow you off the lot." I drove home, fuming at my mistreatment and relieved to be away from the mall cop.

I found Beth in the kitchen and gave her my lament.

"I got busted at the mall for using the women's restroom." I felt indignant and wanted a hug.

She chopped a carrot.

"Yup. You get yourself into all these situations."

No sympathy. I went into my home office and sulked.

The next week, I called a lesbian attorney known for handling LGBT causes. I told her the story, including how I hadn't been charged with a crime, and had nothing in writing about the incident or the banishment. She was outraged at how I had been treated.

My lawyer wrote to the president of the Jacobs mall chain at their headquarters in Cleveland protesting my treatment. She brought up my right to use the restroom, how no one had complained about my use of the restroom, and the dismissal of my Crystal Club ID. She emphasized any problem created was not by me, but by the mall cop who accosted me on his initiative on his sixth day as a security guard. She made several demands: rescind the ban, destroy the report, institute a policy of respect for transgender persons, including restroom use, and educate mall security personnel about diversity.

"Were Ms. Horton to go into the men's restroom, she would be subjecting herself to the danger of being assaulted, and other mall patrons are not required to either forego restroom usage or subject themselves to danger as a condition of shopping at Eastland Mall," she wrote.

* * *

During this legal limbo, I traveled to Phoenix for a joint conference sponsored by EQUAL! National, and ABLE, the Lucent group for employees with disabilities. Our agenda was to expose the groups to each other and gain perspective of what the other group faced. I was happy to see our transgender contingent had grown to six of us.

I learned we are more alike than different. People with disabilities, similar to gay and transgender persons, often live in closets. Many can pass as able by hiding or disguising their disabilities. Others are forced to be visible. Those who can pass must wrestle with whether to come out and disclose their disability.

After the conference, I felt good and wanted to treat myself to a spa visit. I called a nearby Hyatt. They assured me they accepted trans clients. Wearing a nice dress, I drove over and checked in.

"I'd like the aloe facial treatment, please." Upon request, I handed over my driver's license and she gave it back.

"The changing room is down that hall on your left."

The door she sent me to read: Men. I dropped my smile. She had seen the M on my driver's license. Fortunately, being a spa, the men's changing room was empty, and I enjoyed the privacy. After a delightful facial, I returned to the changing room and dressed. I pulled a chair up to the mirror to redo my makeup when I heard the door open. A man walked in and did a double-take, thinking he was in the wrong room.

"Oops, sorry."

"No," I said. "You're in the right room. Come on in."

It felt surreal to hear him use the urinal around the corner as I finished my makeup. On the way out, he smiled and waved.

* * *

The next month, my attorney and I received a letter from the mall's lawyer.

> *While the Company does not agree with many of the allegations contained in your letter, it does believe that the provisions of this letter should end any dispute which may exist between the parties. Specifically, Ms. Horton is not banned from shopping in Eastland Mall. Second, with respect to Ms. Horton's use of restrooms at Eastland Mall, she should use only the family restroom at Eastland, which is gender neutral and which is located just off the food court. Third, security personnel at Eastland have been made aware of Ms. Horton's status as a transgender shopper and of the fact that she is not banned from shopping in Eastland Mall, and they will conduct themselves accordingly and in an appropriate manner.*

I met with Meral Crane and unburdened my soul. Meral had seen things like this many times. She knew what to do. She wrote me what she called a "carry letter." Such a letter, written on letterhead from a licensed clinical counselor, relates that she knows me and I am in treatment in her program. It stated I was "not dressing to cause public nuisance nor trying to hide [my] identity for illegal reasons."

I put a copy of Meral's carry letter and the attorney's letter in my purse in case of any future problems at Eastland or elsewhere. Nearly twenty years later, her carry letter remains in my wallet, and I never needed to show it.

* * *

That fall, Out & Equal, presented the Outie Awards at a festive banquet. Three San Francisco supervisors were announced as cowinners of the Trailblazer Award for granting domestic partner benefits to all city employees.

They certainly deserve that award, I thought. I remembered when Out & Equal had put out the nominations call for the Outies, seeking individuals and companies who had made substantial contributions to LGBT equality in the workplace. One of them, the Trailblazer Award, would go to an LGBT person. I was busy and forgot about it.

As the awards droned on, my mind wandered. A few words from the speaker caught my attention. "…and as a woman…"

Wait a minute, I thought. *I am a woman. I'm not some man who likes to wear women's clothing. I'm not a part-timer who feels like a man sometimes and like a woman other times. At my core, I'm a woman. All the time.*

When I taught TG 101 workshops, I illustrated the difference between gender identity and gender expression using a model I learned from a panelist. The model was a measuring tool with scales, like on a fancy home stereo with bass, midrange, and treble sliders. "Gender identity" was who you felt you were inside, woman on one end, man on the other end, and gender fluid crossdressers and non-binary people somewhere in the middle. "Gender expression" was how you presented to others, Barbie on one end, Rambo on the other, and androgynous people in between. Most people were somewhere between Barbie and Rambo. The third scale, "sex," was what you had between the legs, female at one end of the scale, male at the other, and intersex in between. The fourth slider, "sexual orientation," was who you loved, with attraction to men at one end, women at the other, and bisexuals in between.

I wasn't a hairstyle-obsessed, math-hating Barbie doll. My gender expression ran the gamut from dresses and heels to yard work and home repairs. I loved to cook and to make computers dance. I disliked tea parties and competitive male power games. On gender tests, I scored in the middle between men and women. My sex was still male, and I remained attracted only to women.

What changed was my gender identity. I had always identified as a crossdresser, as bi-gender, somewhere between a man and a woman. Now I realized my identity was all the way to the woman end of the scale. This was a new feeling, a welcome feeling. My gender identity as a woman would not change, even when I presented as a man.

I relished my time as Mary Ann, yet I had many social and legal obligations as Mark. Beth wanted her husband. Matt and Adam needed their dad. Even as I rejoiced in my identity, I decided to keep my self-identification as a woman to myself. My gender expression would remain fluid.

A familiar name jolted me back to the awards presentation. Lucent's Director of Diversity won the Champion Award, a non-LGBT person who has made a significant contribution to workplace equality. She had been the one who added transgender language into the EEO policy and determined our benefits were covered. I was so happy for her. I gave her a big hug, crying tears of joy.

I wanted that Trailblazer Award. I kicked myself for not following up. *Next year*, I thought. *Trans policies are important. I work hard for them. I deserve that award.*

23
Avaya

2000

The first of July was a typical hot, sticky Ohio summer day. I sat in my home office in Bexley, looking out the window at Sherwood Road, the same tree-lined view I had always seen…with one big change. Yesterday, I had worked for Lucent. Today, I worked for an Avaya group of two.

Jim, from Lucent's POST group, and I were the only staff assigned to provide the email and POST directory service for Avaya, processes that required sixteen Lucent workers. It was absurd. My new management told me Avaya was one-quarter of the size Lucent had been, so we had to find a way to do it with one-quarter of the resources.

We'd both been assigned to one group as technical staff members and reported to our director instead of a manager. Jim didn't want to be a manager. After years of trying for a promotion, opportunity knocked.

I flew to Newark and drove to Avaya headquarters in Morristown where I walked to my new boss's office. I mustered my skills from Babson to present him with a business case to promote me to technical manager.

"It took eight people to support the Lucent Corporate Email (LCE) service and eight more to support the POST directory. I understand we have to be smaller, but we can't do it with two people. We need too many skill sets. I'd like to set up a small team with me as manager. I'll get it done."

"You really want all that responsibility?"

"I sure do."

"Okay, I'll promote you to technical manager. You'll need to recruit people for the openings. I'll help you with the paperwork."

I was ecstatic. I named my new group Avaya Corporate Email and Directory with the catchy acronym ACED.

My boss gave me a big raise to go with my promotion—the most I'd made to date. *Woohoo!*

He said he was being outsourced to IBM, along with most of Lucent's and Avaya's IT departments, and would not be my boss for long. The IT staff had to interview with IBM to be hired to do their same jobs as IBM employees. To Avaya, they were only contractors. "As a contractor, I'm the lowest of the low. I look up and see whale scum."

I thought outsourcing was an ill-conceived idea once you looked past the cost savings. Less quantifiable was the cost of poor service. Flexibility to meet the needs of the business turned into fighting with IBM over what was included in the contract. Morale was low, and nothing got done.

Our IT staff wanted to stay with Lucent or Avaya, not go to IBM. Most had no choice. Jim and I were lucky to stay put. Directory was too sensitive to outsource, and IBM's email group only supported Microsoft Mail, not the UNIX-based email Avaya's R&D staff used.

My boss moved on to IBM. He shared with me how he survived outsourcing.

"Every day I come into work. I ask them, 'What do you want me to do today? Do you want me to solve business problems? Do you want me to sweep the parking lot?' Whatever they want me to do, I do it. Then I head home and laugh my way to the bank."

His words impressed me. I needed to stop worrying about petty office politics and refocus on the needs of the business. That mindset served me well over the years.

My new boss, Fred, was based in New Jersey. Thank God, I didn't have to move there. Avaya had two small sales offices in Columbus and their work had nothing to do with me, which is why it made sense to work from home full time.

We were given a deadline to separate Avaya from Lucent. We had to have our Avaya email system with 32,000 users moved from Lucent's servers and onto Avaya's servers within six months or people wouldn't be able to access their email.

In my first managerial challenge, I needed more people on the job. We needed three technical staff for email and Jim needed two more for directory operations. I stated my business case and Fred agreed.

I set out to build a team with no central location, making it easier to recruit people to work from their virtual office at home. This was unheard of in 2000, but we had no other way. We put out the word, and Jim and I found several good people.

I needed a UNIX expert for the R&D side and advertised the job through my network, both internally and externally. I thought Sue, my friend from It's Time, Ohio!, would be a match. She applied for the job. Besides being a strong trans activist, she was an experienced UNIX developer and unhappy in her current job. She had transitioned, and working for a trans boss made it safer for her to be out at work. Working from her home in Cleveland was the icing on the cake.

Until 2000, Microsoft Mail wrote email into mailboxes on file servers, which were glorified PCs. When someone dared send an email outside the local MS Mail cluster, it went over the Internet with uuencode attachments. Having written uuencode, it was gratifying, but MS Mail was a primitive system, largely unchanged since the 1980s.

Microsoft made a huge leap with new servers running Windows 2000 and a new email system called Exchange. It could speak the current Internet standards with other email systems. Microsoft email addresses matched our handle@avaya.com structure. We were offered the existing MS Mail servers in Avaya New Jersey locations, but that would have entailed building new servers for much of the company. We decided to take the leap and build a whole new Exchange system for Avaya. We had six months to design, build, and roll out our new system.

* * *

In 2001, shortly into the new year, Jim gave me bad news. "I'm leaving Avaya to go back to Lucent's POST group." He was the team lead of the directory, a key contributor. We got some software support for POST from Lucent, but his skill was important to integrate Exchange's new Active Directory system with POST. He told me this news in the middle of my first performance review process as a manager. I had rated Jim's performance excellent. Now I had to give out raises and had a dilemma.

Sue had been underpaid in her previous job, and I was able to give her a small raise when I hired her. She needed a big raise to get close to what her pay band indicated she should make. Jim was leaving, and the pay raise would disappear with him. He was a lame duck. I had a certain amount of money to divide up among the team as I saw fit. I gave Jim a zero raise and Sue a big raise.

Jim came to me to discuss my decision. Needless to say, he was most unhappy. Lucent would be matching his Avaya salary. How could I rate him as excellent and not give him a raise? I understood his position and held my ground—one of the worst mistakes I ever made.

After Jim left, Sue asked to become the team lead of POST. A month later, the POST team ran into snags with the software, and we asked for support from Lucent. They had agreed to this during the split; however, it was not in writing. A new tech manager ran Lucent's POST team. Not only didn't she want to support Avaya, she was nasty about it.

Fred, took this business issue off my hands and went into intense negotiations with Lucent. We went months with no help. Sue had to figure out the details on her own. Fred eventually signed an expensive contract with Lucent for POST support.

Jim was part of the Lucent POST team when all this happened. I guessed he told his management how he felt about us, which factored into the frosty reception.

I had my hand slapped—hard—and learned a valuable lesson. Relationships with people are the lifeblood of success and are not separate from the needs of the business. I resolved to do better in the future.

We had a great team, and we were diverse. Rick was liberal and a solid Texan. Sue and I were openly trans, and Noel was gay. Siva, from India, imparted his cultural influence. An introvert, he kept his head down and embedded himself in his technical work. When I came out to him as transgender, he didn't understand it until Sue used the Hindi term, *hijra*. "Oh, eunuchs," he muttered with disgust. I was the boss, and he kept his opinions to himself from then on.

Our team meetings were often by conference call. Sue and Noel knew me as Mary Ann; the others knew me as Mark. I thought it amusing to hear Rick and Sue argue about my name over the phone.

* * *

Spencer Johnson's book, *Who Moved My Cheese*, became popular reading in corporate America. It told the story of four mouse-sized people who came to work every day to run the maze for cheese. Their pile of cheese dwindled, and they had four different reactions. One of them went into a new part of the maze to find "new cheese," different but satisfactory. The book taught people to deal with change in their lives by finding and savoring the new cheese.

The world hurtled through changes, and I felt stressed out at work adjusting to my new job at my new company. Knowing that small adjustments could lead to appreciable outcomes, I decided to replace my car's LUCENT 1 license. Johnson's book inspired me to adorn my Camry with NU CHEEZ. Whenever I felt stressed out, I'd look at my car and remember the book. "Savor the new cheese," I told myself. In the coming year, that message helped me hold on to my sanity as I soon went through several major changes, any one of which could have led to depression.

* * *

We had too little time to move 32,000 users to a new email system. Like the Calvin and Hobbes cartoon characters, I felt as if I had ridden a little red wagon off a cliff. We made the deadline. It wasn't enough. User complaints barreled in. The brand-new system from Microsoft didn't work right. We spent six intense weeks getting the bugs ironed out.

By mid-May, the situation settled down. I breathed a life-giving sigh of relief. I was beginning to like my job.

* * *

Avaya had one-quarter of the Lucent employees, and EQUAL! at Avaya was also smaller. We formed a new national leadership structure with Ken as the national president. We did our best to keep the Lucent structures and programs in place, even as our funding had been drastically reduced. Plus, we were all busy with the split.

When Out & Equal called for Outies nominations, I remembered how I'd felt the prior year about the award. I reached out to Ken and suggested Avaya nominate me for the Trailblazer Award. Ken thought it was a great idea and had me write up a draft nomination. He and Avaya's director of diversity submitted it to Out & Equal. I appreciated their follow up and would have to wait and see if anything came of it.

Due to budget cuts, the traditional annual conference for EQUAL! at Lucent fell to the wayside, and in its stead, Avaya held an annual diversity conference in June attended by people from all seven employee groups. Sue, Noel, and I flew to Morristown. The conference felt watered down, and I took heart in appearing as Mary Ann on company business.

Fred called me on Friday, pulling me out of an inclusion workshop. "Avaya has a severe budget problem. Orders are coming in much slower than expected, and we have to slash expenses. You are to return home, today."

"Fred, if we change flights, it will cost more than tonight's hotel. It's cheaper to stay overnight and return as scheduled tomorrow."

"Okay, but no more travel."

I felt as if he had pushed a boulder onto my chest. Avaya was collapsing. EQUAL! might vanish. My job, which I enjoyed after enduring a precarious start, could be in line for the chopping block.

Many trans women count their surgery date or their transition date as a second birthday. I counted from the day in Phoenix I had first spent as a woman. Friday, June 8, 2001, was my fourteenth Mary Ann birthday. It was bittersweet.

As I lamented to Noel and Sue in the car on the way to dinner, they spontaneously broke into song. "Happy birthday, dear Mary Ann. Happy birthday to you."

Avaya made an announcement the next week. Everyone had upgraded their equipment for Y2K. Our customers were set for years. "Orders are down. Our revenue is appropriate for a much smaller company. We are offering a '5 + 5' package to encourage people to retire early. We will credit an extra five years to your age and five years to your experience to determine your retirement eligibility."

I had heard of these sweet deals. People would take a package, then find another job and keep working. After AT&T and Lucent separated in 1996, a similar package had been offered. The leaders of POST in the AT&T and Lucent groups took the packages, creating openings in both groups. They filled each other's jobs and wound up with both a pension and a salary.

Avaya followed the tradition of AT&T and Lucent when it downsized. Normally one needed twenty-five years of service or be fifty-five years old to qualify for retirement. Now I needed twenty years of service or fifty years of age by the deadline, August 1, 2001.

I did the math. I started in July 1981, at age twenty-five. I would have twenty years and one month of service. I was eligible. This meant a pension payment for life, a great opportunity.

Asking around on my network of Avaya employees, the consensus was clear. "You can take the deal and get a pension, or stay and get laid off. Don't be stupid. Take the package." I took it.

Having less than a year of company service, Sue was offered a small cash buyout. "I considered staying out of loyalty to you, but if you're leaving, so will I."

Now I felt like a heel. At Jim's expense, I had given her a big raise with more lifetime earning potential, and it was going down the drain. I felt bad for Jim and the decision I'd made.

Avaya offered me a lifetime payment of about a quarter of my salary. I knew I would find a comparable job in no time, and in the interim, I could consult. I thought I was hot stuff.

Right off, I got a consulting nibble from a Chicago attorney related to my expertise with text editors. Another company had filed for a patent for an editor Undo command in 1979, causing his client grief. Could I show "prior art" that there was an Undo command in an editor before 1979?

This seemed like a no-brainer. Vi had an Undo in 1978. I had created an Undo for the UNIX editor at Wisconsin in 1977. I researched online and found an Undo command at the University of Michigan in the early 1970s. I wrote up a document outlining my findings, and I wrote it up as Mary Ann. I offered to testify in court. He seemed skittish about having Mary Ann testify. I provided him with the evidence by email and asked for a meeting to discuss it.

In July, I flew to an Avaya early retirement workshop held in Naperville, an hour's drive west of Chicago. Ironically, travel was allowed again. I offered to meet the attorney at the airport while waiting to board my return flight. He agreed.

Driving back to Midway airport, I hit traffic. I called the lawyer to let him know I'd be late. As I fought through traffic, I stayed on the phone, advising him of my progress. We chatted as he waited for me at the terminal gate, my newfangled flip phone pressed to my ear. I became distraught as the window for catching my flight grew near. I rushed to return my rental car, still on the phone, and when I reached the gate, the agents were ready to close the door. I managed to shake the attorney's hand as the agent rushed me onto the flight. I felt like my exit must have left a bad taste. I never heard from that company again. At least they paid my invoice.

24
Transition

As an Avaya retiree, my pension was not enough to live on. I'd always been in great demand and figured I would have no trouble. I updated my resume and posted it on several job search websites. I also applied to dozens of jobs I sourced online. I didn't get a single response. Quite a few large companies had downsized and thousands of well-qualified workers applied for the same jobs. The tech bubble had burst, leaving me in a sticky mess.

Before retirement, my routine each morning had been to "boot up" as either Mark or Mary Ann, depending on the day's calendar. If Mark was expected at work or school, I'd go into boy mode: men's clothes, deep voice, hair brushed back into a ponytail. If Mary Ann was expected, I'd go into girl mode: women's clothes, makeup, higher voice, hair down and with bangs. Now that I had stopped work, I realized how much the distraction of a day job had influenced presenting as Mark. Most days, I defaulted to Mary Ann and wanted to find work as Mary Ann. It would be a momentous change.

I had honored my promise of appearing as Mark for the boys' school functions. Matt was off at Ohio University in Athens about ninety minutes away. It didn't matter to him anymore, but he stuck up for his brother. "Adam's concern about high school is real. The kids would harass him if they knew about Mary Ann." If Adam had a play or concert, I'd go in boy mode.

The main reason I didn't transition was on account of Beth. She didn't like me making permanent changes, and I felt sure she wouldn't accept a permanent transition to girl mode.

* * *

Adam turned sixteen and passed his driving exam. Karen found him a car, and I added him to our auto insurance policy. "I'll pay for your insurance at first," I said. If you get a ticket or have an accident, you'll pay half. For your second one, you're on your own." I had the same arrangement with Matt, and after three years of perfect driving, I still paid Matt's insurance. Adam seemed motivated and drove with extreme care.

A few months later, I was in my home office as Mary Ann. At 4 p.m., Adam said goodbye and began the seventy-five-minute drive to Karen and Andi's house. Ten minutes later my phone rang.

"I've been in an accident. Mom said to call you because you're closer."

"Are you okay? Is anyone hurt?"

"No, nobody's hurt. The police are on their way. I just don't know what else to do."

"I'll be right there."

When I arrived at the accident on a country highway, he pulled me aside with obvious embarrassment. "What do I tell the officers about who you are?" Are you my aunt? My mom?"

"You're my son. I'll handle it."

I went up to an officer. "Hi. I'm Mary Ann Horton. This is my son, Adam. He called me and I came to help."

While we waited, I asked Adam what happened. He needed to change lanes and checked his blind spot. He demonstrated by turning his head to the right, then returning forward as if he were in slow motion. "The car in front of me had stopped to turn left and I couldn't stop in time." In his effort to be careful, he'd rear-ended a car.

Insurance covered the damage. At sixteen, he had to pay half his insurance, which of course went up. For the rest of high school, he worked part-time at McDonald's. When he graduated from Purdue, he asked me to stop paying my half. It was important to him to be financially independent.

* * *

Tech jobs remained at a standstill and I went to plan B. Consulting seemed the way to go. I set up a small business to create a professional appearance. I built a website, offering my services as Red Ace Consulting Services, in part, because I could get the domain: redace.com.

I'd been teaching my own Transgender 101 class to LGBT groups, nonprofits, and churches for a few years. Now that I needed work, I planned to turn it into a paying gig. I found a few corporate education jobs, teaching TG 101 and what to expect when a colleague transitioned in the workplace. I focused on workplace issues like dress codes and restroom use. When someone came to work in their new gender, after about twenty minutes of novelty, I advised everyone to welcome their coworker with their new name and pronouns, and then get back to work.

In reply to the question of restroom use, I would ask, "How would you feel about seeing me in the men's room? Workers should use the restroom matching the gender they're presenting. I call it the principle of least astonishment." I would follow up with this analogy. "Fifty years ago, there were separate restrooms for Blacks and Whites. When they integrated, a few White women didn't like sharing them with Black women, but in time, they got over it. This is the same issue."

I discovered some of these nonprofits and small businesses needed websites. I set up a discount web hosting service for them, creating an ongoing revenue stream. It covered expenses and made a tiny profit, keeping the IRS happy. I rebranded the company as Red Ace Technology Solutions, enjoying the inside joke that the acronym was RATS.

* * *

I had forgotten all about my award nomination, part of my former life with Avaya. An email from Out & Equal jolted me out of my chair. They had chosen me as the winner of the 2001 Trailblazer Award! What an amazing honor.

On a sunny, Thursday afternoon in October, I made the two-hour drive to Cincinnati for the conference. I only packed for Mary Ann. The mile markers ticked by as I jammed to Elton John on the radio. Beth would join me Saturday.

I wheeled my bag into the Holiday Inn, located across the Ohio River in Kentucky. I loved the sound of the fountain burbling in the center of the expansive lobby. A tall redhead with a welcoming smile greeted me at the conference registration table.

"Mary Ann, it's such an honor to meet you. I'm Heidi, the conference chair. I'll be introducing you at the awards ceremony."

I liked being acknowledged. Heidi and I retreated to one of the lounge tables to chat. She worked for Procter & Gamble in Cincinnati. In addition to her day job as a finance manager, she was a leader in GABLE, P&G's employee resource group, and involved with the awards process. She made me feel like I was the big shot.

Saturday night, Beth and I rode down the hotel elevator dressed to the nines for the awards banquet. Out & Equal's first-class dinner program featured printed programs, lesbians in tuxedos, and canned music. A gay comedian emceed and did his standup routine centered on gay men with lots of jokes about drag queens.

When the awards were presented, Heidi gave an effusive introduction detailing my accomplishments and why I deserved the Trailblazer Award, which she presented to me. I gave my acceptance speech, thanking Lucent, Avaya, and a list of people who had helped make it happen. I finished my speech with my most important words of appreciation.

"A special thanks to my wife, Beth. I can say 'wife,' can't I? Same-gender marriages rock. Beth has put up with *a lot* from me over the years, and she's always been right there, supporting me with her time and her love." I knew this was a stretch, as Beth had been mixed about my work. I hoped she might warm up to it after the award and some kind words.

I beamed as the room burst into applause. I soaked up the moment, feeling a new high. Beth's happy face glowed. My feet didn't touch the floor all night.

After the program, Beth and I celebrated in the lounge. Her smiling face further lifted my spirits. The emcee entered the bar and spotted me. He approached us.

"If you don't mind my asking, I'm confused. I know a lot of gay men who do drag. How are you different?"

"I hear you. You see, some days I'm Mark, and some days I'm Mary Ann. I'm not a gay man. I love my wife no matter what I'm wearing. Drag queens are performers. I'm not performing. Drag is something you do; transgender is something you are. This is who I am."

His eyes lit up and I knew he got it.

* * *

That Monday evening, I changed back to Mark to attend Adam's high school band concert with Beth. Tuesday morning, I awakened as Mary Ann. Wednesday evening was Adam's night with Karen. Beth and I sat on the backyard patio, chatting and enjoying a glass of wine.

"I've been thinking about looking for work as a woman." I'm sure I sounded tentative, thinking she would push back, but she surprised me.

"You know, I'd have a lot more respect for you if you had to deal with being a woman *all* the time, not just when it's *convenient* for you."

Her emphasis was not lost on me. I heard what I wanted to hear: "It's okay to transition."

Then she added a caveat. "Remember, though, I never signed up for being married to a woman."

Once again, I heard: "It's okay to transition."

"Why don't we give it a three-month trial?" she said. "You can see what it's like full time."

"That sounds good to me."

My transition to full time began the day prior when I had presented as Mary Ann and would stay as Mary Ann. When I consulted to help other transsexuals through their workplace transition, I recommended careful planning, something I discovered I had not done.

We made love with me as Mary Ann. She tried hard, but it wasn't working for her.

The next day, she admitted, "I'm not really attracted to *you*," meaning Mary Ann. "I don't want to do that anymore."

I felt so happy being Mary Ann twenty-four/seven that I didn't mind being cut off. I felt attracted to her, but sex was far less important to me than transitioning. "We'll be like an old married couple," I said. I liked the idea. She nodded.

I gave Matt and Adam one final school event each as their dad. I saw Adam act in a school play and went to Matt's homecoming football game at Ohio U. I didn't say a word about my transition.

When I called Matt later to tell him, he said "I thought I detected a different voice when you came to homecoming. I'm okay with it."

Adam came home from school and saw me in the kitchen making a tuna casserole.

"I finally did it; I transitioned. I'm going to be Mary Ann all the time now."

Adam paused. I could tell he searched for the right words.

"I don't want you going to school or church as Mary Ann."

"This is who I am now. If you have concerts or plays, I want to see you."

"If people see you as Mary Ann, I'm gonna get harassed."

"I'll be inconspicuous. I can wear my big plastic glasses. Nobody recognizes me in them."

He hung his head. He had a choice to make. He never gave a bit of trouble at school. He knew if I had to appear at the principal's office, Mary Ann would show up. A little extra motivation never hurt.

* * *

Sarah called me with news. "I found a local dermatologist who does laser hair removal. It's way faster than electrolysis. He has a special introductory price for four treatments, and then you're done. I've had two treatments, and I'm getting great results."

Every morning, I resorted to concealer, Pan Stik makeup and powder to disguise my beard shadow. Many of my friends had gone for electrolysis, which sounded expensive, painful, and like it could take forever. I remembered my friend's advice, that my dark beard hair made me a good candidate for laser hair removal. I made an appointment.

The doctor showed me his diode laser device. It looked like a gun on a hose, connected to a machine, kind of like a medical gas pump.

"All the hairs will be removed, and about seventy percent of them will grow back. You'll come again in six weeks for a second treatment. It will kill thirty percent of the remaining hair follicles. The third treatment will kill thirty percent of what's left. The hair reduction will be permanent. Your fourth session will touch up minor regrowth."

After his initial examination, he handed me off to a pleasant young nurse. She gave me a tube of EMLA cream to numb my face.

"Rub this in forty-five minutes before the procedure. Push it into your pores with your fingers and then cover your face with plastic wrap."

That evening, I told Beth. "I'm tired of wearing thick foundation every day. I've made an appointment for laser hair removal."

"What's that mean?"

"After four treatments my beard hair will be gone. I won't have to shave, and I won't have to wear all this makeup."

"You know how I feel about permanent changes. You won't be able to look like a man anymore."

"I haven't wanted to look like a man for a long time. I'm doing this for me."

She sighed and retreated to her home office.

Two weeks later at 9:00 a.m., I drove across town with my lower face and neck shiny from the cream and covered in plastic with a hole cut for my mouth so I could breathe. It had a bitter smell. I dreaded whatever pain I might feel. I was a bundle of nerves as the nurse set me up on the exam bed. The diode laser had an intensity setting from 0 to 60, which she set to 30.

"We can adjust this the next time. Let's see how it goes today."

The square business end was about the size of my fingertip. She said it would feel like a rubber band snapping on my face, which didn't sound all that bad. Her assurances fell short. Even with the EMLA cream acting as a topical anesthetic, it hurt like hell.

As she moved the wand over my face, she pressed the button for each square. *Zap, zap, zap*—like a staple gun moving along my face, one small postage stamp-sized square at a time.

I soon learned I could tolerate the pain on certain parts of my face, but the bony spots over my chin and the sensitive area around my lips hurt like hell. Then she got to my upper lip, sixteen super painful zaps. I had to ask for a timeout so she could scrape me off the ceiling.

After forty-five minutes of torture, she had treated my cheeks, mouth, chin, and neck—all the facial beard areas. I smelled like burned hair, and I was goopy from the topical anesthetic. Mercifully, she spread aloe cream on my face and told me to put ice on it when I got home.

At home, I looked in the mirror. My face burned with pain and had the appearance of a checkered tablecloth. I saw little black squares of singed hair burned into my skin. I took it easy the rest of the day.

I bought a flexible ice pack that could be wrapped around any shape. It was about a square foot and had blue and white cherry-sized cells. I used it to cool my face.

On a cold, rainy day in late November, I returned for my second treatment. We decided to increase the setting to 40. I figured it would hurt like hell anyway, but it would be over in forty-five minutes, and I could suck it up for that long.

Youch! It hurt way more than the first time. I drove home with my checkered flexi-pack on my face. I was happy to get home.

In perhaps not my smartest move, I'd agreed to be a speaker that same evening at Columbus's first annual Transgender Day of Remembrance. This small event would be held on the steps at City Hall. Three speakers had been invited; I was the only one to show up.

By default, I became the keynote speaker. The gay media there covered the event and I tried not to think about my plaid face. I gave my speech in the cold rain and included a personal story.

"NYNEX is a phone company, similar to Lucent where I used to work," I said. "A transsexual NYNEX employee, Chanelle Pickett, worked in IT. She was fired when she tried to transition on the job. During her transition, she couldn't find another job. She wound up in the sex trade.

"One of her customers strangled her to death. His defense was 'deception.' The killer argued he didn't know the transgender person was not a 'real woman,' and thus, his brutal and violent response was justified. He claimed it was okay to kill this person because she was transsexual. Her killer got only two years on an assault and battery conviction.

"If NYNEX had a transgender-inclusive diversity nondiscrimination policy, Chanelle Pickett would be alive today. We have a long way to go and we have to act. Many of us are scared to go out on the streets."

The *Gay People's Chronicle* from Cleveland took my photo and printed it with their coverage of the event. It was the worst picture of me ever taken with my face singed from the laser treatment and my wet hair plastered to my head. I cherished that photo like a proud badge of honor, having helped kick off what came to be an international day of mourning observed on November twentieth, often recognized by a candlelit vigil for the dozens of transgender people who had been murdered in the prior year.

Photo by Kaizaad Kotwal for the Gay People's Chronicle

A few days later, my face felt better and I made a happy discovery. After two laser treatments, the few whiskers I had left allowed me to skip using foundation. I put on a little eyeliner, mascara, and lipstick, and was ready to "face" the world. Thank you, Sarah.

At my third treatment, we decided to set the dial at 50. Since fewer hairs were left, there were fewer to absorb the hot laser and it hurt less. We got crazy on the fourth treatment and set it at 55. Treatment on my upper lip had me holding in my screams, whereas other places didn't hurt much at all. I'm convinced my good result was a combination of my dark hair, the diode laser machine, and the intense setting.

25

Let's End it Here

2001

My dad's friend Larry called me. In a somber voice, he said, "Your dad and Betty came to visit us here in Flagstaff this weekend. I'm sorry to bring bad news. Your dad died in his sleep last night."

I was shocked. I knew Dad had been in a lot of pain from his lung cancer surgery. I hadn't spoken with him in several months and had no idea he might be near the end of his life. I left messages on their answering machine, but he'd never called me back. Now I'd never have a chance to talk to him.

"By the way, did you know they got married? She's his widow."

They got married and didn't tell me.

Ugh. This was too much to process. I would do whatever was needed, and didn't know what that would be.

Larry gave me a task. "Can you help me find Big John, his executor?"

First, I sent Betty flowers with a nice note. After telling Beth, I called Mom and gave her the news. I knew she'd be relieved because even after all these years, she held onto her paranoid belief that Dad would come after her.

Big John had moved to Phoenix and I had a little trouble tracking him down. When I got him on the phone, I gave him the bad news.

"I'm so sorry to hear about your dad. I'm not his executor anymore. He has a lawyer doing that."

I felt useless with no direction. I dreaded going to Dad's funeral. I knew Betty was mad at me, and had no way of knowing if she had calmed down. I called Larry to let him know about Big John and to see how Betty was doing.

"Not good," he answered. "It's after 9:00 a.m., and she's been drinking. She's consumed with grief and not doing much."

"I want to make sure my dad's wishes are respected. Did he ask for anything?"

"He had a favorite place at the golf course where he worked—the space by the clubhouse between the first tee and the eighteenth green. He had a lot of fond memories of visiting with his golfing friends there. He wanted his ashes scattered on that spot."

"And will there be a memorial service to scatter his ashes?"

"I wouldn't count on it. Betty doesn't seem interested. She's talking about selling his golf clubs. They were his most prized possession." He added, "I'll see if I can get you some of his ashes."

His comments provided a small ray of hope. All I could do was wait and find out what I needed to do. A few days later, I got a collect call from "Elizabeth Horton." This was Beth's legal name, but it turned out to be Betty. She laid into me.

"Why did you call John? Why did you tell your mother? Let's just end it here. I don't want to see you ever again."

"Betty, what does his will say?"

"I don't have to show it to you. That's none of your business."

Huh? This was bizarre. "I have a right to know what's in his will. I'll contest it if I have to."

She was speechless. Then I heard the click; she hung up on me. In my shock, I decided it was important to me to make sure Dad's wishes were carried out. After what Larry told me, I sure didn't have any confidence Betty would do it. A part of me felt paralyzed, unable to do anything. I would have had a hard time flying out for his funeral. I was Mary Ann now, and once there, that fact would make a bad situation worse. I shrank into inaction.

After my brain fog lifted, the emotion of my dad's death didn't hit me as I imagined. According to everything I've seen, heard, and read, the death of a parent is one of the worst things anyone ever goes through, only I did not experience that raw feeling. My fear of dealing with Betty occupied my mind and I was relieved we were done. I missed my dad, and I wanted to talk to him. I wouldn't be leaving any more phone messages.

In her weekly email, Mom told me she had applied for Dad's Social Security benefit. As his ex-wife, she automatically got fifty percent of his monthly payment. Betty took offense at this, even though it didn't interfere with receiving her full widow's benefit.

A week later, I received another unexpected call.

"I'm the attorney who wrote Bill and Betty's will. I'm calling because you wanted to know what's in it. First of all, you have no legal right to see his will."

Great. I could feel the world caving in on me.

"That said, I'm going to tell you about the relevant parts. The will leaves everything to the trust, that's the important document. There is a lot in the trust that doesn't concern you. The important part is what I'll call 'disinheritance language.' "

My stomach tightened into a knot as the attorney read some legalese about nothing going to me.

"And you're not the only one. This language appears about all the children."

I couldn't believe it. Betty had three kids. Dad had me. We were all in the same boat. I recalled a visit when Betty had shared her intentions for her will. "I was going to leave everything to the San Diego Zoo," she said, "but when I asked them for free tickets, they wouldn't do it. So now it's all going to the Boys and Girls Club." It had never occurred to me that comment could matter. Betty had her house, and Dad had nothing. I wasn't concerned about him leaving me any money. I would have been happy with a few photos or mementos. As I saw it, this was about dignity, his and mine. And our dignity had been squashed, another bug under Betty's heel.

Larry sent me a small jar of Dad's gritty cremains. He'd heard Betty knew a couple with a house on the thirteenth hole. They held a party there and scattered his ashes behind the house—right golf course, wrong spot. I resolved to scatter these ashes in the place Dad wanted. It's illegal in California to scatter ashes in a setting like that, though I knew it happened in all sorts of places. The cremains sat on a shelf in my home office. Other than following through with his wishes, I had no reason to visit San Diego. Years later, I returned and waited for evening. Watching over my shoulder for the golf police, I spread the ashes all around his favorite spot.

* * *

> To: Mark
> From: Mom
> Not much news here this week. Yesterday we had sunshine and 62 degrees, warm enough to get the "old heifer" lawn mower started. Took over 2 hours of effort. Then the real work began. The grass was 8-10 inches tall so I mowed a 1/3 row width, even at that it jammed repeatedly, another 3-1/2 hours. Afterwards, I could hardly move around. Now I am full of aches and pains + hayfever. I have taken to bed and expect 3 days to heal enough to function again.
> Hope all is well with you and yours.
> Love,
> Mom

Signing my weekly emails to Mom as "Mark" felt wrong. Being out meant being out to everybody. Over the years, Mom had remembered my borrowing her clothes when I was a kid and had asked once or twice if I still wore dresses. I'd lied to her and told her what she wanted to hear.

I was still in the three-month trial period Beth had suggested, and I felt it was important to get through all the sticking points before making anything permanent. It happened in the middle of an otherwise normal newsy November email.

> I just got back from Milwaukee. I've been at a gay/lesbian/bi/trans conference, managed to go there on-the-cheap. Beth is in Florida this next week. First travel we've both done since 9/11. Security is a real pain.

Her response came back the same day:

> Why would you attend a gay/lesbian/bi/trans conference? Are you one of them? If so, which one(s)?

I felt committed. I spent two days composing my coming-out email to her, agonizing over every word.

> Dear Mom,
>
> This is hard to do. I'm shaking as I type this.
>
> I have struggled with my gender identity since I was a small child. The world expected me to be a man, and I have tried very hard to meet those expectations. In many ways I've done very well. But it is not who I am at my core. When I try to function in society as a man, it does not work. I become more and more uncomfortable, depressed, and unhappy. I have found, over many years, that when I dress and act as a woman, I am at peace. I am much more relaxed, and people who know me tell me I seem much happier.
>
> Through extensive reading, conversations with many other people, counseling, and much soul searching, I have come to the inescapable conclusion that I am a transgender woman. My body is an ordinary male body, but my mind is wired much more like a woman's than a man's.
>
> This is not a choice I make, but rather a discovery about myself. I've chosen the name Mary Ann—it seems to fit and feel comfortable.
>
> I know this must be hard for you to hear, Mom. I've been so afraid to tell you, afraid of rejection, anger, misunderstanding. But it's time I was honest with you. I look quite a bit different than the last time you saw me, and

you'll notice that the next time we see each other. I hope you'll be able to find it in your heart to love me and accept me for who I am.

Mom, I love you.

Mary Ann

I sent the message and waited on pins and needles for her response. It took three long days.

I don't want to leave you dangling, so I will answer back now. Of all the rest, a trans is the lesser of the evils, though I am not thrilled about it. I have known many queers and faggots in my life, and I know a little bit about them.

You say you look quite a bit different. What DO you look like? If you ever had one of those operations, you would be very sorry, they don't work and you could never undo it and would have to live with it forever.

The political rhetoric is that they are born that way. That shuts everybody up and absolves them of any responsibility. So many of the shrinks are queers themselves and they promote that notion heavily—it's politically helpful. They even claim there is a difference in the brain.

All things considered, you turned out amazingly well. You went ahead and worked very hard to do the right thing to NOT BE a scoundrel. And everybody is proud of you—you have done wonders! I guess you finally found a group who will accept you ok in the CULT. I guess it is better than nothing.

I'm very tired, and shoulders beginning to ache, so I'm going to quit for now. I love you, too, son, and you are a wonderful person, but I really don't think you need this crap.

Love, Mom

Much of this hateful rhetoric was typical Mom. She viewed anyone accepting of LGBT peoples as a cult, brainwashed into believing a ridiculous idea. In her paranoia, she hated almost everybody, and she often decided men she hated were queer. I was used to her rants, so this didn't bother me much. My reaction was relief. This could have been "I hate you, go away," or "You are evil and wrong and blah, blah, blah," for pages. Her hatred didn't seem directed at me.

> Mom,
> I've attached a picture—I hope you like it!
> Love,
> Mary Ann

Photo by Fabulous Fay Bass

Her reply waited until the usual weekly email.

> Hi!

My, what a gorgeous gal! It's all dark and I can't see anything. All I can see is somebody smiling. Are you wearing a dress and high heels? Are you wearing makeup? A wig?

Do you sit around the house in women's garb in front of your sons? If you get the job, will you go as a woman?

Personally, I think the whole thing is hilarious. I can't wait to see a picture of the whole you. Especially in your high heels and stockings! WOW!!

Love,

Mom

Her message wasn't as bad as I'd feared. I'd developed an activist's thick skin, and it came in handy here. I painted the picture for her.

Mom,

I think you're getting the wrong idea. That's easy to do. When people hear the word transgender, they picture somebody in six-inch heels and boas. When they see we're ordinary boring people, the image changes.

Let me paint a mental picture for you. I haven't worn a wig in years, my own hair is long.

If I wear makeup, it's usually eyeliner and mascara. Sometime if I really need to look good, I'll do the full makeup with foundation, but that's pretty rare. My ears are pierced, and usually I'll have French hook dangly earrings. (Posts hurt when I use the phone.)

If it's a casual or technical day, I'm usually in a polo shirt, leggings, and sandals or tennis shoes. If it's a professional or dressy occasion, think knit top or sweater, black pants or long skirt, and flats. If I have to be super professional (job interview or something) it's a skirted suit, nylons, and my most professional pair of black pumps with 1-1/2" heel.

> Do I sit around the house in women's garb in front of my sons? Well, tonight I'm in a baseball polo shirt, stirrup pants, and black tennis shoes. All four of us are here. I suppose that's women's garb, it's mine and I'm a woman.
>
> If I get the job, will I go as a woman? Yes. Full time includes work. This is my biggest challenge, but it's important for me to face the discrimination women face to ensure this is right for me. I'm very careful not to overextend, but to be real.
>
> Love,
> Mary Ann

Mom and I went back to our regular weekly emails. She never accepted me one-hundred percent as a woman. Cards and packages would come addressed to: "M~ Horton" or "My kid." At least we respected each other's views with some tolerance.

* * *

I loved being a woman. I could keep nail polish on until it flaked off. I could wear a dress any time I felt like it. I was excited about trans activism, job hunting as Mary Ann, waking up every day and not having to think about which way to dress.

Beth checked in with me. "How are you liking being Mary Ann all the time?"

Her remark caught me by surprise. It was December 2001, a reminder of our trial period.

"I like it just fine."

"Okay."

Her short reply left much unsaid. I didn't realize this was the beginning of the end. We got along fine and I loved her. In my mind, I thought we could go on like this forever.

"It's been three months," she said. "I don't want to be married to a woman."

"I understand. I want to continue a warm friendship."

Beth withdrew. Our emotional connection withered. We

behaved like good friends, eating together, being parents. Neither of us moved out from the bedroom of our beautiful master suite. Our intimacies had ended some time ago and I missed our close connection. Being a woman was so important to me, I was in denial about my crumbling marriage.

26

Mary Ann's Job Hunt

I felt grateful Beth was able to include me on her health benefits at Lucent. According to the paperwork Avaya filed, those of us who took the package were laid off. This allowed me to collect unemployment compensation until I found work. I had some savings. I needed to find a job.

The jobs I was used to were impossible to find. I signed up with Kelly Services to gain experience working as a woman. Kelly sent me downtown to the convention center for a day to check people in at the registration desk and print their name badges. The people were nice, and I enjoyed it. The day's pay wasn't even enough to affect my unemployment check.

Next, they sent me for a day to a Rent-A-Center to file papers. It was super easy and boring as heck. The manager told me if I ever wanted more work like that, I could contact him directly instead of going through the temp agency. I thanked him and didn't mention my PhD in computer science. These jobs proved how much I liked working as a woman. Full speed ahead!

In December, I saw a newspaper story about Bank One, a fast-growing local bank. Bank One was insourcing IT, exactly the opposite of what Lucent and Avaya had done. They had fired IBM and needed to hire dozens of UNIX engineers. The article quoted the director: "We have no idea where we'll find them all." I knew at least one available person with UNIX skills.

I found the job opening online and applied along with hundreds of others. A good friend who worked in the same building got me the name and number of the director.

When I called, his admin answered the phone. Her tone was condescending. "We have hundreds of resumes. He's working his way through them."

"I'm a perfect match for these openings. Would you please show my resume to him?"

"Okay. Goodbye."

That was the last I heard from her.

I considered seasonal Christmas work. I loved Brookstone—so many cool gadgets, and I applied there. I handed my application to a store associate, and said I'd love to start by Black Friday. Soon, I was in a back room with the store manager.

"Yes, we need seasonal help." She asked a few standard questions and decided to hire me. She gave me her card and wrote down a separate telephone number. "Call this number to take a routine ethics test."

I was pumped. I went out to my car and called from the parking lot. The routine test asked questions about whether I would steal from the company and whether I had ever called in sick when I wasn't. A few days later, I called the manager to follow up.

"We got the test results back, and it's recommending we don't hire you," she said by way of apology.

"I don't understand. I'm an ethical person."

"One of the questions was whether you intend to leave in the first six months. You answered yes."

"I told you I was looking for seasonal work."

"Well, that's the reason."

"So how do you hire seasonal help?"

"It's not a perfect system."

I couldn't imagine this would have happened to someone who wasn't trans.

I came home from a fruitless day of job hunting to find an email from Mom.

> I don't think you're going to get a job. This is the way people in the world (outside the "cult") think, and feel, about this:
>
> a) Having your "proclivity" tells them you have a screw loose, and they don't want to entrust their business to

someone they can't depend upon. Blabbing it tells them you have another screw loose.

b) You would be a mammoth distraction to the work force, cutting their efficiency and therefore, the company bottom line.

c) They would be repulsed just having you around. Bosses tend to want their people to be enjoyable, and who will represent the company favorably. You have aligned yourself with the lowest of the low.

It saddens me greatly that you waste all that you worked so hard for getting thru school, and still are working hard for. You can't get them for discrimination because they won't tell you. They just will give the job to someone else "more qualified."

You might be able to get employed in a group of like-minded people (the cult) someplace. I think the State of Oregon & City of Portland government have many of them and they take care of each other.

Wishing you the best.

Love,

Mom

My heart sank to read such depressing, hostile comments. My desolate mood sunk even lower.

I applied for a UNIX position with a Columbus consulting company. The general manager called me. I hated starting with a phone call with someone I didn't know. My girl voice sounded male and the other person couldn't see me. After a successful phone screening with their technical guy, she told me the way they worked was I would only get paid when I brought in consulting revenue; the rest of the time I'd be "on the bench," and they would have training to keep me busy. We talked about my background, and she suggested we set a high asking rate for clients to pay with room for the actual rate to be negotiated down if necessary.

She said, "We'll have a face-to-face meeting Tuesday to meet the team and sign the paperwork." She didn't name a time for the meeting.

The emailed paperwork arrived within an hour. It included a cover letter addressed to "Mr. Mary Ann Horton." The contract had an asking rate slightly lower than we'd discussed. I figured she was testing me to see if I would let clients backslide.

I replied to her email, "I am a woman, and Ms. Mary Ann Horton will do fine." I reminded her of the higher figure we'd agree to on the phone. "Would you please update the paperwork and resend?"

An instant later, she called me back—livid. She informed me I would not like working there, and I needed to think hard about that over the weekend. I couldn't believe she was so bent out of shape about a small difference in my asking price, which left me to conclude she was mad about my gender. I tried calling back Monday to set up the time for the face-to-face meeting and could not get through. She would not return my calls. What a disappointment.

* * *

I responded to an ad from a small company offering training for would-be webmasters. Solid Computer Decisions guaranteed a job offer to anyone who took all seven weeks of training and passed each of the seven tests. It wasn't great, but it was work. I applied.

The boss was an older, ex-military man who gave me the same written screening test they gave their students. When I handed it in, he smiled at me. In a syrupy Texas accent, he drawled, "Isn't that just the easiest test you've ever taken?"

I nodded.

"I read your resume and I'm impressed. I'm sure somewhere, there's a plaque with your name on it."

I thought of Usenix's Lifetime Achievement Award, presented to the developers of Berkeley UNIX, hanging on the wall of my home office. Mark's name was on it, along with more than one hundred others.

"I run the Columbus office, but SCD is headquartered in Charlotte. We're opening new offices all over the country. I want you to teach the CIW program," he said, referring to the Certified Internet Webmaster course.

I accepted. I was happy to be working again. Best of all, I was working as Mary Ann.

I hadn't taught much since grad school, and thought back to the truism: the teacher is one step ahead of the students. The CIW sequence consisted of seven progressive classes, each lasting a week with two idle weeks before the next class. I needed the full two weeks to prepare for the next class. I was only paid for the thirty hours I spent in front of a class and no pay for the other two weeks. I could still collect unemployment for the weeks I wasn't being paid.

Class preparation was intense. First, I had to read the material to ensure I knew it the way CIW wanted it taught. I had to pass the online test of the material, and I didn't always agree with their test answers. Next, I had to do the class exercises and make sure they worked. CIW classes directed students to specific websites, and often those websites had changed since the book had been printed. This meant the exercises the students were expected to do in class didn't work. I had to figure out a work-around using the current website.

I took extensive notes on my copy of the class materials. Friday evening, I visited the classroom to set up the student PCs. On Monday morning, I arrived thirty minutes early to deal with any surprises.

I felt I had to try to pass as a woman at work. I took great pains to have my makeup right, to dress professionally, and to use my girl voice, not easy when I talked all day. It was hard to fit the mounds of material into the thirty hours. I drank a lot of water during the class, and still sounded hoarse.

There were only six students in my class. There was a recession, they wanted a job, and their butts filled the chairs. They had no computer experience and acted as if they wanted to be somewhere else, even though they took out five-figure student loans to pay for the classes. One student played solitaire on his class PC all day. Another couldn't follow the material and didn't try. The topic for the seventh week was coding in Java, an advanced topic I wasn't optimistic any of the students could master.

I wasn't the best teacher. A good teacher doesn't cover all the material, only the important stuff. She expects the students to read to get the rest. I spent too much time talking and too little interacting. The students were bored and not learning. I hoped I'd get better with experience.

One day, my boss called me into his office. I was self-conscious and thought for sure someone had read me as trans.

I asked and his answer shocked me. "Oh, everybody knows. Nobody cares about that."

He blew off my concern with a wave of his hand. Despite my best efforts, I felt quite a letdown to realize I wasn't passing as a woman.

"I need your help," he said with an ingratiating smile. "I have a nephew who shared with my sister that he's gay. She wasn't sure how to react or how to be supportive."

I coached him about his relative.

Later, thinking about whether I would ever pass, I remembered these wise words from Be All. "What's important is to be accepted." SCD had accepted me, and that's what mattered.

After completing two weeks of classes, I was ready for a relaxing weekend. Reading the Saturday morning newspaper, I came across a startling bit of news. Solid Computer Decisions had declared bankruptcy. The doors were locked. The office was closed. All classes were canceled. I had taught two weeks of classes and been paid for one. My second week's paycheck would not be coming. I considered myself luckier than the students, who were on the hook for their loans with no further classwork and no job. They were the ones hurting.

* * *

I'd held onto one set of boy clothes, like a file backup. Six months later, I was curious about how I would feel. I dressed in the men's shirt and pants, combed my hair back, put on a ball cap, and drove to a supermarket. Pushing my shopping cart into the store, I felt self-conscious. It reminded me of a time, before I found Alpha Omega, when I'd ventured into a grocery store in a dress and a wig. Now this felt wrong.

"Excuse me, ma'am."

I was so self-absorbed I didn't realize I had blocked the entrance. I moved forward and a young man wheeled his shopping cart past me. I put a few item in my cart and pondered the deli case.

"Can I help you find something, ma'am?" the clerk asked.

This wasn't working. I got called "ma'am" twice. I didn't pass for a man anymore. My smooth face, even without makeup, turned out to be an important cue for strangers trying to determine if I was a man or a woman. The laser hair removal had done its job. I decided there was no going back. At home, I dumped the boy clothes into the trash. It was my final purge.

* * *

That spring, Beth told me she was looking for a house. She formed a close friendship with a local male realtor. They went out to dinner, and she came back with a telling smile on her face. This was more than a professional dinner. Someone new had entered her life. I felt betrayed.

I'd been in denial about our marriage falling apart for months. Her happy expression set off alarm bells in my mind. *Whoop! Whoop!* Reality crashed in loud and clear. I had to accept that Beth was leaving me. I sat down, fatigued with heartache.

Beth found a house in Bexley a mile away, and made plans to move that summer. I hoped I'd see her often.

Beth had another significant change on the horizon, kind of a redo of what happened with my job at Avaya.

"Lucent's orders are dropping off fast," Beth said. "They're going to have a massive downsizing and I was offered a severance package. I haven't been there twenty years, so they're offering me a few months of pay."

"Are you going to take it?"

She made a wry grin. "I want to get out of that madhouse as soon as possible." With a twinkle in her eye, she added, "Some of us are forming a human factors consulting company."

Beth moved out, and Adam and I had the big house to ourselves. I resolved to stay another year or two so he could graduate from Bexley High. Despite my best wishes for our continued friendship, Beth and I rarely saw each other.

* * *

June arrived, and I'd given up on my December job application at Bank One. Life is full of surprises and one of them was a call from a manager. They had my resume in hand and wanted to interview me.

A former Lucent colleague was the technical screener. I was sure he remembered me as Mark, so he knew I was trans. I was anxious and flustered. He was nice on the phone and asked easy technical questions. On one, he gave me an Internet IP address and asked me to divide it into two parts. This required binary arithmetic. I'd been doing these calculations by hand since they were invented in 1993. My stomach turned and my mind raced, stressed from having to perform on the phone interview. He reassured me and told me to take my time. I got the right answer. A year later, I heard about a website that did the math for you.

After I passed the phone screening, the manager invited me to an in-person interview. After working in the non-descript Bell Labs building and the tiny SCD office, I was blown away by Bank One's modern and beautiful four-story office building on the north side of Columbus. Four pairs of wings branched off the atrium into huge cube farms that housed six thousand workers. It was like a skyscraper turned on its side with windows lining the exterior walls, and a quarter-mile-long central atrium. It felt like being in a fancy shopping mall.

I interviewed with the manager, who told me he led a group of UNIX system administrators. The group designed, installed, and configured new UNIX server environments for deploying large banking system projects.

Since Bank One had fired IBM, their new IT organization had created a new set of UNIX and Windows IT standards, and deployed them throughout the bank. It was a "greenfield design," unconstrained by older legacy systems. I was delighted and impressed to see they had taken the opportunity to do it right.

A year ago, I might have turned up my nose at system administration. After all, I was a developer with a PhD and management experience. A year of unemployment changed my attitude. A job with Bank One was a huge improvement over teaching, and I wanted that steady paycheck.

My colleague interviewed me over lunch. I was bug-eyed over the spacious cafeteria. From my seat, I could see through the sweeping floor-to-ceiling windows to the staff dining outdoors. Beyond them, a pond dotted with lily pads gave off a relaxing vibe.

When we concluded, I got up to go to the next interview. "Mary Ann!" My colleague chased after me. I had left my purse under the chair. I wasn't quite used to the working-as-a-woman thing yet.

I met with the HR recruiter for my final interview. She went over the usual information about benefits, payroll, and the hiring process. She asked if I had any questions. I figured this was the time to come out.

"I'm transgender. It won't be a problem. If you have any questions or concerns about it, I will be happy to help."

She said it wasn't legal to ask about gender during hiring, but now that I had opened the door, we could talk about it.

"I've guided other companies with employees who have transitioned," I said. Bank One had a diversity group called Eagle One. "I can ask their leaders to step in if you need an internal resource."

"Well, then, I think you'll find this interesting. When we started the hiring process, I was sitting in the director's office going over resumes. He was reading through your accomplishments and he started to smile, and when he got to the section on publications and saw your book, *Portable C Software*, he laughed a little."

I chuckled to myself. I published that technical book in 1990.

"His face lit up and he said, 'Wait a minute. I have that book and it's by *Mark* Horton.' He got the funniest look on his face and said, 'Ohhhh. What do we do?' And I asked him if he thought she could do the job and he didn't even blink. He said, 'Yes, I guess that's all that should matter,' and we set your resume aside as someone to contact."

I got a call back, this time to meet the director who had my book. He invited me into his office.

"I'd like to hire you as a senior UNIX engineer."

He wrote a salary on a slip of paper. It was twenty-five percent less than what I'd made at Avaya and a lot more than I was making at the time. I crunched my face in what must have been a pained look. I handed him a paper from my briefcase.

"This is my salary history."

He was quiet for a few seconds and wrote another number, about 80 percent of my previous salary.

I took the offer. Apparently, women really do make 20 percent less than men.

Bank One paid me every two weeks no matter how much or how little I accomplished. My former boss's words became my mantra as I laughed my way to the bank. Petty office politics and gripes didn't bother me. I now had a positive attitude toward my job and my employer. This outlook proved to be the secret to my future success.

27
Legally Female

2002

I had to consider housing plans. Beth and I owned our Bexley house together and I needed to buy out her half of the equity. This meant refinancing the mortgage.

I didn't need to live in that fancy house with its half-hour commute. If I waited two more years, the Bexley house would have appreciated enough for me to sell it and buy a house closer to Bank One that would be modest enough to forgo a mortgage. There were houses worth half as much all over Columbus, many near Bank One.

I found a great interest rate to refinance the loan. They were happy with my credit, but there was a small snag—my legal name. They would not make the loan to Mary Ann. This hit me like a bucket of cold water.

I had done everything as Mary Ann for nearly a year. I used a trick Beth taught me to add "also known as Mary Ann Horton" to my passport, by showing I had used the name for years. Bank One had hired me as Mary Ann, and opened my employee checking account in that name. I had credit cards in Mary Ann's name as an authorized user of Mark's account. The bank with the low interest rate refused to accept my passport notation. *Rats!* I completed the loan as Mark and resolved to take the proper legal steps to document my new identity.

* * *

Beth came by to divide up the Christmas ornaments.

"Are we getting divorced?" I asked.

"I think we should. We're not a couple anymore."

"I hate to lose you, but I suppose it's the right thing to do."

This breakup would be different from my divorce with Karen. There was nothing to fight over, no child custody issues. We each had our own house, car, job, and bank accounts. I had a lawyer draw up a dissolution agreement. She used a standard template intended for a man and woman, editing in the details.

"In Re the Marriage Of: Mary Ann Horton, f.k.a. Mark R. Horton, Plaintiff, and Elizabeth A Horton, Defendant...The Court further finds no children have been born as issue of their marriage. Defendant is not currently pregnant."

This didn't sit right with me. I complained to my attorney.

"We are two women. At our age, neither of us could be pregnant. Why are we singling her out?"

"It's standard."

She meant that the law treated me as the husband, and only the wife's pregnancy status mattered. I hated it.

"Would it be all right if we said that neither party is currently pregnant?"

"I suppose that would be OK."

The final paperwork read "Neither Petitioner is now pregnant."

We signed the paperwork in January. It was official; we were no longer married. The finality of it hurt. I felt sad to see Beth go.

* * *

I had long realized I wasn't a typical transsexual. Most true transsexuals knew from their earliest memory they needed to be in the other body. I recalled Harry Benjamin's scale for "how transgender are you?"

I hadn't realized anything was different until age nine when I became interested in clothes (number 2 on the scale). I progressed to 3 in 1987 when I fully presented as a woman in Phoenix and to 4 in 1997 when I came out. Now I recognized myself as 5, going full time. There was an obvious trend toward 6, wanting sex reassignment surgery (SRS), but I wasn't ready for it, nor was I sure it was what I wanted.

I felt it was time to see Meral Crane in her role as a professional gender therapist. We knew each other well. I had the utmost respect for her and trusted her to be my guide as I journeyed through the gender maze.

I wasn't sure how far I needed to go to be my authentic self. I wanted my legal name to be Mary Ann Horton. I needed an F on my ID so I could use a public restroom. I'd been wearing breast forms in the pockets of a mastectomy bra for years, and I tired of it. They were comfortable, but it was inconvenient if I wanted to swim, wear a pretty bra, or to feel whole in my body. To avoid the bra, I tried sticking the forms directly to my chest with medical glue. That worked well from a visual and practical standpoint. Afterward, it was impossible to clean the forms properly. Repeated applications of glue only made them ickier. Silicon breast forms were expensive, and I felt lucky to afford an extra set of clean breast forms for everyday wear. I wanted actual breasts.

Transsexuals could get hormone therapy to start breast development, the only way to have natural breasts. It would take a couple of years and results were inconsistent. Some trans women opted for implants if hormones didn't produce results.

Only a few doctors knew the medical protocols around transgender hormones. They would not prescribe them without a letter from a mental health professional, attesting the patient was transsexual, grounded, and stable. Breast growth is permanent, and doctors don't want to be sued by patients who might later change their minds. Meral knew me well and obliged. She sent me to Dr. Elio Ventresca with my letter.

Dr. Ventresca was a tall, attractive man about my age, in general practice. After a few visits, I liked him so much I made him my primary care physician. He prescribed Premarin, the same estrogen drug given to cis women for menopause. It was made from pregnant horses fit with a diaper bag to catch their pee. The name is a shortened version of "pregnant mare urine." I didn't care much for the concept so I hoped the results would be worth it.

"We'll start you off with a small dose and gradually increase it over the first year," he explained. "You won't notice much growth at first. It should take about two years to reach your full growth. Some women see a lot of growth, some very little."

At the time, most health insurance policies excluded coverage for anything related to a sex change, including hormones. Even though Premarin was covered for menopause, many of my trans sisters reported denial of coverage for anyone marked "male" in their records. I expected a fight from the insurance company. I was fortunate. My prescriptions went through with no problem. I went home with a bottle of little purple football-shaped pills.

* * *

The next step was to legally change my name. In theory, it was easy. Ohio law was clear: anyone living in the same county for twelve months can change their name to anything they want. They must publish the name change in a local newspaper thirty days in advance. The name change can't be for fraudulent purposes, such as trying to escape debt, and the judge had the discretion to grant or deny the change.

Meral coached me. "You have to be careful how you do it. It depends on which judge you get. Some of them don't want to do it." Meral gave me a letter of recommendation with a cautionary request. "Don't give this letter unless you have to. I don't want them getting used to it."

I filled out the paperwork and published my upcoming name change in an obscure newspaper designed for such legal announcements.

On November 14, 2002, I appeared in court in my best skirted business suit. I was assigned to a magistrate—one of the better ones, I was told. He took me into his office for added privacy.

"Why are you changing your name?

"I'm a transsexual. This is the name I've been living with and using socially for years."

"Do you have any children?"

"Yes, I have two sons."

"Are you under a doctor's care?"

"Yes, I see Dr. Elio Ventresca and Ms. Meral Crane."

"And have you brought letters from them indicating that your name change would not be harmful to the children?"

Shit. This was a new wrinkle.

Meral's voice echoed in my mind. "Don't let them get used to these letters."

I decided to be bold, not to let him bully me.

"I wasn't aware that I needed to."

He paused and then continued, "Are you making this change for any fraudulent purpose?"

Ha! It worked. I mentally pumped my fist.

"No, sir."

A few questions later, I had an official court order signed by the judge on duty. It stated, "Therefore, it is ORDERED the name of Mark Randolph Horton be changed to Mary Ann Horton," along with a list of places to notify of my name change. I immediately notified some of my contacts. I had one important step to undertake before sending out masses of letters.

I needed an F designation on my driver's license. After my harrowing experience with the mall rent-a-cop, I looked over my shoulder whenever I needed to use a public restroom. It was common knowledge that the gender marker on my driver's license was my passport to the ladies' room. Any business owner or police officer could demand to see my license at any time.

In those days, the standard process for a gender marker change was to go through two years of hormones, full facial electrolysis, live full time for a year as a woman, and get approval from two specialists. Only then could we make an appointment with a surgical specialist for SRS, or bottom surgery, as we called it. A dozen doctors in the US, Canada, and Thailand performed these operations. Once the surgeon completed the surgery, he would write a letter.

This golden document was the ticket to a gender marker change. It attested that the surgeon had performed "irreversible genital surgery." All fifty states would accept it to change a driver's license; forty-seven states to update a birth certificate. People born in Idaho, Tennessee, and—you guessed it—Ohio, were out of luck. These states refused to update birth certificates. I was born in Washington—good for me. Many of my trans friends were Ohio natives—not good for them.

Today, surgery is no longer required in many states to update documentation. A simple administrative form at the DMV allows anyone to officially change their gender marker to F or M, and in a few states, X. Some states require a doctor or hospital to attest "appropriate medical treatment" has been given without specifying the treatment.

This proof-of-surgery path was a long and daunting road to womanhood. However, the trans community held a well-kept secret—an orchiectomy, the removal of the testicles. Orchies were a common step on the path toward SRS, to get rid of all that nasty testosterone without the expense of total SRS. An orchie didn't require a specialist. Any urologist could do it. The urologist sometimes wrote a letter attesting to having performed "irreversible genital surgery." It was good enough to convince the bureaucrats to change the trans women's gender markers.

I wasn't ready for an orchiectomy. Meral and I had a long discussion.

"I had a vasectomy after Adam was born. Wouldn't that be as good as an orchie?"

"We can try it," she agreed.

A boomer might say I was bold. Some might call it badass. I just wanted to get on with my life. Time to do an ask.

I made an appointment to see my urologist and wore my skirt suit. Nobody blinked in the waiting room.

The doctor was an attentive professional with a well-kept beard. "How can I help you?"

"Maybe you remember, you performed a vasectomy on me in 1985. I've changed a bit since then, and now I'm living my life as a woman. I need to update my documents, and I hope you can help me. Would you be willing to write a letter so I can change my ID?"

He seemed sympathetic. "It seems like a reasonable request. I mean, look at you, you've done all *this*." He gestured toward my updated appearance.

I had come prepared. Meral and I had drafted a letter together with all the expected verbiage. I offered it to him. "Here's a sample letter. Of course, you can change it as you see fit." I gave him Meral's contact information.

Meral later told me about their conversation. She convinced him this was the right thing to do. He wrote the letter. Thanks to his kindness, I had my ticket. I did the happy dance. *Yay!* He did change one thing. He removed the word "irreversible" because technically, a vasectomy can be reversed. I prayed this wouldn't matter.

I took the letter and my court order to the Ohio Bureau of Motor Vehicles. I'd heard the BMV had adopted a strict computer system, and only a certain bureaucrat in a state office could change gender markers. There had been trouble with BMV office clerks making changes on their own, and conservatives had put a stop to it. My letter and court order were passed to the powers that be, and thankfully, were accepted. I walked out with my new driver's license bearing a new female photo, my new female name, and my new female sex.

I handwrote a heartfelt thank-you letter to my urologist. Through his kindness, that wonderful man paved the way for my future.

I wrote a form letter requesting an update to my documentation, and sent it with my court order and driver's license to utility companies, banks, professional organizations, my Avaya pension managers, the Columbus Clippers for my baseball season tickets, and more.

I decided to hold off updating my Washington State birth certificate. I felt the only reason the birth certificate mattered was if I wanted to marry a man. I was not into men. I could marry another woman again someday and might need to prove I was born male to pull that off.

28

Musical Theatre

One winter Sunday, I went to Show Tunes at Union Café. I arrived by myself at 6:00 p.m., and planned to leave around 8:00 p.m. when it would get busy. I found a small four-top table.

By 7:30 p.m., the place had filled, and I felt guilty taking a table by myself. I saw two women and a man looking for a table and invited them to join me.

"I'm leaving soon anyway," I said.

"I'm Todd. This is Jody and Maddy," he introduced the group with a warm smile. "We just came from the live Broadway performance of *Chicago*. We enjoy musical theatre."

Union Café is loud when it's crowded, and with everyone talking, it's hard to hear the music from the videos. Todd and Jody talked on one side of the table. I chatted with Maddy.

"I'm a music teacher," she said.

"My son is into music. He sings in his high school choir and he's been in school musicals."

"Where?"

"Bexley High."

Todd and Jody leaned forward.

Jody asked, "What's your son's name?"

"Adam Horton."

Their eyes lit up. "Let me reintroduce myself. I'm Mrs. Hepp," Jody said.

"I'm Mr. Decker."

I recognized the names of Adam's choir and theatre teachers.

Uh-oh. I was in girl mode. I knew I didn't pass. I had outed myself to Adam's teachers, a big no-no. This group was nice, and we were in a gay bar, friendly territory, so I tried not to sweat it. We had a great conversation about Adam, whom they both adored.

"Did you have a long drive from home to Columbus?" Jody asked.

"I live in Bexley. It's only about ten minutes."

She looked a little confused. I was relaxed and having fun, and in the moment, I failed to make the connection with Adam's seventy-five-minute commute from Karen's house to Bexley.

I didn't have Adam that weekend, Karen did. When he came to our home in Bexley after school the following Monday, I felt nervous with anticipation.

"I had a surprise encounter on Sunday," I said.

Adam rolled his eyes. "Hold on. Let me tell you what happened in school today. Mr. Decker was all excited after class today." He imitated Mr. Decker's musical voice: "I met…your mother." Adam sighed and lowered his head. "I had to explain he'd actually met my father. He looked all surprised, and said, 'Well, then, your father is a really good actor.' "

"Is it okay that your teachers know about me?" I asked.

"I guess. Mr. Decker is really open-minded."

Adam had a look of resolve. I was relieved neither of us had encountered any trouble. Both teachers turned out to be cool about me, and they liked Adam, so they kept his secret.

* * *

Adam thrived in his senior year. He sang in Mrs. Hepp's show choir, played baritone sax in the marching band, and excelled at math. His favorite class was musical theatre. Mr. Decker told him "theatre" should be spelled ending in "re," not "er."

I wanted to come to school to see his performances. Adam was dead set against it, certain he'd be harassed for having a trans parent. Perhaps it was devious of me, but I decided I could anonymously sneak in. I'd wear my glasses with over-sized plastic frames and sit in the back. I wanted to video the performances, and was told it wasn't allowed. At the fall performance of *Dracula*, a thoughtful coed remembered I had asked about videotaping and sought me out to say an official audio recording would be available later. So much for being inconspicuous. However, it did not turn into a problem for Adam.

Even though I'd met Todd Decker at Show Tunes, mostly I knew him from the stories Adam told me. Apparently, Decker, as Adam called him, was a colorful character. Adam had taken to writing down memorable "Decker quotes." Todd was a gay man, and his quotes were the sort of witty repartee you hear from the queens in the community. His frizzy hair and constant smile reinforced his image.

One cold January day, Adam came home from school bubbling with excitement.

"We're going to France!"

"You're what?"

"This summer, Decker is taking us to the Fringe Festival in Paris. He won it last year. All I have to do is get a part in our summer musical." The chosen musical was *Once on This Island.* I'd never heard of it. "It's *The Little Mermaid* set in Haiti one hundred years ago. The original tragic fairy tale, not the Disney cartoon with the happy ending."

I was impressed. "How are you going to pay for this?"

"We'll raise the money ourselves. It won't cost you a cent."

Uh-huh. I mentally rolled my eyes.

After playing small parts in other shows, Adam set his sights on a lead role. He auditioned for the part of Papa Ge (pronounced "Papa Gay"), one of the four gods in the play. Papa Ge was the villain, the "sly demon of death." A few days later, he came home from school all charged up, announcing he'd won the part.

A month later, I was leaving a Stonewall board meeting when my phone rang. Adam greeted me with more excited news on his tongue.

"I would like to invite you to a dinner at school."

"What? I thought I wasn't allowed at school."

"Well, you are for this. This is for the theatre group. We are inviting a bunch of rich people to come to a dinner at the school. We'll be performing a song from the musical. You don't have to spend any money. I just want you to be there."

I was stunned. He wanted me to come to school? As Mary Ann? It was only for this event, but it felt wonderful to be included. Of course, I agreed.

I showed up at the event, planning to hang in the background. It was clear the only people there were Mr. Decker, and the theatre students and their parents, who all knew one another. I was startled to see Karen and Andi. We had long been polite in one another's presence so I sat with them and tried not to attract any attention.

The event had a silent auction to raise money for the trip to France. Items were donated by parents, along with many treasures handmade by the students. I bid on a tropical photo, autographed by everyone in the cast, and hung this beloved memento at home.

"Do you want to get involved with the theatre parents?" Adam asked me. "All the students in Decker's class are fine with him being gay. It's a really open and accepting atmosphere. I think the parents would be okay too." I rejoiced at my good fortune and agreed to come to a parents' meeting.

Sitting in a circle at the meeting, the leader asked us to introduce ourselves and tell one thing about ourselves that nobody knew. The other parents mentioned their hobbies, travels, or family. When my turn came, I should have said, "I am Adam's father," but I chickened out and said something lame about computers. Adam told me later the question had been designed to let me come out to the other parents. It didn't matter. They were all warm and accepting. We shared our mutual excitement for our kids, and we planned how to raise money for the trip to France.

Adam worked in the school cafeteria, which earned him a free lunch and allowed him to save his lunch money. He bought candy bars in bulk and sold them at school for a dollar each. He took a summer job waiting tables. All the money went toward the trip.

I was now an accepted part of the theatre group. I came to rehearsals for the spring musical, *The Scarlet Pimpernel*, and had a blast. At the dress rehearsal for the foppish number "The Creation of Man," all the male characters were in fancy dress and makeup, and so overdone, they almost looked like drag queens. I asked to take Adam's picture, and he posed for me with a queen's flirty pucker. I treasured that picture and carried it in my wallet to show LGBT friends, rather than spill a thousand words about our great relationship.

In one fundraising event that May, the troupe of students and parents held a parade through the streets of Bexley. The dads fashioned a float from a truck and a flatbed trailer. Adam played electronic keyboard and the group sang as the parade moved down the street. We stopped at intervals so the cast could perform a musical number in the middle of the road. We held up coffee cans to collect donations from passersby attracted to the commotion. Some of us knocked on doors to ask for contributions. I was so "out" at this point, I didn't care who knew, and in this context, neither did Adam.

As we passed near our house, I knocked on the door of one of Adam's old friends from elementary school. I hadn't heard about his friend for years, and I hadn't seen his parents since long before my transition. His dad answered the door. I assumed he recognized me, and I had no fear. He was speechless. Here was this neighbor he knew, dressed as a woman, babbling about the musical, and asking for a donation. Dumbfounded, he opened his wallet and dropped in some cash.

The cast performed the musical on the school stage in May with spectacular results. Everyone commented on the quality of the performance, saying the kids were beyond high school level. I was thrilled to hear Adam, as Papa Ge, cackle his robust, evil laughs.

* * *

I was so proud when Adam graduated. Matt and I sat together in the balcony of the school gym and Beth joined us. Adam couldn't wait to start Purdue that fall where he planned to study engineering. The next day we all sat together at Christ Lutheran Church. Harassment was no longer an issue.

Adam turned eighteen in June, marking the end of my child support obligation to Karen. The county sent a statement to each of us, showing how they would charge me for two extra weeks and refund me later. Karen didn't like the county's calculations, saying they would refund me too much money. The county wouldn't listen; they defended their numbers.

My calculations matched Karen's. I called her and suggested an easy way out. Rather than arguing with a deaf bureaucracy, I would send her the difference when I got my refund. She agreed, with hesitation. When I sent her the check, our relationship defrosted. We no longer had anything to fight over. Both boys were eighteen, and no custody or money issues remained.

Adam summed it up for me later. "When you transitioned, Mom said she had a lot more respect for you." Karen and Andi sent me an attractive sculpture of two female figures embracing. It was nice to know they now thought of me as a woman, not as some evil, defective man.

* * *

A pleasant couple had been asking to buy the Bexley house all year. I waited for Adam to graduate from Bexley High before letting them buy it. In turn, I bought in Westerville, close to work at Bank One, a modest house I wouldn't mind leaving one day. I wanted to move back to San Diego, and I knew owning a luxury home in Ohio would make it hard to make the leap to expensive Southern California.

I joined Lord of Life Lutheran, a church much closer to my new home. I appreciated their harmonious welcome of LGBT people. Redeemer was great, but the LGBT energy at Lord of Life blew me away. A gay man redecorated the sanctuary every season, and I felt its fabulous vibe wrapped around me every Sunday.

When Adam left for college that fall, I was alone in my house. I realized I'd been through several big changes in the last two years. I'd lost my job, changed my career, lost my father and been disinherited, changed my gender, divorced, moved to another house, and become an empty nester. Thank God I had my NU CHEEZ license plate to remind me to "savor the new cheese" and to hold on to my sanity.

That July, a problem arose with Adam's play and the trip to France was called off. Mr. Decker would not disappoint the kids. He arranged to go to Edinburgh, Scotland, for the Fringe Festival there. The kids were super excited about this new adventure.

A few parents went as chaperones. I heard lots of progress reports. The troupe put up posters, posted buzz on social media, and talked up the performances. There were only a few actual theatre stages in Edinburgh, and many performances were put on in improvised settings. *Once on This Island* was performed in a spacious hotel conference room with a stage on one end. Our parents' group had the performance recorded on video. It was amazing. I still enjoy my DVD.

In one final big change, Beth decided she no longer wanted any kind of a relationship. I felt sad at this turn of events. By the end of the year, she had ghosted me.

29

Dating While Trans

2002

Dating is hard. Dating while transgender is harder. Way, way, harder.

I hated being single, and hadn't been in this position since before meeting Karen. All that awful loneliness came back and it troubled my soul. I spent way too much energy searching for someone to share my life.

At TG 101s, I was often asked why I changed genders if I'm attracted to women. It's a great question. I explained how sexual orientation was different than gender identity. I wasn't a gay man who wanted to be a woman so I could fit into the world as straight. It doesn't work that way. Gay men don't want to be women, even if some of them do drag occasionally. Trans women don't transition for romance. It's hard to transition, and love is a terrible reason to do it. Changing gender alters every part of life: work, family, health, given names and pronouns. It's far easier to be a man in a same-sex relationship.

I'd met a lot of trans women over the years. Nearly all of them were attracted to women before their transition. After transitioning from male to female, they were about evenly split in that half were still attracted to women and half discovered they were now attracted to men. When I read about Alfred Kinsey's 1948 study, *Sexual Behavior in the Human Male*, this started to make sense.

Kinsey found about fifty percent of men were exclusively heterosexual, ten percent exclusively homosexual, and forty percent had some homosexual attraction and may have been bisexual. This fit with my own observations. If about half the trans people born male I'd met were attracted only to women, they stayed that way after transition and identified as lesbian. If most of the other half were attracted to both men and women, perhaps they were able to choose the socially acceptable half of their orientation, shutting off the part that's attracted to women and choosing men instead.

I was in the half that liked women. I identified as lesbian, but while lesbians were polite, they weren't into me. Most lesbians I met at LGBT events were the types one would associate as being butch, sporting short haircuts and exhibiting masculine gender expression. Or else they were what I thought of as "dykie," meaning they also preferred a relaxed look, but still spoke and acted more traditionally feminine. I was a femme with long hair, wore skirts, and enjoyed being a girl. I rarely saw femmes, lesbian girly girls. I was attracted to femmes, but they weren't into me either. I felt like I had a scarlet "T" plastered on my forehead.

My situation was further complicated due to the fact I hadn't had bottom surgery. In my day-to-day life, everyone seemed to assume I'd had bottom surgery. I knew better than to tell them the truth. People got weird if they knew I still had an "outie." They were beholden to the trope that a trans person was a man until the day of their bottom surgery, then instantly became a woman.

Disclosing I was transgender ended many budding romances. Anyone I dated also had to know what I had down there before we got too serious. Once my partner knew, they would have to keep the secret. We would both be in a new kind of closet.

Dating straight women was out of the question for the same reason Beth chose to leave. Straight women saw no reason to venture outside the socially acceptable custom of partnering with a man. I'd been through two divorces. I wasn't going back there again.

I thought I might find my soul mate in the bisexual community. Bi women tended to be femme and more open to trans women. I went to some bisexual groups. They were small, mostly male, and there were no unattached women. A few cis women who came regularly to Crystal Club events identified as bi, but were there to support a partner.

Some trans women date other trans women. I was open to the possibility, except I didn't find myself attracted to any of the trans women I met.

Mostly I made it a point to get myself out there. LGBT space was a safe space. I went to every LGBT event I could in hopes I'd meet somebody. I was there to make a case for trans inclusion. I kept my eyes open. Being active also kept me busy, so I had less time to pine away from loneliness.

I hit Internet dating sites. The most active local site for LGBT people was Out in Columbus. There were versions for most cities. The local site was the one that hopped because the company was based in Columbus.

Online dating was hard enough without being trans. Out in Columbus was intended for gays and lesbians, and the categories were "women interested in women" and "men interested in men." There was no box to check for "trans interested in women." I soon learned if I put "transgender" in my profile, no lesbian would respond. When I didn't include it, a potential date would get mad when they found out. I got used to being ghosted as soon as I disclosed my trans status. It was depressing.

Wanting to be honest but subtle, I conjured the phrase "out trans lesbian." It was vague enough to have spurred conversations. I'd mention being trans around the third email, which ended a lot of budding romances. It hurt. At least I found out before getting emotionally invested.

* * *

The LGBT friendly Grapevine bar/restaurant was the Columbus hot spot for trans women to hang out *en femme*, since the owner had officially welcomed the Crystal Club in 1996. During a Ladies' Night Out, a nice butch hit on me. She turned on the charm, making it clear she was interested. I was stunned. Butches weren't my thing, but she was interested, and I enjoyed the attention. We exchanged contact information, and as we left the Vine, she kissed me. It was so nice to be kissed as myself. She suggested she wanted to get together for some hanky panky.

Uh, oh. I had a dilemma. I had "outdoor plumbing," and there were stories about people going ballistic when they made a discovery in intimate situations. I knew I'd better speak up.

"Well, you should know, I haven't had the surgery."

"That shouldn't matter."

Wow. She hadn't turned me down.

She invited me to a celebration of her son's birthday at her house a few days later. That sounded wonderful. She would send me the details. When I didn't hear from her, I asked if she wanted me to come.

"Sure, I guess you can come. It's a casual thing, not a big party."

She sent me her address, and I put it on my calendar.

When I arrived, the party was low-key, yet the tension was so thick I felt frozen. She was polite, no flirting, no electricity.

After an hour or so of casual group chitchat, I was alone with her in her family room. She had a pained expression and shared her feelings.

"You're nice. I like you. But the thing you have to understand is this: I gotta have pussy."

Women often needed a few days to process the reality of my physical body. This woman changed her mind. The rejection hurt. I wasn't confident it would have worked out with her, yet twenty years later, we're still Facebook friends.

I met an attractive femme on Out in Columbus, and we formed an emotional bond. As we emailed back and forth, we learned about each other's kids. Many women had ghosted me and to remove that possibility, I suggested if one of us decided to break up, we wouldn't disappear and be honest about the reason. She agreed, writing she couldn't imagine doing such a thing. The next day, I came out to her as trans. She responded: "I know we promised we wouldn't vanish, so I owe you this letter. I cannot imagine myself with a transgender girlfriend. I hope you have a good life. Goodbye."

I was getting used to rejection. I learned to create an emotional buffer until we passed the trans disclosure. I felt unwanted and alone. It sucked.

I communicated with one woman who got past my revelation of being trans and not having had surgery. She was a soft butch, confident, with short hair, not too masculine or feminine. Upon sharing my address, she responded, "We're practically neighbors." She wanted to get together.

One evening she called and asked if she could come over. I was glad to expect her company. She arrived with a bottle of champagne and two glasses—what a nice gesture. We sat on the back patio and enjoyed the bubbly.

She leaned over and kissed me. I was startled. This was going awfully fast and she knew my status. I thought, *what the hell?* One thing led to another, and before you could say "trans lesbian," we were upstairs in bed. I had some doubts about how we should proceed, which proved to be no problem. I didn't have to do a thing. She was all over me and relished my something extra. I had a blast being seduced.

When we were done, I felt a little self-conscious about my body's role in our tryst. On the contrary, she had a tell-tale smile. With a twinkle in her eye, she confided, "I sure learned something about myself tonight." It didn't turn into a relationship, but she was a good soul.

* * *

One way to keep my mind off being single was to stay busy. Bank One continued to send me to the Out & Equal conferences, and the 2002 conference in Orlando sounded like fun. Our group stayed at a Disney hotel, held our conference in a Disney hall, and partied in Disney style.

Pleasure Island in Downtown Disney was a nightclub neighborhood with everything Disney-esque. While waiting for the bus to the event, I chatted with other conference-goers. Talking with a gay man from another company, I bemoaned being single. He felt alone as well, as his partner was back home in Colorado. On a whim, we decided tonight would be a "date." We knew we were safe, as I was lesbian, and he was gay and not single.

At forty-six, it was my first and only date with a man. At first, he was chivalrous and kind. We sat together on the bus and chose our venues together. We decided on the Adventurers Club, an African safari lodge with trophies on the walls and bush-helmeted staff behind the bar pouring drinks with a heavy hand.

We went to a club to dance, and soon realized neither of us was any good. I was all dressed up, and my high heels weren't a good match for dancing.

At the bar, my date found a pack of gay men and bantered with them to my exclusion. I wandered around Pleasure Island on my own, finding little pleasure. We joined up again later, and with nothing else to interest us, we headed to the hotel shuttle.

By now, my feet were killing me and discovered they were bleeding. I had to find a place to sit down, pull a Band-Aid from my purse, and contain the damage. Oblivious, he kept walking to the bus. Barefoot and carrying my shoes, I hobbled to the bus by myself. I saw him chatting up the gay men, and once again, felt alone and forgotten. So much for dating guys. At last, I understood why women were so frustrated with men.

30

Transgender Health Benefits

2002

When asked how many transsexuals there were, 1990's experts quoted prevalence from the *Diagnostic and Statistical Manual-III*, the psychologist's handbook of mental health issues they could diagnose and treat. The *DSM-III* stated that one in 30,000 people born male were transsexual, as were one in 100,000 born female. I didn't buy it. Meral Crane's program alone had helped hundreds of Ohio residents transition to females. I felt it had to be much more common.

Lynn Conway didn't buy it either. She was a well-known PhD who invented very large-scale integration (VLSI), the technology to design and build complex computer chips. She transitioned in the 1960s, was promptly fired by IBM for being transgender, and spent decades in the closet. She came out in 1999 and became an outspoken transgender activist.

In a 2001 article published on her website, Conway floated an interesting idea: one could divide the number of male to female (MTF) surgeries performed to date in the US (at least 32,000, she estimated in 2001) into the US population of age-appropriate people assigned male at birth (about 80 million). This suggested that one in 2,500 people born male had the surgery. She reasoned the prevalence had to be at least one in 2,500 and perhaps as high as 1 in 500, given that many transsexuals never have surgery or hadn't had it yet. She also estimated that between 1,500 and 2,000 MTF surgeries are performed each year for US residents.

As an activist, I wanted health insurance to cover these surgeries. The petitioners were almost always denied. Insurance companies would say: "at $50,000 per person, it would cost too much." Most of us thought these estimates were way too high, and we didn't have good data to suggest otherwise.

There was also an ick factor. Straight people didn't want to think about medical mayhem to body parts that carried a strong emotional component. A small, albeit loud, group of anti-gay activists railed against anything that would imply acceptance of people who, in their view, were immoral. It was far easier for benefits managers to keep transgender people on the exclusion list and not think about it.

In practice, this meant that transsexuals had to pay out of pocket, cash in advance, for their surgeries. A surgery cost about the same as a new car. Saving for surgery was like paying cash for that car. People got a car loan more often than paying cash, but the loans are secured by the car. Getting a loan for bottom surgery isn't easy. If you don't pay, the bank can't repossess your vagina.

Dr. Conway's estimates inspired me. I decided to find the real numbers by performing a proper study. After all, I had a PhD and could do basic math and statistics. All I had to do was to survey the surgeons and analyze the results.

The transsexuals in Meral's group often discussed their surgical options. Each person needed to choose a surgeon, and those who had procedures shared their stories. Only a few surgeons were seriously considered. Most trans women went to one of seven surgeons: three in America, two in Montreal, and two in Thailand. Typically, they spent about $13,000, half that if they went to Thailand, neither of which came near to $50,000.

Pricing for FTM surgeries was more complex. Everyone got top surgery (breast removal and chest contouring), but only a few had bottom surgeries. The FTM bottom surgery options were expensive, and the results weren't great. Hysterectomies were also common, and any OB/GYN could do them. This made them difficult to track.

I consulted several expert activists and made a list of fifteen surgeons we felt most Americans went to for either MTF or FTM surgeries. I sent them a short survey, asking how many of each surgery they did in 2001, the total amount they charged for all those surgeries, and what percent of those were on US residents. Twelve completed my survey. Most researchers are delighted with a 25 percent response rate, and I had 80 percent.

I followed up with surgeons who didn't respond. One doctor's receptionist reminded him of the survey, and felt he would complete it, so I waited. A week later, I got a cryptic email: "The doctor didn't realize what you were wanted. Now that he understands what you're doing, he's not willing to participate." In lieu of his response, I estimated his surgeries at 150 per year, based on a comment from a woman in Meral's group who thought he did "two to four per week."

In a surprising wrinkle, two years later, I read Jenny Boylan's wonderful memoir, *She's Not There*. In an afterword, her friend told how he went with her when she had her surgery. Describing the surgical practice scene, he stated he performed eighty MTF bottom surgeries each year. His price was on his website, giving me all the information I needed. With data from thirteen of fifteen surgeons, I could extrapolate the other two.

From this survey data, I calculated the total annual cost of MTF and FTM surgeries, top and bottom, at $15 million in 2001. The total spent on transgender surgeries that year worked out to five cents per US resident. Using other data to add in the cost of hormone prescriptions, appointments and lab tests for the hormones, and therapy, an insurer would spend seventeen cents per insured person, about .004 percent of the total amount spent on medical premiums. I could find that kind of silver under my couch cushions.

Approximately 1,170 MTF and 430 FTM surgeries were performed on Americans in 2001. The calculations showed that only one in 240,000 had it in any given year. For any one person, it's a once-in-a-lifetime event. About one in 3,100 people will have the surgery at some time in their life.

These numbers were astonishing. Transsexualism was far more common than stated in the *DSM* and being transgender applied to a significant portion of the population. If a company paid for transgender health benefits, the added cost would be negligible. There was no reason to fear an expensive surgery when it so rarely occurred. A company with 24,000 employees would pay for one surgery every ten years.

I wrote an academic paper and submitted it to the *International Journal of Transgenderism* for publication. They rejected it for being too long and not detailed enough. I found them unhelpful in making the paper more readable. I tried splitting it into two papers, one on prevalence and one on cost. After three years and repeated inquiries, I decided I had been ghosted. Instead, I published it online on tgender.net and washed my hands of the process.

My research showed there was no cost-related reason for companies to deny transgender health benefits from their insurance plans. A typical policy had a list of coverage exceptions, for example, "services related to sex change" or "sex reassignment surgery." This language had been added in the 1980s, when somebody found out surgeries were starting to change from "experimental" to "medically necessary," and soon became standard.

I wanted to do something about this injustice. Lucent had added the coverage, and it seemed reasonable for other companies to do the same. I resolved to get the word out.

* * *

Out & Equal offered workshops at their annual conferences, and they were always looking for new topics. I usually attended and knew the right audience would be there. In 2004, I decided to put together a workshop presenting my research results. I wanted my presentation to be interesting, not a bunch of numbers from the white paper. I wanted to wake them up, not put them asleep. I needed to find a way to spice it up.

Bank One and Chase Bank merged in 2003, and my friends from Chase's Employee Resource Group were eager to help. We kicked around some ideas and added a game show element for fun. During the course of the workshop, I explained how I had estimated the number of transgender people. I showed the *DSM* was wrong and that about .03 percent of the population would have a transgender surgery in their lifetime.

Another juicy nugget turned up in a book on sexual habits by a husband-and-wife research team, Drs. Janus and Janus. In the middle of a list of highly personal "have you ever" questions, they asked, "Have you ever cross-dressed?" Six percent of men and three percent of women answered yes, giving an inclusive measure of people who could be considered transgender, at least number 1 on the Benjamin scale.

The small numbers of transgender surgeries, compared with the much larger numbers of transgender people elsewhere on the Benjamin scale, showed that post-op transsexuals were only the tip of the iceberg. The numbers inspired me to create my favorite graphic, the "rainbow ice cream cone" slide. Then I explained how I arrived at seventeen cents per insured member.

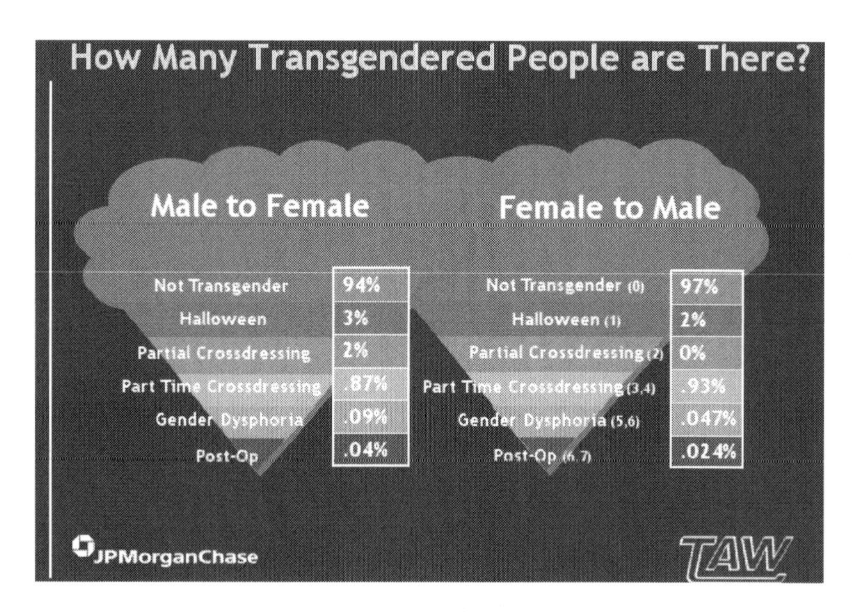

The best part of the workshop was a parody of *The Price Is Right*. We had four pill bottles of different shapes wrapped in paper to hide their identity. They represented commonly used medications: insulin for diabetes, Diovan for high blood pressure, Viagra for ED, and estrogen for trans women. We drew laughs showing a phallic-looking shoe polish bottle, labeled "Viagra".

We displayed four prices per dose, ranging from a few cents to tens of dollars, and invited a volunteer on stage to try to match the prices to the medication. They always got it wrong. The estrogen, even though it's the most common transgender expense, wound up being the least expensive of all the drugs. We had fun, and drove home the point.

The Human Rights Campaign gave a workshop at the same conference, talking about their Corporate Equality Index (CEI). They raised the bar by asking more from companies to achieve their coveted 100 percent rating. I, along with other activists, lobbied them to require trans health benefits. HRC listened. I was impressed with their project's commitment to transgender equality in the workplace.

There was still plenty of well-deserved controversy about HRC in the trans community, and we were happy to discover this branch of HRC appeared to be different. They pushed beneficial employee policies for LGBT workers and were open to trans inclusion. Their requirement for a trans-inclusive EEO policy was set in place, and it worked. Dozens of companies now had meaningful trans-inclusive policies, up from the original four in 2001. HRC proved they could give a helpful nudge, and from that, I saw a golden opportunity.

I wanted companies to voluntarily offer the same benefits to trans employees they offered to cisgender workers. To me, that meant coverage for five benefits: mental health counseling for gender dysphoria, prescription coverage for hormones, office visits for the hormones, lab tests to monitor hormone levels, and medically necessary transgender surgeries.

These benefits, or their equivalent, were covered for cisgender people. Menopausal cis women took the same hormones as trans women. Plastic surgery to correct injuries, disease, or birth defects between the legs was covered for cis people. I stopped short of asking for electrolysis, breast augmentation, and facial feminization surgery coverage because these were deemed cosmetic for cis women.

HRC inched the bar a bit higher, stopping short of my ask. They gave full credit if an employer health plan covered at least one of the five benefits on my list. If they offered no coverage, points were deducted, and the company lost its 100 percent rating.

ERG leaders took the message back to their companies and asked them to cover trans health benefits. The HRC 100 percent score proved a huge carrot. I had provided data projecting a low cost.

The city of San Francisco, always at the forefront of LGBT rights, announced new data. In 2001, they had offered hormonal and surgical coverage to their employees as part of their standard medical plan. Fearing it would cost a fortune, and that transgender people would flock to city employment for surgical coverage, they charged an extra $1.70/month per employee to cover estimated costs. After five years, having collected $4.3 million to cover the transgender benefit and spent $156,000 on seven claims for surgery, they realized the cost was tiny, and dropped the surcharge.

I gave the workshop at Out & Equal from 2004 to 2008, teaming up with colleagues from Chase Pride, cheering as the movement took off. In 2009, the CEI tracked 49 major businesses with trans-inclusive health benefits. This rose to 278 in 2013 and 1160 in 2022.

In 2008, the World Professional Association for Transgender Health (WPATH) weighed in. WPATH, a professional medical organization that set the standards for trans medical treatment, issued a bold new statement on medical necessity. Not only were my five "equal" procedures considered essential for transgender health, they went further. Electrolysis, facial feminization surgery, and breast augmentation could be medically necessary for some transgender patients. To WPATH, these procedures were not cosmetic or experimental, and they thought it would be discriminatory not to cover them.

When HRC raised the bar again to require benefit plans to fully comply with WPATH's standard, companies didn't blink. Within a year, full coverage became the standard. Once again, HRC's 100 percent score proved to be one tempting carrot.

Today, it has become standard for large companies to cover all medically necessary transition-related health services. Many states, and the Affordable Care Act, legally require coverage, and consider lack of coverage to be discrimination based on gender identity. We keep marching on the long road toward equality.

31
Women's Space

2003

As an activist, I showed up at LGBT groups, business diversity meetings, church groups, women's groups, lobby days. My message was consistent. "I am a woman. I am transgender. I want to support this group, and be included and accepted as a woman."

I sensed hesitation from some women's groups. They preferred to have supportive conversations and made decisions by consensus with women only—the whole point of getting away from men and male energy. I was never one to let my jumpy nerves stop me, even when I could potentially face rejection. I did my best to be positive and to work with the group, and in return, the women were receptive, which made me feel good. Every group needed new members and had work to be done. I thrived as Mary Ann and was accepted as a woman.

I started working with the National Organization for Women (NOW), strong supporters of lesbian rights, like me. Most of the work involved keeping the group running. I signed on as treasurer of Columbus NOW and set up their bank account. The statewide group, Ohio NOW, met often in Columbus, and I got to know the state leadership. I made friends in NOW, and they were early clients of Red Ace's web hosting service.

I showed up at numerous organizations as an openly transgender woman and through my continued presence, became the face of transgender Columbus. When somebody needed a trans view on something, they would ask me.

I was often asked: "You've lived life as a man and as a woman. Have you seen any difference?"

"I took a 20 percent cut in pay." It was the truth.

“Do men treat you differently as a woman? Do they not take you seriously or talk over you?”

“I keep expecting that to happen. It doesn’t and I’m not sure why. Maybe it’s because I learned to be assertive as a man. Maybe it’s because I know what I’m talking about and bring value to the table.”

“I know somebody at work who is transitioning. What can I do to support them?”

“Reach out to show they have your support. Get their new name and pronouns right. Include them in a group of women.”

My friends would return from an event where the discussion turned to transgender topics and tell me they met a new person who said, “Oh, I know a transgender woman, and she’s really nice. Her name is Mary Ann.”

Often these groups asked me to present TG 101 workshops. After covering the basics, I told my personal story. I started to hear from my transsexual friends about how my visibility had caused them problems. Listeners would hear my story and assume I was typical. Many trans women knew from their earliest memory they were trans, and this was an important distinction. They would have to reeducate those who thought all trans women were “just like Mary Ann.”

I had to clean up my act. When I told my story, I made a point of saying, “I’m not a typical transsexual. Every journey is different, and every trans person is an individual.”

* * *

In 2003, Lutherans Concerned invited me to appear in a Sunday school video presentation featuring LGBT people speaking about their relationship with the church. The video would be filmed at Christ Lutheran, my former home church behind the Bexley house, and made into a DVD for use by Lutheran congregations nationwide. I jumped at the opportunity.

The filming went swimmingly well, and I was happy with the DVD, *It’s All about Being Church*, (2007). I was featured in Chapter 4: “Transgender Voices and Church II.” In the process, I met some women from Christ Lutheran who were supportive of LGBT people. One invited me to a women’s tea at their church. I was so happy to be included in a women's event at a straight church, I accepted at once.

The next thing I knew, I was on the planning committee. Christ Lutheran wasn't a congregation I could be out in at the time I lived at the Bexley house, and I felt the time was right to be involved. I was sure everyone in the planning group knew I was trans. It never came up. I dug in, looking for things to do. When the leader introduced the planning committee, she offered praise. "This is Mary Ann. She's a hard worker. She gets lots of things done." That felt good.

I learned something about myself too. I'm not a creative party planner. Something deep inside me cringes when I'm supposed to be coming up with ideas for an event. Give me a script or a task, and I'll do it.

* * *

Some of the biggest women's events in the country were the lesbian music festivals. These were women-only events, celebrating the joy of being in "women's space" without the overbearing presence of men. The most ardent lesbians have long dreamed of living in a space without men, and the festivals allowed a few days of living the dream. Some went so far as to spell the word "womyn" so "man" wouldn't be part of it.

Women's space was a frontier for trans women. Trans women, like me, were often nervous going into woman's spaces. We could be arrested for using a restroom. We could be excluded from a social group.

Some lesbians have strong feelings and proclaim in no uncertain terms that trans women are men and are the enemy of women. Some of the early "radical feminists," as they called themselves, even coined the term "transgender exclusive radical feminists" or TERF. The term has since become an impolite word; however, I loved the irony that it originated from the radical feminists.

"The Michigan Womyn's Music Festival won't allow trans women into the event," Sarah said. "They've kicked post-op trans women out. The TERFs running it announced their policy, only 'womyn born womyn' are welcome."

Ohio also had a big women's festival, the Ohio Lesbian Festival

(OLF), less than an hour from Columbus. Trans women expected the same treatment as in Michigan and didn't go.

My friends from NOW raved about the OLF and encouraged me to go. I drove to the festival unafraid of being kicked out. Once on the grounds, I was warmly accepted. I fit right in at the workshops. I helped "woman" the NOW booth. I picnicked with my NOW friends and listened to the music. A few of the women went topless at the festival, but I couldn't. I wore breast forms in my bra.

One of the workshops was led by the doctor who delivered Matt and Adam. She confirmed she was lesbian when I spoke with her after the workshop.

"Twenty years ago, you delivered my sons."

"How are they?"

"They turned out great. You know what? I didn't realize it then, but in the delivery room, both parents and the doctor were lesbian."

Walking among the exhibiter booths, I saw my best friend, Katheryn. We were both startled to come across one another. She had made her trans wife stay home, thinking she wouldn't be welcome. Her face lit up. If I was welcome, so was her wife.

A friend of mine led the Buckeye Regional Anti-Violence Organization (BRAVO), a group I supported, and I discovered she led the festival committee at OLF. I had always tried to make a good impression, and I'd earned her respect.

"Thank you so much for making this a trans-inclusive event," I told her.

"And it always will be, as long as I'm in charge."

I liked to think that as the most visible trans woman in central Ohio, I had some influence in her strong affirmation. I loved the Ohio festival, and I went each year I lived in the state.

* * *

I couldn't change my voice enough to pass as female and whenever I tried to use my girl voice on the phone, I was usually called "sir." Since it didn't work and I was used to this, I decided to use my natural voice rather than forcing a higher tone to try to pass. Once I'd opened up to a cis woman I'd just met.

"No matter what I do with my voice, on the phone I'm always 'sir-ed.' "

Getting "sir-ed" and "ma'am-ed" were verbs used in the trans community.

The woman said, "They just hear your voice. Talking with you face to face, I'm having a completely different experience."

Another time, a cis female friend and I went to the ladies' room, chatting away about our day. As we sat in adjacent stalls, another woman came in. Hearing my voice, she called out, "Is there a man in here?" We both clammed up, embarrassed at the misunderstanding.

Today I avoid speaking in public restrooms so I won't make other women uncomfortable. Having a face-to-face interaction removed doubt and was key to being accepted as a woman.

* * *

Stonewall Columbus was awarded an advertising spot with the American Advertising Federation, a group that donated their time and resources to shoot a few TV commercials as public service announcements. We were asked for ideas for Stonewall commercials.

I suggested a commercial showing a business meeting where an unseen person is speaking in a male voice. Eventually, the camera focuses on the speaker, a trans woman.

A few weeks later, they decided on two commercials. One would be about a same-sex wedding. The other would be in a boardroom where you heard a male voice without seeing the speaker. At the end, the camera would switch to the speaker, a woman. *Gee, where did they get that idea?* The boardroom was a nice touch.

I was invited to audition for the part, and with a dearth of applicants, I was selected. The director asked me to bring formal business suits and selected a dark green skirted suit. I showed up in my suit with clean hair and no makeup. I met several actors and actresses, all dressed in formal business attire to play the board members. They were professionals, and I felt underqualified. They treated me as if I were their acting peer—what a treat. They whisked me away for makeup and hairstyling. A professional makeup artist made my face look great and styled my hair into a businesslike coif. The director came in and looked startled.

"Oh, no. She looks too good. I want her to look severe. Change the hairstyle."

The stylist obliged, and I came out looking like I could have clicked my heels into a group of workers and scolded them about their half-assed work. I dubbed the look the "boardroom bitch."

The commercial was fast and simple. In a deep voice, I read from my financial report, proving with facts and figures why I needed more budget. The camera panned around the faces of the members sitting around the conference table. The chairman smiled and nodded, loving my report. The other board members faces were crestfallen, knowing they had lost. The viewers were to assume the speaker was a powerful man.

The camera then cut to the chairman. "Excellent report, Aurora. And if you don't mind me saying so, that's a fabulous pashmina you're wearing."

Next, the camera cut to me. In my deepest voice, I said, "Thank you, Samuel."

The chairman moved on to other business as the voice-over narrated the tagline: "Until the world is a little more like this, we're here. Stonewall Columbus, in pursuit of equality, fairness, and safety, for the entire gay, lesbian, bisexual, and transgender community."

I loved hearing "and transgender" in the Stonewall tagline. We'd worked hard for that.

The cast, crew, and I had a spirited discussion about the word "pashmina." I had no idea what a pashmina was, and neither did most of the cast. We finally changed it to "scarf" so the viewers would get it.

Each time I delivered my line, the director encouraged me to speak slower and with more bass. I tried and tried again, but it wasn't low enough for his satisfaction. In post-production, they electronically lowered my voice.

At the end of the shoot, the stylist was kind enough to give my hair more of a street look so I didn't scare any small children the rest of the day. This was my first and only brush with TV stardom. I had a blast.

These commercials aired at 5:30 a.m., too early for me. I received digital copies and watched them whenever I felt like it. The ads were bold at the time, and though most workers wouldn't find themselves in this position, I lived this reality in my day job.

A few weeks later, one of my colleagues at work called out to me. "Mary Ann? Hey, were you in a TV commercial?"

"Yes. Did you see it?"

"Yeah. I had the TV on this morning, and I saw this commercial. I said, 'Hey, that's Mary Ann.' "

Cool. Somebody actually saw it.

Activist that I was, I made sure I uploaded both ads to YouTube. (Search for "Stonewall Columbus Boardroom.") I notified The Commercial Closet, a group that monitored ads on television and other media, and evaluated whether they presented the LGBT community in a positive, negative, or neutral light. Many positive ads have shown a same-sex couple as part of a family. There have been negative ads, like the ones showing whiskered men wearing dresses and wigs to get a free Bud Light at a bar on ladies' night. I was disappointed to see our ads were rated neutral.

There has been much controversy over the years about straight, White, cis actors playing diverse roles in Hollywood. White actors played Chinese and Indigenous parts in the 1900s. John Goodman, a cis male actor, and Felicity Huffman, a cis female actress, played trans lead parts in major motion pictures. Hillary Swank, a cis actress, played trans man Brandon Teena in *Boys Don't Cry*. Jeffrey Tambour, a straight cis man, played a trans role in *TransParent*.

Meanwhile, talented trans actresses like Andrea James and Alexandra Billings struggled to get trans roles. It wasn't until Laverne Cox broke the barrier with her role as trans inmate Sophia in *Orange Is the New Black* that trans actresses began to be seriously considered for trans roles. Finally, when the TV series *Pose* hit the mainstream, we saw more than one trans woman playing a trans role. It was a sweet bonus that many of these trans actresses were women of color.

Trailblazer

As far as I know, I was one of the first trans actors playing a trans part on TV. There have been many talented trans actors and actresses since then, and they have done a much better job. It was fun while it lasted.

32

Relationships

2003

After a day of helping Adam pack for college at Purdue, I took a well-deserved break. I sat at my computer and caught up on my email. I looked at my Out in Columbus dating profile. A new message blinked at me.

"Hello. I read your profile, and I believe we could be a good fit. Would you be interested in talking? Sue."

Wow. It felt wonderful to be approached. She had newly identified as lesbian and decided to reach out. After a few emails, we met for coffee. She was a techie and terse in her messaging without coming on too strong—a great match for me.

Sue was unique. She stood six feet tall with a stocky build. Her permed gray hair looked grandmotherly, but at forty-nine, she was about my age. She had an attractive smile and an outgoing charm that won me over. She was an IT worker at a local insurance company and had been single for most of her life. She loved bird watching and playing with her cats. Sue and I hit it off, and soon became a couple. At first, she was nervous about me being transgender. It took a few days for her to process it.

Sue and I were a success. We were together for about two years, living together for the last year. When we broke up, it had nothing to do with me being trans. She concluded she was asexual and living with someone wasn't for her. She moved out in 2005, and we remained friends.

* * *

The November 2004 election was more noisy and obnoxious than usual. The Ohio ballot featured Issue 1, a state constitutional amendment defining marriage as the union of one man and one woman, championed by Rep. Bill Seitz from Cincinnati. Issue 1 brought conservative voters to the polls in droves. Ohio voters passed the amendment nearly two to one. They also managed to squeak George W. Bush ahead of John Kerry, making Ohio the decisive state in Bush's reelection. Perhaps Issue 1 kept Bush in the White House.

Our LGBT community mourned the election. Not only had the hated Bush been handed another four years, our state constitution enshrined discrimination. We were miserable.

With Christmas approaching and holiday offerings of Dr. Seuss's *How the Grinch Stole Christmas*, I noticed a parallel between the Grinch and Seitz. Both were hateful. Both tried to stop something from coming, but it came anyway in the hearts and minds of the people. Christmas came because the Whos sang and celebrated. Gay marriage would come too.

The word "marriage" was used to describe same-sex unions. Gays held "weddings," men had "husbands," women had "wives." They weren't legally recognized, but the First Amendment allowed us to speak the words. Some gays and lesbians were afraid to use the words, instead choosing terms such as "commitment ceremony" and "partner."

I wanted to encourage open use of the same words heterosexuals used for their unions to help acclimate the public. I believed society would get used to us once everyday conversations mentioned marriages, wives, and husbands among same-sex couples. Hearts and minds would soften, and legal recognition would soon pass.

One night I made a parody of Seuss's *Grinch*. The words flowed to a degree. Two of my friends helped. We worked on it until everything clicked. I posted the poem to my webpage and sent it to my email lists. It went viral. I googled: "How the Grinch Stole Marriage," and dozens of pages popped up. It felt wonderful. The full text is on http://maryannhorton.com/grinch.html.

As I browsed the booths at the Ohio Lesbian Festival that summer, I heard my name over the loudspeakers. I went closer to the stage and was thrilled to hear a woman performing my poem. She added musical effects and commentary, suggesting George W. Bush was the Grinch. After her set, I shook her hand, encouraged her to keep it up, and to let people know the Grinch was Seitz.

* * *

I met a cute femme nurse on Out in Columbus who didn't seem concerned about me being trans. She lived in Apple Valley, about an hour's drive away. We sent warm emails back and forth for days. We had a casual coffee and seemed to hit it off.

I invited her over to my house on Friday, December 23. In the pre-Christmas calm, I anticipated a quiet, relaxing evening. I'd cook a nice dinner, and we could settle in and cuddle while watching a lesbian movie on my new home theater projector screen. I gave her my home phone number and directions to my house.

Friday came, and she called with a problem. She said she was excited to come over, but her car was making a troublesome noise and she wasn't sure her mechanic friend could fix it in time. Then she had another problem, a crisis at the drug rehab program where she worked. She had to take a client to Portsmouth, a three-hour drive each way. She emailed she would drop him off at 4:00, and then we could talk in private on her drive back. She wouldn't be back until 7 p.m.. She suggested we get together Monday instead.

"Do call on the way back," I emailed. "Hang in there; it has to get better."

Four o'clock came and went. I broiled the fish I'd planned for our nice dinner and ate it alone. At 10:00, I sent another email. "Sorry we didn't connect today. Must have been one hell of a day. Wish I could have given you a hug to help you through it. I hope you're okay. I'm free Monday—if you've recovered maybe we can get together?"

The next day, I googled her. She didn't have much presence on the net, but one item caught my eye. The Ohio Board of Nursing had disciplined her six months earlier and put her on restricted duty. The infraction? "Theft of medication for use by self."

I never heard from her again. I counted my blessings.

* * *

Out in Columbus was buzzing. The July 4th picnic at Buckeye Lake was on. "Over one thousand women are coming," the panicked organizer wrote. "Can the picnic site handle them all?"

I made my famous fried chicken for the potluck. I had high hopes. Maybe I'd meet somebody. I arrived at the lake and counted about twenty women. The organizer invited every woman on Out in Columbus. What she didn't do was set up an RSVP option to know how many would show up. She had no idea how many ever saw the invitation. For some reason, she assumed everyone would come.

I scanned the crowd. The women I met, though friendly, weren't femmes and didn't interest me. Then I saw a feminine woman who took care with her appearance. She sat in the shade of the picnic shelter, wearing a frilly sleeveless top and pale blue shorts. Her face was fully made up, and her short gray hair was spiked into a stylish do. She sat quietly, unlike the boisterous butches playing corn hole.

I struck up a conversation. Ramona was a nurse and spoke with an intelligent air. I felt an instant connection. At the end of the day, I asked her out.

Ramona and I soon became a couple. She was proud to be seen with me—what a wonderful change. Being trans wasn't a problem for her. The first time she saw me naked, she laughed without thinking. I felt a wave of body shame. Maybe she was nervous. We soon got over it and once she got used to my body, she liked it. "You're the best of both worlds," she said. Over time, she decided she was bisexual, and that's why it worked for her.

33

Let Her Pee

2006

The 2006 Out & Equal conference was a milestone for workplace activism in many ways. Chase Pride sent an impressive delegation of about forty LGBT advocates to the Chicago conference, including Katheryn and myself, to receive the Workplace Excellence Award.

Martin Luther King Jr.'s daughter, Yolanda, was one of the keynote speakers. She took questions after her talk, and I waited my turn.

"My name is Mary Ann Horton. I'm from Columbus, Ohio. Thank you for speaking to us. As a transgender American, and one that works with other transgender people, I'm often asked about the bathroom issue. People say, 'Well, it's not right for people that used to be men to use the women's bathroom.' Advocates ask me: 'What can we do to help people work through this?' I'd like your view on the answer I've given them. Tell me if this is a fair analogy.

"I tell people, 'Fifty years ago we had restrooms for White people and Black people. It wasn't right, but that's the way it was. In time, we worked through that, and we realized that it's okay for people of different races to share the same bathroom. And this is the exact same issue with trans people, just in a different context.' Is that a fair analogy?"

"I believe it is. I believe it is," Ms. King said. "It's the same kind of dealing from, I think, moving from a personal response. I mean, what you just said is extremely accurate. Because they are similar issues, similar concerns, and it's that same kind of phobic, in that instance, racist, but it's that same kind of bias that's operating. It comes from the same place. I think the approach you're taking is appropriate. All the best to you and the work that you're doing."

Yolanda King, an activist and Black woman who personally experienced segregated restrooms in the South, confirmed on the record my talking point was valid. I was on cloud nine.

The next day, Rosalyn Taylor O'Neale gave a workshop. She was an articulate, professional, African American diversity specialist who also had experienced segregated restrooms. I asked her the same question. She responded by entertaining us with a four-minute speech, enthusiastically agreeing with my premise.

"I just don't understand why some people care who pees with you. First of all, women pee in stalls. So it's not like we're all out there somewhere, squatting in some hole together. We go in, we sit down, we close the door. Not only do we close the door, we lock the door. And if the door doesn't have a lock, we put our foot against the door!"

Attired in an elegant dress and high heels, she demonstrated this by holding her foot up against an imaginary door, drawing enthusiastic laughter.

"We ought to wear stickers. 'Let her pee!' There you go, we got a movement. 'Let Her Pee!' "

I bought the audio CDs of these presentations and put the clips of my questions and their answers on the Transgender at Work website. Visit: http://tgender.net/taw/restroom.html to read the recap and hear the recording. The trans restroom issue continued to be debated in red states, and I sent the resource to activists fighting for the basic right to use a public restroom without fear of arrest.

George Takei, who played Hikaru Sulu on *Star Trek* and voiced a part in Disney's animated version of *Mulan* in 1998, also gave a keynote address. My ears perked up. I'd drawn inspiration from trans themes in *Mulan*. I recalled the scene where Mulan, on the first day spent as a man, had to quickly come up with a male name. "Um, um, I have a name. Um, um, it's a boy's name. Um, um, my name is Ping." I felt that line on a personal level, having had much the same experience during my makeover in 1987. Mulan also featured Christina Aguilera's song "Reflection," which profoundly fit the trans sentiment of someone staring in the mirror and not recognizing themselves.

Disney was decidedly not LGBT-friendly when they made *Mulan*. Curious about his experience, I asked Takei what it was like at Disney doing a transgender-themed movie in 1998. His answer deflated me.

"If you resonated with what you felt were transgender themes in *Mulan*, I'm happy for you, but I can assure you Disney did not consider *Mulan* to be transgender-friendly at all."

Thankfully, Disney has made strides toward equality, thanks to groups like Out & Equal.

* * *

In 2007, six years after transitioning full time, I wondered how far my transgender journey would take me. I hadn't had any surgery. I wanted real breasts, and years of hormones hadn't produced much growth. After three years of high-dose estrogen, at first with pills, then sticking myself in the butt each week, I had at best an AA cup. I still needed a bra with pockets and silicone breast forms, which limited my wardrobe options. As a tall woman, I needed breasts that fit my size.

I went through a phase where I planned to accept my body. At the Ohio Lesbian Festival, a T-shirt for body acceptance reading: "No silicone, no saline, no sir," resonated with me, and I went looking for a size 40A bra. I was amazed to see Sears had them, and I bought out their supply of three bras. I wore them for a few months. I hated being flat-chested.

Hormones had not provided the result I wanted. I had minimal breast growth and plenty of negative side effects. My sense of smell grew more intense with acrid odors like urine becoming more intense. *Yuck.* My skin seemed thinner, more easily hurt and slower to heal. My fingers grew numb in the Ohio winters, making a simple dash from the car into the grocery store worthy of gloves. Hormones did not affect my mood or libido.

I also struggled with whether to have bottom surgery. Having progressed from a Benjamin scale 2 through 3, 4, and 5, it seemed inevitable 6 would come sooner or later. Did I want bottom surgery? The process wasn't pleasant: full genital electrolysis to get rid of hair that would otherwise wind up inside me after surgery, a painful recovery from the procedure, and for what? To accommodate penetration by a hypothetical man.

My answer was always no. What I had downstairs may have also limited my wardrobe, but it worked adequately, and Ramona said she liked it the way it was. I deferred going through with any surgery.

Ramona didn't like having to keep my surgical status private. The decision wasn't up to her and I stood firm. "People get weird if they know. It's none of their business," I insisted. I had to be careful what I wore, lest any unwanted bulges appeared. If I wore leggings, I had to wear a long tunic top. Skirts couldn't be too tight. We all have our figure flaws, I rationalized.

After long deliberation, I decided I wanted bigger boobs I didn't have to put on in the morning. I felt ready for top surgery. Augmentation cost a few thousand dollars, which I could afford.

Meral referred me to a sympathetic plastic surgeon.

"Are you taking hormones?" he asked.

I gestured at my chest. "I was on them four years. This is all I got."

"That's fine. I don't want you growing any bigger after the surgery. You might end up with lumpy breasts."

I knew how big I wanted to be, having carried around a B-cup insert in my bra for years. The doctor measured my silicone boobs.

"I'd say these are about 375 milliliters each."

"How about I bring you a 750 ml bottle of wine to use?" We laughed.

On the appointed day, Ramona drove me to the outpatient surgery center. I brought the sports bra I would need to wear for weeks afterward. At the center, I was ushered into a sterile exam room where the surgeon greeted me. I must have looked startled when he proceeded to draw all over my chest with a black marker. He explained why it was important for me to sit up as my chest would shift once I was flat on my back.

"Since you had little breast development, the implants will be sub-pectoral—beneath the chest muscles. Otherwise, they'd look lumpy. I'll insert two empty implant bags, and then gradually fill them with saline until they look right. You'll wake up in the recovery room."

"I'll be there when you wake up," Ramona promised. She conversed in fluent nurse-ese with the staff nurses and assured me all was well.

When I woke up, I felt groggy with little pain. My chest was wrapped in bandages and my sports bra was on over them. Ramona was there to reassure me. She laughed at all the loopy things I said.

I had to sleep on my back in my recliner for a few days. I'm not a good back sleeper and was glad I had taken a week off of work. After the first day, I didn't need pain meds. Two days later, I was allowed to shower. What a relief to wash away the ick. My boobs were black and blue, and sore. It would take a while for me to appreciate them.

Two weeks later, my doctor had me take off my top at our follow-up exam. I told him I was surprised at how stiff they were; I had expected more bounce. He reached right out with both hands and grabbed my boobs. He moved them around, up and down, side to side. It was a strange feeling. "You have a lot of movement," he pronounced. Apparently, that was a necessary part of the exam. "You have sub-pectoral implants and the chest muscles hold them in place. They'll relax. And always wear a bra. It will help keep your breasts from going south."

Once my breasts healed and the muscles stretched, they still didn't move much. I found I could go braless and my bust looked supported. I still wore a bra most days; I could hear his voice in my head, like my mother telling me to wear clean underwear.

Fifteen years later, my enhanced boobs have kept their shape. Having top surgery was one of the best decisions I've ever made. I'm happy with the result, and I would never go back to being flat-chested. Ramona and I kept my plumbing status private.

34

Coming Home to San Diego

2007

Every cold winter in Columbus, I longed to be somewhere warm. Ramona and I decided to spend Valentine's week in San Diego. I wanted to show her the place I considered home. I also wanted to start planning to move there for retirement, which I hoped to do in five years.

I planned to save enough to sell my Ohio house and buy a house in San Diego. An ordinary California house was triple the cost, like jumping to warp speed. To pull it off, I needed a detailed plan that included an intense effort to save.

To ensure a good impression in San Diego, I drove us down Coast Highway with its picture postcard palm trees and ocean views. We stayed at a vacation rental in Mission Beach, a block from the ocean. I hoped Ramona would like San Diego and be willing to move out there with me. It seemed promising as she took in the waves, beaches, and beauty of a typical sunny San Diego February day. After freezing in thirty-degree Ohio weather, we were treated to seventy-degree days all week.

We hung out with Betty's daughter, Lu Ann, and her husband. At first, Lu Ann seemed guarded. Once she got to know me as Mary Ann, she took me under her wing. Even though Betty had written me off, Lu Ann and I were still friendly, and as stepsisters, we wanted to develop a relationship. She showed us around the local real estate market.

Her husband wrote mortgages and knew property values.

"The time to buy is now," he said. "The recession has brought prices down. They'll go back up, and the gap between Ohio and San Diego prices will get worse."

"What do you suggest?"

"You could buy a house and rent it out. When you're ready to move out here, you'll have a house."

"Won't renters be hard on my house?"

"If you want a different house to live in, you'll already be in the market. Sell it and buy another one."

His coaching made sense.

We landed in Ohio with a foot of snow on the ground. Matt and his wife drove us home from the airport. Driving through our unplowed street proved difficult and he had to let us out in front of our house without going up the drive. We dragged our luggage like sleds up to the house.

It felt good to be home. The cold and snow? Not so much.

Ramona was euphoric about our week in San Diego. She endorsed a move out there—the sooner, the better.

I made a house-hunting trip in April. Lu Ann let me stay in her guest room. She seemed a bit uncomfortable at first and restricted me to one end of the house. After the first night, she relaxed. I was her step-sister, not a weirdo.

"Are there jobs?" I asked her.

"Biotech companies are growing like crazy in San Diego. There are plenty of IT jobs out here. I'm sure you could find something."

Hmm. What an interesting idea. What if I bought a San Diego house and we moved now? The kids were grown. The job market had picked up. It might work. I asked Ramona about finding work. "No problem," she said. "Nurses are in demand everywhere. I can always get work as a travel nurse."

I decided to put my resume on the Internet. It couldn't hurt to try. I perked up over a few nibbles. Most of the inquiries came from headhunters—recruiters wanting to pitch me for one of their openings. I spoke with them and did my best to sell my strengths. The jobs were usually contract-to-hire, where I'd come on as a contractor for six months, and maybe, if they liked me, they'd hire me. I'd have to pay my own benefits and move to San Diego on my own dime.

One day, my phone rang and I heard the magic words: "I am the hiring manager."

A personal call from the hiring manager. I'd better pay attention to this one.

"I saw your resume. You have lots of experience with UNIX, system administration, and IT. We need that here at San Diego Gas and Electric."

Blech. A utility company. I pictured working with a bunch of macho guys in boots and jeans who climbed telephone poles. A lead was a lead. I kept the conversation alive. He had some hesitation about committing to an interview in San Diego.

Amylin Pharmaceuticals, a San Diego biotech, needed an IT guru with skills more closely aligned to mine. Our phone interviews went well, and they decided to fly me out for an in-person interview. My excitement grew as the reality sank in. I was coming out in July for a second house-hunting trip and we scheduled the interview for the same week. I called SDG&E and arranged to interview with them after I concluded with Amylin.

As my plane approached San Diego, I looked out the window at what I hoped would be my future home. Gliding over beautiful Balboa Park, I saw a huge array of tents and canopies. I thought it was a farmers' market. I found out later I'd passed over San Diego's LGBT Pride Festival, a good omen.

I rocked the interview with Amylin. I felt the company and I were a good fit, and they seemed to like me. I was optimistic they would be my ticket to San Diego.

On Friday, I arrived at SDG&E's location in Mission Valley, a nondescript sign reading "9060" and a road that went up a hill so steep, the car strained to get to the top. A security guard confronted me. I told him I was there for an interview. He checked my ID, wrote down the license plate number, gave me a stick-on badge and instructions to the next gate.

I motored to the gate and pushed the call button. "I'm Mary Ann Horton, here for an interview." After a pause, the gate opened and I parked in the lot. I looked around from the gorgeous hilltop setting, the cars threading along the freeway in Mission Valley amid beautiful greenery and the blue, cloudless sky. The dry, ninety-degree July weather felt good against my skin. The door to the building was locked. A guard inside buzzed me in.

My tour of the building was limited to the lobby, the restroom, and a conference room. I didn't have a good feeling. I felt daunted by the amount of security. The air conditioning wasn't working—at a utility!

I felt a connection to the hiring manager, who was my height, about my age, and personable. He joked about his Southern accent. He turned out to be easy to understand once I got to know him. He was from Iran and in part, had come to America to get away from the Ayatollah. Showing me the organization chart, he introduced himself as the software team supervisor. Joining him was another supervisor and their boss. I thought it strange that no technical people interviewed me.

The Energy Management System Operations (EMSO) department ran the Energy Management System (EMS), the computers that control the electric transmission power grid. This was a big deal—the freeway system of the electric utility. It was about to become a bigger deal with new government regulations taking effect to ensure hackers couldn't break in and shut off the power.

They asked me softball questions about scripting, backups, and how my boss saw me. I knew I'd aced it, perhaps so much that they might deem me overqualified. I looked forward to getting an offer from Amylin and saw SDG&E as a potential backup.

The next day, Lu Ann and I looked at houses in her town of Poway, half an hour north of San Diego. I chose ordinary, affordable houses comparable to my Westerville house. I would need a mortgage, one I could pay off before I retired.

We toured several houses that were either in escrow or had drawbacks. One house wasn't available to see until Sunday. It looked great on paper, and better in person. I spent half an hour videoing the house and yard while the realtor drew a floor plan.

The house, located on the end curve on a cul-de-sac, was roomier than most and in fair condition. I could envision the potential. The dark living room would make a great home theater. The pie-shaped yard had a pool on one side and a brown lawn on the other. A spacious addition had room for a home office, family room, and dining room. The steep hill behind the house provided great privacy. Clambering up the hill like a mountain goat, I had a fabulous view of the valley. I imagined building a deck up there, a place to sit and enjoy the sunset. This was the right house, and I was thankful for Lu Ann's help in finding it.

Back in Columbus, I showed Ramona the videos. We talked about the houses and agreed on the one I'd seen on Sunday. I made an offer and went back to work. I waited to hear from Amylin and SDG&E. I didn't have to wait long. My phone rang Tuesday. SDG&E's offer wasn't a raise from my salary at Chase, but the numbers worked. They offered a full relocation package. I thanked them and waited to hear from Amylin.

Amylin took two weeks to get back to me. "You interviewed really well. We had another good candidate who was local and avoiding relocation costs tipped the scales."

As a trans woman, I felt vulnerable working with a group of macho guys at SDG&E, and wasn't looking forward to a hot, dusty environment. I forged ahead, the decision made, I accepted the position and we set a starting date in early September. We were moving to San Diego—not in five years—in a month!

Ramona and I had only a few weeks to prepare. In a whirlwind of activity, I applied for a mortgage, had the Ohio house inspected, and we cleaned out all the junk we didn't want to move.

I felt strange leaving a city I'd called home for 26 years. I loved so many things about Columbus. Matt and Adam. Ramona's family. My many friends. My hairdresser, who gave me one last perm. We said our goodbyes. Clippers baseball games. Show tunes at Union Café. Every place I went, I stopped to appreciate its value, knowing it was the last time I'd be there.

On our last Sunday in Columbus, Ramona and I went to church to donate our heavy coats to the needy. We wouldn't need them in San Diego. I shared the news of our move with Pastor Jim.

"Have I got a church for you!" His face lit up like a little kid's on Christmas morning. "I visited my son in San Diego when he was in the military, and attended First Lutheran. They feed the homeless, and they're Reconciling in Christ. They're awesome."

As my plane lifted off, I thanked God for my new adventure.

* * *

I went to my first day at SDG&E filled with doubts and a sense of foreboding. Everybody knew I was trans. Would I be accepted as a woman? Would there be a bunch of homophobes? Would I be taken seriously? Would I be working in the back of a truck?

First days are always important, and I wanted to look nice when they took my photo for my company badge. I wore full makeup, and my cranberry jacket and skirt. I managed a pleasant smile. My freshly permed hair dominated my photo.

My new supervisor welcomed me and wasted no time showing me around. I saw where I would be working and met my coworkers.

The EMSO room was a large bullpen set up for about two dozen workers. My boss and the other leaders had offices with doors. Everybody else had a cubicle.

When I was shown mine, I was overcome with joy. It was twice the size of my Chase cubicle, plus it had a window. I had been given a desktop PC with a huge flat-screen monitor. A laptop in a briefcase had been placed on the desk. I was used to having only a laptop and a boxy tube monitor I'd paid for myself.

My boss gave me the building tour and tested my badge in all the readers to make sure it worked. He showed me the data center where the EMS servers were racked and the control room where the operators ran the San Diego County power grid.

The control room was quite a sight. *Yowza!* The ceiling reached two stories high. Two walls were filled with a huge, curved "map board," illustrating the entire San Diego power grid. Embedded in the map board were small red and green lights showing all was well in all the substations. It looked like something out of NASA.

It was then I realized why this building was called MCC, or the Mission Control Center. We were in Mission Valley. This control center ran the power grid. I was literally working at Mission Control.

Operators staffed a curved row of workstations with a second smaller row behind it for supervisors. Each operator used a Sun workstation with three monitors to control the grid.

I blinked. It was 2007, and the power grid was running on the Sun workstations I remembered from Bell Labs in the early 1990s—modern ones with flat-screen monitors and USB keyboards in the familiar Sun layout.

We went back to the EMSO room and my boss introduced me around. Four women worked in our room and two of them wore skirts. The guys were dressed in jeans and business casual shirts. My coworkers seemed like good folks, and most of them were techies, like me.

Everybody knew in advance I was transgender and nobody brought it up. I was sure management had made it clear I had their support. As with Bank One, my history with the UNIX vi editor had made me a legend from the start because most of them used it in their daily jobs. My fears were soon put to rest.

I was happy to discover two of the women on our team were technical. These two expressed their welcome by taking me to lunch on my first day. We sat on a café patio and talked at length about SDG&E, the EMS, and the people who worked there.

My boss took me under his wing and trained me on the EMS. He took me through the architecture, the operation, and some of the basics about activities we performed from time to time, such as moving operations to the backup site to rehearse for a disaster.

* * *

Pastor Jim's recommendation was right on. Ramona and I tried a few churches and though all of them seemed fine, First Lutheran felt special. Several gay and lesbian couples were members, and they rolled out the red carpet for us. First Lutheran had been Reconciling in Christ since 1989, and marched in Pride every year. They also hosted a soup kitchen to feed the homeless twice a week. We became members that Easter.

* * *

Our senior systems guy announced in November that he was going upstairs to work in distribution. His backup took on the role of bringing me up to speed. This new arrangement didn't last long because in December, that person announced he had accepted a job in Sacramento with California ISO, the gargantuan electrical operation responsible for the entire California power grid. He and his wife had a baby on the way and wanted affordable housing in which to raise his family. He was gone the first of the year.

I did a gut check. I was the senior systems person on the team, whereas everyone else worked on the database. I knew I'd better step up and be a leader. I asked for extra training, attended meetings, and wrote EMS monitoring software. My supervisor took notice and sent me to training with the software vendor in Florida. Once back, I presented ways to smooth operations and increase reliability. Not only did my boss support my initiatives, he appointed me to the team that would implement our new compliance work, intended to keep the hackers out of the EMS and the auditors off our backs.

I received a raise to go along with my responsibilities and within a year, I was promoted to their highest senior technical level. In little time, the pay cut I'd taken to come to San Diego turned into a pay raise. After another year, I topped what I had made at Avaya, my previous peak.

* * *

Ramona felt homesick. As much as she loved San Diego winters, she was a Buckeye through and through, and she longed for Ohio. After a year in San Diego working temporary nursing jobs and not settling into any of them, she wanted to return. In the middle of the winter of 2009, she drove back to Columbus. I missed her but hoped it would be temporary.

Searching online for resources, I happened upon a group called Lesbians in North County (LINC), a lesbian social group. It seemed like the perfect outlet I needed to make friends. They met every Friday evening in a Unitarian church in Vista, forty-five minutes from Poway.

I arrived at my first meeting not sure what to expect. Some lesbian groups didn't want any trans people there. Others were welcoming. I was nervous going in the door.

The women introduced themselves. We sat in a circle and went around the room, each woman checking in with what was going on for her that week. Some of the women talked quite a bit, and it was easy to see it might take the whole meeting time to get around the circle. When my turn came, I came out as trans to make sure I'd be welcome, and felt assured by their warmth. I mentioned my partner, Ramona, to put people at ease that I wasn't looking for a date. I became a regular at LINC. I formed many friendships and it became the center of my social circle.

I set up a home theater in my living room. I painted the entire wall with special movie screen paint that reflected light like a theater screen. I mounted a projector on the ceiling, added a five-speaker sound system, and a small stage with footlights. It was like going to the movies. When I switched the input, it became my TV.

I loved the projection setup. It seemed like a lot for one person when I could fill the room. I started hosting movie night parties at my house. Friends from LINC and church would arrive with potluck food, and we'd visit for a few hours. Then we'd crowd chairs into the living room, pop some popcorn, and watch a movie. It was fun, and I enjoyed sharing my nice home and fancy TV with my friends.

Ramona came back to San Diego later in 2009, and we were a couple for a few more years. We broke up for good in 2011. She went back to Ohio and, sadly, I was single again.

35

Goodbye, Mom

2011

I went up to Portland to visit Mom for a few days. She expressed difficulty living alone and trying to take care of her house in the suburbs. At eighty, Mom was tough, independent, and paranoid, and she wouldn't trust anyone to help her. I saw a few areas where I could pitch in and make her life a little easier.

She relied on dial-up Internet and complained it took forever for the photos I sent to download. She didn't want to pay for cable and didn't want the installers on her property, even if I paid for it. She watched over-the-air TV for hours on end and scrutinized the TV schedule for movies.

The world had moved to broadband, and I was amazed when she accepted my offer to install cable Internet so she could watch Netflix. To keep her blood pressure down, she let me work with the installer as they dug up her yard. I presented her an inexpensive Internet phone, saving her from paying a landline phone bill.

I was still afraid of her, and I could tell her temper simmered beneath the surface waiting to boil. Overall, I was relieved the visit went well, and I felt closer to her because of it. I wore a skirt when I took her to dinner at Olive Garden and she seemed okay with it. After dinner, we went to the ladies' room together, a big step for her. She smiled and chatted as if nothing were unusual.

Mom explained her finances to me and it progressed into an end-of-life discussion about what she wanted done. "I don't expect to live much longer." She was serious. I felt disturbed to hear this news and wistful sentiment that she bothered to organize everything for when that day would come.

After the first of the year our weekly emails took on a more serious tone.

They did the pictures in the stomach and a biopsy. It held its own sort of for a while, but now it is progressing rapidly. My gut area is as big as 9 months pregnant, it's almost impossible to put on shoes & stockings. I can eat about 3/4 cup of food. I suppose intestinal blockage. 2 legs swollen from hip to feet, I think heart failure as I get winded over the smallest action. I spend all my time in bed except for necessities. My upper body is skin & bones, shoulder bones and ribs sticking out, and skin hanging in droops. Pretty grotesque. I am taking it day by day.

It is my intention to start emailing you daily. It will be CI-SA, shorthand for CHECKING IN-STILL ALIVE, in case I can't type a message.

I am very sick, got to go now. Bye.

As the weeks passed, she complained more and more about her stomach.

CI-SA

I am very sick this morning. My belly is so big and taught it feels like it will burst. I didn't take a pill yesterday. With stomach cancer, there is no quality of life. It is one of the deadliest of all cancers.

Whew, this is awful! Just lay in bed all the time, and sleep a lot. I don't know why mother nature keeps me on. There are uncertainties about doing it myself. I wish it would just happen.

She planned to take her own life if she thought it would work. Even if I'd been strongly opposed, there was nothing I could do.

I'm so sorry it's awful, Mom.

> If you decide to do it yourself, you go right ahead. You have every right. And if you decide not to, that's OK too. You're a grownup and you can take whatever path you choose. I love you either way.

On April 16, I was startled to read this message from Mom.

> Recent Thoughts
>
> Back door open 8 inches for Blue to go outside & potty.
>
> Key in car ignition—other keys in side pocket in purse.
>
> Garage door opener—in shoe on floor of car, passenger side.
>
> Call Mortuary first thing for notification and advice.
>
> Don't call 911. I don't want the arrogant medical community involved. They will make all the money off it they can.
>
> Thank you ever so much for all the many things you have done for me. I appreciate every single one of them. You are a kid to be proud of!!
>
> I love you very much.
>
> Mom

I steeled myself. Now she wasn't hedging. I hated that she was going to end it all. I'd promised to take care of her affairs and would respect her wishes.

That Thursday, two days before a scheduled movie night, she sent the dreaded email.

> I am taking the pills tonight. I wish you were here. Can you come? Please hurry.

I dropped everything, canceled the movie night, and took a Friday morning flight to Portland. A cab dropped me off at the house, and I went in the back door. I saw Blue, her toy poodle. His tail was down and he whimpered as he paced back and forth inside and outside of the house. I walked into her bedroom, dreading the thought of finding her dead in her bed.

She lay motionless on her back with a shower cap on top of her head. I gulped and walked to her bedside. I touched her face. Her eyes opened, and she screamed. Startled, I screamed too. Her well-made plans had gone awry.

"Mom, it's me."

"Oh, I guess it didn't work."

She was coherent and distraught to be alive. Suicide by pills was not going to work. We needed to figure out something else.

"We'll need to get you to a doctor tomorrow to figure out what's going on with your stomach," I told her. She was right, her bulging belly did make her look pregnant.

We talked and visited all day. She showed me her DNR (do not resuscitate) order and a suicide note on her fridge. I set them aside, not wanting to read them. After we had dinner, I retired to her guest room and slept well.

I woke up refreshed at 5:00 a.m. Saturday, and heard a strange noise coming from her bedroom, like a growl. Stepping in, I found her propped in the corner of her attached bathroom. She let out a low moan. She had used the toilet in the middle of the night and didn't make it back to bed; she was out of it. I couldn't lift her. I got her as far as the middle of the floor and paused to catch my breath. Then she stopped breathing.

My first inclination was to call 911 and do CPR, in my mind, the right thing to do. Then I remembered her DNR order. She had gone to a great deal of trouble to end her life. It would be wrong for me to try to bring her back. If I did, she'd be furious with me.

I forced myself to wait and think it through. I could see she was gone. I needed to follow her wishes. I found some peace knowing she got what she wanted.

She had pre-arranged a cremation through a local memorial society at a thrifty price. Mom could have taught Jack Benny, the world's stingiest miser, how to save money. At her insistence, I read *The American Way of Dying*, Jessica Mitford's exposé of the funeral industry. She would not want to pay a dime more for a funeral than she had to.

Following her wishes started a comedy of errors. I called the funeral home at 6:00 a.m. and left a message. The funeral director called me back at seven. After telling me he was sorry for my loss, he said they don't pick up the deceased. I should call 911. They would call the authorities later to pick her up.

Mom didn't want me to call 911. I had no choice. "My mother has died. We need you to pick her up for the mortuary."

Within a few minutes, I heard sirens. A fire truck and an ambulance pulled into her cul-de-sac. All the neighbors looked out their windows. My mother, who valued her privacy and made plans for the mortuary to pick her up without a fuss, would have been mortified. I felt like a fool.

A breathless team of medics and firefighters rushed in, ready to save her life. They took one look at her lifeless body and relaxed. They asked if she had a DNR, and I directed them to the order on the fridge and the suicide note she'd taped to her headboard.

They read the note and showed it to me.

"I am going to take my own life with morphine pills. This decision is mine alone in a normal state of mind. If I am discovered before I have stopped breathing, I forbid anyone, including doctors and paramedics, to attempt to revive me. If I am revived against my wishes, I shall sue anyone who aided this."

She sure knew how to get her point across.

One medic asked if she had any prescriptions in the house. I pointed him to the cluttered dining room table, half covered with bags and pill bottles. The paramedic's jaw dropped. Mom had dozens of filled, unopened prescriptions on the table, hoarded, just in case. They included four or five unopened bags of oxycodone, filled at the cost of over two hundred dollars each. What a waste of the money she prized. Three separate bottles of morphine pills were in the collection, all empty.

The medics were kind and thorough. They gave me the wristwatch she was wearing and prepped her to go. I took a moment to say goodbye to her, telling her how much I loved her. I'm not an emotional person. I tried to cry and the tears wouldn't come. Maybe I would feel it later. I felt emptiness as they carried her lifeless body out the door, and a bit of relief. I no longer had to be afraid of my mother.

Blue and I took a few minutes to regroup. The poor little guy had watched his person die. He cuddled with me for comfort. I was his person now.

I had a lot of arrangements to make, which she had laid out in detail. It was Saturday morning, and dealing with lawyers and banks would wait until Monday.

I needed to make some calls to let people know she had passed away. Her favorite relative had passed the previous year. I saw an elderly cousin on the list. I left a message at her place of work. She returned my voicemail within a half hour.

"Okay, first off. Virginia has a son. Who are you?"

Mom had only talked about Mark. She barely acknowledged my new name to me, and she never did to any relatives.

"That's me," I replied. "I'm transgender. I've changed my name to Mary Ann."

"Okay." Ever the businesswoman, she moved to the point. "So, what happened?"

I called Matt and Adam next. They both wanted to come out to help. Matt was studying for law school exams and couldn't come. His wife and Adam flew out to help me go through her things. After a week, we had it sorted out.

Mom had an eight-year-old Toyota with 6,800 miles. It looked like a new car. It would replace my fourteen-year-old Camry. I loaded it with as much as I could fit inside, set up Blue's crate so he could see out the window, and began the long trip to his new home in San Diego.

36

“Nice ‘n’ Easy”

2012

I kept my social life active. I needed to stay busy, and I had to begin the “dating-while-trans” thing again. It was hard. I had a few single dates, nothing that went anywhere. I went to LINC meetings and Meetups, and I kept the movie nights going.

I had two season tickets to the Broadway Series musicals. Without Ramona in my life, I invited friends. Katie had my attention. Everybody at LINC loved her. She’d been coming to movie night for a few months. She was gorgeous, younger, and fun. I thought she was out of my league. I was older and, well, trans. *The Addams Family* came to town in May, and I sent Katie an email asking if she’d like to see it with me “as friends.”

We went to many of the same LINC events. At a staged reading of a LINC member’s play, a half dozen of us came in support. Katie happened to be across the room from me. I’m a hugger, and on the way out, I was hugging my LINC friends within arm’s reach and didn’t get to Katie. As I left, she walked over with an expectant look.

“Don’t I get a hug?” she wailed. I was more than happy to hug her.

A week later, we ran into each other at the annual gala for the North County LGBTQ Center and sat at the same table with other LINCers. I hadn’t heard back from her about *The Addams Family*, and assumed she wasn’t interested.

“Aren’t you going to send me details about the theater tickets?”

“Oh. I never heard back. I thought you weren’t interested.”

“I replied to your email. I’d love to go.”

“Then I’d love to take you.” Inside, I did my happy dance.

I took her to a casual restaurant. Being my mother’s frugal child,

I paid using a two-for-one coupon for the meal.

We had fun at the show going as friends. I thought I felt a bit of electricity between us and sensed she would be receptive to go out on a date. First, though, I asked to see her over dinner and I was delighted when she accepted. I took her to her favorite restaurant, California Pizza Kitchen.

As we sat at the table, I reached across the table and took Katie's hands in mine. I looked into her eyes with all the sincerity and care I could muster. "I would like to ask your permission to date you."

Katie looked confused. She nodded. "I thought we were already dating."

Now I was confused. "We are?"

"When you took me to *The Addams Family*; that was a date."

Oh, man. We'd been dating for two weeks and I didn't know it.

"I'd wondered why you used a coupon on our first date."

Oops. It was time to come out to her. "You know I'm transgender, right?"

"I know."

"Well, I want you to know I haven't had bottom surgery. It's all still there."

"It's fine. We'll figure it out."

What a relief.

Katie and I soon became a couple. We decided to take it slow and I'm glad we did. No U-Haul for these lesbians. Frank Sinatra's "Nice 'n' Easy" became my earworm song for months.

Friends and acquaintances asked her if I'd had "the surgery." It wasn't easy on her, but she supported me, implying I had. We couldn't imagine why people felt it was their business what my privates looked like.

Katie impressed me from the beginning. She had been a quality assurance manager with a small software company for over fifteen years. She owned her home, and lived there with her adult daughter and son, plus each of them had a dog. Katie described the chaos at her home as a "rodeo," and therefore, didn't want me to come to her place. Her work commute to Carlsbad took her west and it was a bit much for her to go east to get to my place. Instead, she drove to my place once a week for our time together. In all, she was a responsible adult who got things done—and a great catch.

Over the next several months, she spent more time at my house. One night a week, then two, then three. She brought her spirited cocker spaniel with her, and I grew to love him as part of Katie's life. Except for the long haul work commute, she loved being with me in my house. She made a game of finding scenic back routes, enjoying the drive through the wealthy neighborhood of Rancho Santa Fe.

Katie introduced me to her kids. They were sweet and welcoming from the beginning. Her parents took longer. Her mother was a conservative retired minister and didn't appreciate her daughter dating a woman. I thought it helped that I served on church council and brought Katie to worship. Her dad once said, "It doesn't hurt that we don't get any more frantic phone calls in the middle of the night about things her husband did to her." They eventually accepted me, and treated us both as daughters.

A year later, we took a long vacation, driving up the California coast while the kitchen was being remodeled. When we returned, she moved in for good. She put her touches on the new kitchen and launched culinary creations that made my mouth water. I enjoyed cooking, but seeing my love in her element was special—and yummy!

Katie made one thing clear. "We can live together, but I don't want to get married."

"I don't want to get married either. I want something more permanent. My marriages haven't worked out."

"I don't believe in it. I was married to a man once, and he treated me terribly."

"I'm not your ex-husband. My job is to be good to you."

* * *

I've always celebrated Father's Day with my sons. They have lots of mothers: Karen, Andi, Matt's widowed mother-in-law, and my partners. I'm the only father they have. I like having Father's Day to myself. Katie's kids never knew me as a man, and have a father, albeit an imperfect one. They see me as another mother and honor me on Mother's Day. It's sweet of them.

As the years went by, Katie and I became more solid. Our relationship wasn't about sex anymore; our aging bodies didn't cooperate and we lost interest. Our love was about our personalities, our lives, the theater, hikes, and our cuddle time in the evening watching TV. I updated my will to protect Katie and all of our kids.

I made a vow to Katie. "I want to die in your arms—in about 40 years."

Epilogue

2019

The UNIX system began at Bell Labs in 1969. My friend, Clem, vowed to make sure its fiftieth anniversary had a proper celebration and chose the July 2019 Usenix conference in Seattle as the perfect venue. I had attended many Usenix conferences in the 1980s as a business trip. This was an important anniversary, and I wanted to be there. Katie encouraged me to go. I emailed Clem, saying I would be happy to help arrange it. Now that I was retired, I had some time to help.

Clem set up the event on his own. He reached out to Seattle's Living Computer Museum and arranged for a Wednesday party. Usenix included a notice in the conference program, and Clem invited seventy-five UNIX old-timers.

Clem wanted UNIX memorabilia brought to the conference, and I was more than happy to oblige. I had collected progressively modern memorabilia during my career and created what I called a museum. I uploaded the archived inventory to stargatemuseum.org.

I looked for appropriate items and scrounged up a floppy disk labeled "Usenet Maps." I didn't recognize the handwriting on the label and didn't know what was stored there. I dug out the ancient AT&T PC from my museum and booted it up. This 1984 box ran MS-DOS and Windows 1.0 with a 5¼-inch floppy drive. I saw about twenty text files with Usenet maps on them. They spanned from the first connection in 1980 between Duke and UNC, to maps from 1986 that could only show the Usenet backbone because the whole net had grown too big to draw. I thought these items might have historical value and would make a great display at the event.

I decided to commemorate the anniversary by doing the same thing I'd done in 1983 and 1984: show up at Usenix and hand out paper Usenet maps. I printed a twenty-page handout for the event and I put a PDF file online at stargatemuseum.org/maps for others to download. Back in 1983, a hundred people picked up a map so they could route their email. Today, user@domain works everywhere.

Clem wanted anything Usenet or Stargate related, so I brought a copy of my Stargate Internet Museum sequence and planned to post sixty sheets on the walls at the exhibit. As it turned out, the hotel's policy prohibited anything attached to the walls, so I put them in display folders for tabletop use instead.

Arriving in Seattle on a rainy Wednesday morning, I was delighted to find a city bus route from the airport to the hotel. A short drizzly walk from the bus stop put me in the hotel lobby an hour after my flight landed. And what a hotel it was. The new Hyatt Lake Washington was filled with amenities. The sweet check-in clerk pointed out the lakeside seating located behind the hotel. My room had all the modern conveniences, including a spectacular lake view as I sipped my morning coffee and read the San Diego newspaper online.

I took the elevator down and thought I recognized Kirk, my office mate and colleague from Berkeley. He didn't have a name badge, so I asked. He heard a male voice and looked at everyone in the elevator except for me. That hadn't happened to me for years. I introduced myself and shook his hand. He looked me up and down, astonished by my transformation. I asked about his partner, Eric, whom I also knew from Berkeley. Eric was at the conference and would be at the event that night.

Clem and I carpooled to the Living Computer Museum to set up. I brought my tote bag of memorabilia, which turned out to be the only thing anyone brought. For me, the main event was taking a grand tour with the curator and seeing all the historic computers up and running. He graciously placed a table in a prime, central location where I spread out my exhibits: the Stargate and Usenet map booklets, the stack of Usenet maps to take home, and my UNIX license plate, which attracted covetous attention from the museum staff. I had playing cards from the twenty-fifth anniversary. Usenix had put together the deck by featuring a different photo of someone they considered important to UNIX's history on each card. I, as Mark, was on the six of hearts. The attendees were fascinated, and I enjoyed explaining everything to them.

Afterward, I hung out at the hotel bar with Clem and other new friends. I drifted off to bed after midnight, feeling great about the commemorative celebration.

The next morning, I wasn't sure what to do. The conference itself was filled with academic presentations from youthful attendees with newer subjects than UNIX on the roster, such as cloud computing and file systems.

My historical items were on display near the Usenix desk. I made a little explanatory sign and stuck it to the wall with an adhesive square. This raised the ire of the hotel staff until I showed them how it came right off with no residue.

Browsing the next table where all the Usenix handouts had been consolidated, I noticed trays of ribbons people could attach to their conference badges. Next to ribbons reading: "I'm hiring" or "Job seeker," I was delighted to see: "My pronouns are," followed by "she/her," "he/him," "they/them," and a blank one to be filled in as desired. The Usenix staff had made a great effort to be inclusive, and I thanked them as I proudly attached a "she/her" ribbon to my badge.

I skipped the Thursday morning sessions. Exciting developments from the 1980s had been replaced by narrow technical talks describing how someone had made a corner of the Linux system faster. Instead, I lounged outside by the lake, enjoying the view and a good book.

I saw other female attendees sporting skinny black pants and comfortable tops on their way to the remaining big event, the conference reception. I decided to scratch my itch and wear a nice dress. I entered the hotel ballroom crowded with a few hundred attendees seeking free food and drinks. Posters of the technical talks lined the room's perimeter, each with a presenter standing by to explain their work and answer questions. I took a glass of wine and worked my way around the room.

Picking up some pasta from the buffet, I joined a table with Clem and three others. After some pleasantries, a memory snapped into place and I shared a personal, important aspect of Usenix. I related the story of how I'd played hooky the first day of the 1987 Phoenix conference to be entirely dressed as a woman. I told them how I purchased women's clothes at the mall and had my makeup done. I choked up. Sitting with them as a female, I realized I had come full circle, surrounded by my friends at Usenix, and felt a sense of closure.

I got a refill at the bar, and joined a table with Kirk and his partner Eric, another couple, and a young man from Denmark. We listened to one another's old stories about UNIX. I shared my Phoenix story, and how I felt about coming full circle. In return, I received a warm sense of inclusion. Eric reminded me he had chaired the Phoenix conference.

"I was so grateful when you and Kirk let me couch surf while I finished my PhD," I said. Those days seemed forever ago, and in between, I had turned my schooling into a successful career.

The Seattle clouds parted to reveal a beautiful sunset over the lake, and the group went outside to enjoy it. We took group photos against the spectacular background.

Photo by Geoff Kuenning

Eric and Kirk joined me as we headed upstairs to turn in after the long day.

"I think I like Mary Ann a lot better than Mark," Eric said.

"That means so much to hear you say that," I said. "I'm so sorry if I ever put you off. I hope I've matured since then."

"I like Mary Ann better too," Kirk agreed.

It felt wonderful to reconnect with people I admired from such an important period in life.

Back in my room, I reflected on my life's journey. I'd grown from a selfish, obsessive teen into a kind, helpful elder. I'd learned to make change by summoning my courage to do a big ask, to focus on the needs of the business, and laugh my way to the bank.

Transitioning had been a monumental part of coming full circle at UNIX, and thinking of the larger picture of my life, I realized it incorporated much more. I had to give credit to those who had supported me in all facets of my life. The more I gave to my kids, in my relationships, at church, and at work, the more I realized what had been given to me. Being my authentic self allowed me to thrive and be my best self. This applied to my role as a parent, a partner, in friendships, within the church, as well as in business.

I learned lessons that made me who I am. The golden rule worked for me: do unto others by being friendly, confident, and clear, and others will respond in kind. I looked for opportunities and put myself in a position to move ahead. Life takes unexpected twists and change is inevitable. When I found myself knocked down and the old cheese disappeared, I learned to savor the new cheese by being grateful, allowing God to show me the way, staying agile, and having the tenacity to carry on.

* * *

2021

Thanks to Katie, I had a change in heart about marriage. At a fancy anniversary dinner, I dropped down on my knees and presented a ring.

"Katie, you are the love of my life and I want to spend the rest of my life with you. Let's make it official. Will you marry me?"

Katie was stunned. She cried. She nodded. I slipped the ring on her finger.

Photo by Kat George

We married in a gracious Victorian house in Columbus, Ohio with family and a couple of friends present. Katheryn stood at my side as my Maid of Honor. My pastor from Lord of Life performed the rite on a beautiful September day.

I'm retired from SDG&E. Katie and I live happily together in Poway, or as I like to call it, Paradise. Katie works from her home office, and we live the good life.

Matt and Adam are grown and married, and now Katie and I have grandchildren to adore. Katie and I visit them often in Ohio. Katie's kids are great; they treat me like another mother.

Karen and Andi married when the Supreme Court allowed it. They've been together more than thirty years, and I doff my hat to them for making it work.

I never had bottom surgery, and I feel I've been in the right body for well over a decade. I updated the gender marker in my Washington birth certificate once same-sex marriage became legal. I am so thankful to be where I am.

I've kept my surgical status private—until now. By writing this book, I've come out of my last closet and released Katie from having to keep my secret. I'm a woman in every other way: mentally, socially, and legally. Years ago, I might have lost friends if they had known about that unimportant lump of flesh down there. I believe we've moved on. Today, I often skip wearing makeup and go *au naturel*. I pluck the dozen or so hairs on my face once or twice a month, like most women my age.

These days, it's normal for trans people to come out using whatever combination of social, legal, and medical steps fit their personal situation. Being out is being empowered. Closets waste energy.

My activism has slowed down and I make an appearance here and there when asked. The pendulum on LGBT rights swings to and fro from state to state, and with pressures at the federal level, it's likely I'll keep my finger on the pulse of action and do what I can. Oftentimes, the help I give is a one-on-one encounter, educating, supporting, and being the change I want to see in the world.

Blazing a trail had been the hardest at the onset. Each step of the way provided new challenges as I cut down obstacles in my path and new ones rose before me. Once the path had been worn, it was easier to widen it, and for both trans people and allies to walk it. I realized the value in setting an example on how to integrate an equal right as a social norm. When all is said and done, educating and mentoring those who followed may be the best gift I ever gave.

I give thanks to God for my loving family and my wonderful life with Katie in Paradise.

Acknowledgments

My name is on this book, but I could never have done it alone. So many people helped, inspired, or supported me in bringing my story to life.

First and foremost, I give thanks to God, in the person of the Holy Spirit, who guided me through my journey and showed me how to make this remarkable life happen. Thanks to all my friends and clergy at Redeemer Lutheran, Lord of Life Lutheran, and Christ Lutheran churches in Columbus, First Lutheran in San Diego, Lutherans Concerned/Central Ohio and North America.

A special thank you goes to my editors. Aaron Alcorn took an early look at my story and gave me valuable advice. Taylor Graham took my mess and structured it into a coherent story. Janet F. Williams coached me, nurtured me, and brought my words to life.

Thank you to my anonymous beta readers. You showed me what was missing and mangled.

Thank you to all my ARC readers for taking time to read and comment on my book. Special thanks to Jamison Green and Beth Allen Slevcove for finding last-minute items to fix.

Thank you to Robin Locke Monda and Jamie Ty for your amazing cover designs, and to my marketing genius Rachel Cone-Gorham.

Thank you to Sarah Fox for her LesBiGaTr graphics and her friendship over the years. Thank you to Mariette Pathy Allen, who tirelessly showed up at every trans event and took beautiful photos, and to Jesse Egner who dug through the files to find a high-resolution version of Mariette's beautiful Capitol Steps photo. Thank you to Chuck Bryant, Geoff Kuenning, Fay Bass, Kalzaad Kotwal and Martha Pontoni, and Kat George, for permission to use the very special photos you took.

Thank you to favorite teachers Mrs. Reames and Mr. James Ringstrom for nurturing my young brain and putting up with my youthful shenanigans, to Professor John Shutz for setting a troublemaking student onto a real career path, and to Sheree Hickman and Sue Harris for inspiring my young girl self.

Thank you to Professor Sue Graham for inspiring and directing my PhD, to Bill Joy for trusting me to take on his vi editor, and to Jim Ellis, Steve Bellovin, Steve Daniel, and Tom Truscott for creating the Usenet social media network that brought me techie fame.

Thank you to Dr. Janet Lucas for bringing joy into my life by delivering my sons and nurturing the lesbian community, to my attorneys Andy Fishman and Jeff Furrow, the custody evaluation team of Dick Fetter, Jerome Meers, and Dr. James Christopher, and Judge Clayton Rose, who kept me with my children.

Thank you to the crossdressers of Alpha Omega and the trans women of the Crystal Club, to Ken Goodnight, Adrianne Walker, JoAnn Roberts, Paula Jordan Sinclair, Alison Laing, Matt Doutre, and Mary Benis, who befriended me, taught me, and inspired me to become a better woman.

Thank you to Margaret Burd who taught me to "do the ask," Mark Cooke, Vicky Jeczen, Evelyn Leeper, to Ron Behea for his story that inspired me to do the ask, and Kathleen Dermody who welcomed me to EQUAL! and put me to work, to Dana Priesing who gave me the "gender identity, characteristics, or expression" language, and especially to Ethel Batten who put the language in Lucent's EO policy and Rich McGinn who signed it into history.

Thank you to Tom Grote and Michael Caven, who enabled my workplace presence as Mary Ann and hosted many wonderful evenings at Michael's Out On Main LGBT restaurant.

Thank you to Jamison Green for your friendship, your expertise, and your wonderful presence wowing the 1998 EQUAL! conference.

Thank you Jessica Xavier, Riki Wilchins, and all the It's Time, Ohio! members who helped launch a movement.

Big thanks to my dear friends Michele Kämmerer, who turned me on to laser hair removal, and her wife Janis Walworth, who taught me the "4 sliders" of sex, gender identity, gender expression, and sexual orientation I used teaching TG-101s over the years.

A special recognition goes to the late Penni Ashe Matz, a dear friend who taught me to educate the world just by being my non-passing self.

Thank you to Daryl Herschaft and Samir Luther of the HRC Corporate Equality Index, who listened to activists like me and drove 90+ percent of corporate America to adopt trans-inclusive nondiscrimination policies and medical benefit plans.

Thank you to Jeff Redfield, Kelly Pinkleton, Karla Rothan, Linda Schuler, and the others on the Stonewall Columbus board and staff, for listening, being inclusive, and putting me to work, to Chris Cozad and Gloria McCauley, who welcomed me to countless LGBT events and the Ohio Lesbian Festival, and to Carol Galetly for letting me help teach her Ohio State students about LGBT.

A big thank you to Elaine Smith, Gail Ritchie, PJ Guinan, Larry Carr, Tom Champoux, Kerry Ryan, and Kai Rush for your welcome at Babson and friendship.

Thank you to Dottie Painter for keeping me out of restroom jail, and for never sending me a bill.

Thanks to the Avaya Corporate Email and Directory team: Jim Hohman, who taught me an important lesson, Sue Davis, who came through for me in the clutch, Noel Siksai, Vince Fresquez, Rick Cook, Dolla Lakani, and Siva Sonti. You all did the impossible on time.

Thank you to Cannon Douglas, my dad's best friend, who mediated through a messy situation when he passed away.

Thank you to Heidi Bruins Green for your warm welcome at Out & Equal and your friendship and to Jason Stuart for teaching me how much we all have to learn.

Thank you to Marc St. Gil, Steve Potter, Tina Giustino, Joel Spieth, and especially my dear friend Karen Hostetler, for throwing me a lifeline into Bank One.

Thank you to Lisa and Bill Koontz, whose inspiring collaboration turned a rough draft of the "Grinch" into a parody poem worthy of a viral sensation.

Huge thanks to Todd Decker and Jody Hepp for boosting my self confidence in that gay bar and telling me how awesome Adam is, and for changing me from an outsider to a part of a treasured family of theatre parents (and for teaching me that "theatre" ends in "re").

Thanks to the wonderful medical professionals who helped me through my transition: Elio Ventresca, Dr. S. L. Robinson, and the wonderful urologist who turned my vasectomy into truth on my drivers license (whose name I'll omit out of respect for his privacy), and especially, thank you to my dear friend Meral Crane, for being my guide throughout my journey to womanhood.

Thank you to Dr. Lynn Conway, whose brilliant observations about the number of trans surgeries inspired me to conduct my research study, and to all the selfless surgeons and experts who responded to the survey and guided me in the extrapolations, and to Jenny Boylan and Richard Russo, for revealing a key piece of data missing from my results.

Thank you to Yolanda King, Rosalyn Taylor O'Neale, and George Takei for taking my questions at Out & Equal and giving wonderful, quotable responses that helped open the restroom to trans people everywhere.

Thank you to my dear friends Clem Cole for almost single-handedly organizing the 50th anniversary commemoration of UNIX, and Eric Allman and Kirk McKusick for opening your home to me way back when, and still being there for me four decades later.

Huge thanks to the mentors and bosses who made my career a success: Dr. Susan Graham, Dale DeJager, John Bagley, Don Massoni, and Parviz Ebrahimzadeh.

Thank you to my family, to my mom and dad for giving me life and for loving me through their own tumultuous lives, to my sons Matt and Adam for making me proud, to my sister Lu Ann Moore and her husband Rick, for guiding me through the leap from Columbus to San Diego.

Thank you to Karen Summers, the mother of my children, for them and for many good years together.

Thank you to Beth Marshburn, who lovingly and selflessly brought Mary Ann to life and gave me and the boys the best years of her life.

Thank you to Sue Kramp and Ramona Nash for our many good years.

A heartfelt hug to Katheryn Neudecker, my bestie, who has been there for me over the decades.

And most of all, to Katie Tucker, my loving wife and partner in life, all my love for eternity.

About the Author

Mary Ann Horton, PhD, is a transgender activist, computer systems architect, Internet pioneer, entrepreneur, author, and speaker. In 1997, she persuaded Lucent Technologies to become the first Fortune 500 company to add transgender-inclusive language to its nondiscrimination policy, and to add coverage for transition care and surgery. Her work, which was soon replicated at Apple and Avaya, led Out & Equal Workplace Associates to present her with the 2001 Trailblazer Outie Award.

Mary Ann founded several transgender social and activist groups. She conducted a research study that proved the addition of transgender medical coverage would cost companies virtually nothing. She has been featured in the Daily Beast, Out Magazine, Google Arts and Culture, Salon, Diversity Factor, SHRM, L-Mag, Nokia, Faces of Open Source, and Out TV.

Mary Ann earned her PhD in Computer Science from the University of California at Berkeley in 1981, where she created the first binary email attachment tool and led Usenet, an early social media network. At Bell Labs, she made email easier to use, brought user@domain.com email to the have-nots, and published Internet standards for email and Usenet.

She is the author of technical reference books including *Portable C Software*, and of the viral Internet parody, "How the Grinch Stole Marriage."

Trailblazer is her debut memoir.

Visit her website, **maryannhorton.com.**

Made in the USA
Middletown, DE
28 October 2022